MISCARRIAGE

MISCARRIAGE

Women Sharing from the Heart

Marie Allen, Ph.D.
Shelly Marks, M.S.

John Wiley & Sons, Inc.

NEW YORK • CHICHESTER • BRISBANE • TORONTO • SINGAPORE

In recognition of the importance of preserving what has been written, it is a policy of John Wiley & Sons, Inc., to have books of enduring value published in the United States printed on acid-free paper, and we exert our best efforts to that end.

Published by John Wiley & Sons, Inc.

Library of Congress Cataloging-in-Publication Data

Allen, Marie, 1954–
Miscarriage, women sharing from the heart / by Marie Allen & Shelly Marks.
p. cm.
Includes index.
ISBN 0-471-54834-0 (acid-free paper)
1. Miscarriage—Psychological aspects. 2. Miscarriage—Psychological aspects—Case studies. 3. Bereavement—Psychological aspects. 4. Bereavement—Psychological aspects—Case studies.
I. Marks, Shelly. II. Title.
RG648.A56 1993
155.9'37—dc20 92-22852

Printed in the United States of America
20 19 18 17 16 15 14 13 12

I wrote this book in honor of Baby Andy. I dedicate it to my children here on earth. Thank you for sharing your lives with me. You are my Greatest Blessings . . .

Terese Noël,
Jordan Taylor,
& Grace Lorelei

I love you with all my heart,
Mom

To my grandma, Leah, whose spirit guided me through the writing of this book and to Jamie, whose life was the gift that began the journey.
Shelly

ACKNOWLEDGMENTS

To Chris Dunne, Anne Nickel, and very especially Peggy Macy (Empty Cradle support group) for providing the acceptance, security, and guidance that enabled us to journey through grief and return to life.

To Gary Winters for assisting us in the process of defining our dream. To Betsy Wheeler for publicizing our invitation to potential participants throughout Los Angeles, opening her home there to us, and finding us space in which to conduct interviews. To Honolulu University for providing us space, too. To Teri Brown for her referral of many of the San Diego participants.

To Tom Diamond and Josh Shade for their statistical expertise. To Kathy McCoy for marketing guidance. To Bill Durbin for overseeing our contract. To Sue Cramer, L.C.S.W., and Antoinette Thomas, Ph.D., for help with our Additional Reading List. To Judy Davis, L.C.S.W., for sharing her personally compiled list of children's literature.

To fathers who sent us personal writings or gave interviews to help others, including Lyall Kitson, Richard Rudiger, Tim Riley, and James Kenneth Watson.

To Martha Durbin, R.N./M.S.N., Peggy Macy, L.C.S.W., Kurt Benirschke, M.D., Harlen Alcorn, Ph.D., Michael Graves, Sharon Calagna, Jody O'Konski, Steven R. Drosman, M.D., Barbara Drosman, Bleema Moss, M.F.C.C., Judy Davis, L.C.S.W., Susan Cracroft, Reta Shulman, and Gerald Spector, M.D., for support and guidance on our manuscript.

To Robin Rue at Anita Diamant Literary Agency for believing in and selling a book on this subject. To Ted Scheffler at John Wiley & Sons, Inc., for the vision to recognize its importance and persuading Wiley to publish it. To our editor, Judith McCarthy, for her careful and astute suggestions and for coming through on promises.

To Michael Graves and Mike Marois for their skill as photographers.

To Richard F. Jones, III, M.D., and National President of American College of Obstetricians and Gynecologists, for acknowledging the importance of miscarriage as a loss and supporting this effort by writing our foreword.

To Gregory Allen for his belief in me, help with the computer, and countless hours of love and care for our children over the two years and nine months since the origin of this project. To Reta Shulman, for terrific ideas and emotional boosts. To James Isaacson for allowing me to witness the beauty of his journey in grief and the privilege of touching his heart. To Patti Aretz for warm arms, deep compassion, and howling laughter. To Martha Durbin, R.N./M.S.N., for love and an incredibly bright mind. To my parents, Thomas Lanny Gipson and Geraldine Dazey Gipson, for life and love.

To Tinette Thomas for being my personal cheerleader. To my mother, Gloria Marks, for her supportive phone calls throughout the writing process and especially for her prayers. To my husband, Gary Winters, who gave me love and support from the moment I met him and whose continual unfolding and belief in us encourage me to grow and to be all that I am. To my daughters, Lorien, Lyndsey, and Hallie, who gave up their mother for the time it took to write this book and who are my most precious teachers of love and joy.

CONTENTS

FOREWORD

In the quarter century that I have been a practicing obstetrician/gynecologist, I have seen countless women stricken by the loss of their babies, both born and unborn. The tiny life they carried flickered out; they were left to grieve alone.

Although medical art and practice has become increasingly sophisticated in treating women whose full-term babies are stillborn, there has been little emphasis on dealing with the loss experienced by women who lose their babies earlier on. This is no doubt due, in part, to the controversy surrounding the definition of life—when the miraculous division of cells can be regarded as first embryo, then fetus, then unborn child. Regardless, women who are pregnant, at whatever stage, know themselves to be hosts of more than merely potential life. Often even before conception they change their life-style—they quit drinking and smoking, they take vitamins and improve their diets and exercise habits—they make plans, they dare to dream, they *feel* different. They become mothers.

And it is this emotional dimension that gives women who miscarry the right and the need for support, validation, and compassion. We who are involved with these women must be sensitive to the devastation that miscarriage inflicts on their psyches. We must understand that bonding between mothers and their unborn babies takes place long before others can see that they are pregnant, long before ultrasound can prove that life exists, long before the father and other loved ones can feel the stirrings of young life as the baby kicks and moves within its mother.

We must be acutely aware of other dynamics as well. Domestic violence, substance abuse, and untreated disease can and do result in miscarriage and leave a woman shattered. Underlying treatable and physical problems can result in the loss of a pregnancy. And there is the pregnancy that ends for unknown reasons.

Whether or not there is an explanation, there is a loss. Women take these losses very personally and are certain, somehow, that they are at fault.

The unique focus of this book lies in its emphasis that women who miscarry must not and need not be left in emotional isolation.

I am pleased that this timely and sensitive reflection on miscarriage is now available to grieving women and to those who are involved in their lives. Grief, unless expressed and validated, will persist. It is my hope, therefore, that the personal insights expressed within will provide some comfort and direction and will contribute to the catharsis vital for the resolution of grief.

My congratulations to the authors.

—Richard F. Jones, III, M.D., FACOG
President, The American College of
Obstetricians and Gynecologists

OPENING NOTE TO THE MOTHER

Dear Mother,

Regardless of the length of time you were pregnant, you carried a real, living being in your womb. That little being, your baby, died. What you are feeling is grief, a complex, yet normal, response to loss. We will give you information about the feelings you may experience in response to your loss. Although the future appears dark, you will survive. You will find your strength along the way. You will see the light of day again. Together we'll hold steadfast through the tears.

Shelly and Marie

PART ONE

MISCARRIAGE

CHAPTER ONE

A Beginning

In 1987, our unborn babies died. The months to follow contained the darkest hours we have ever known.

We had both always been under the impression that miscarriage was no more than a brief disappointment, and people treated ours accordingly. By all indications, miscarriage was not a serious loss—especially at only 10 and 14 weeks of pregnancy. But we were devastated.

Separately, each of us believed herself to be the only woman in the world who felt profound grief over the loss of a miscarried baby. Both of us feared that we were crazy to be feeling as we did, torn apart by an event that the world minimized. After all, it was "only" a miscarriage. We didn't trust that we had a right to grieve. Weeks went by and still we did not feel better. We were stuck and couldn't heal.

We sought books on the subject. Our public libraries and bookstores had no books concentrating on the emotional experience of miscarriage, which seemed to validate that the emotional experience was not a big deal.

What we did find helped us in many ways. But in other ways, what we found also fortified our previous impressions that we should not have felt so bad over "mere" miscarriages. Miscarriage as a loss was merely touched on in some books. Others clumped miscarriage with the loss of full-term babies. Stillbirth* was referred to as the "death of a baby." Miscarriage, on the other hand, was referred to as the "loss of a dream." What did that say about our babies? Were they hallucinations? We felt that our babies and our losses were not valid and our grief was not justified next to babies and losses that were verifiable as "real." Suggestions for healing, such as holding our babies and obtaining footprints and photographs, were not options we would ever have. Our needs went unattended; the nuances of our invisible tragedy went quietly unrecognized. Some books emphasized diet, nutrition, and exercise. But in the face of the death of our babies, we were looking for a meaning in living.

*You can refer to a glossary in the back of this book for definitions of this and other medical terms used throughout the book.

The two of us met later that year and forged a friendship. With caution and growing trust, we risked exposing to each other the pages of our private journals. What we discovered amazed us. Some of the words and expressions on our pages were identical. Marie asked, "Now do you know you're not crazy?" Shelly answered, "No, now I know we're *both* crazy!"

We wondered if other women also experienced deep grief over their miscarriages. And if they did, was deep grief over miscarriage rare, commonplace, or something in between? We knew that *if* other women felt as we did, there was a great need for the education of society on the emotional impact of miscarriage. Someone needed to delve into the secret places in the hearts and minds of these women and make it known that they are suffering and in need of care.

Our self-doubt, our suspicion that other women experienced miscarriage as a profound loss, and our care about their presumed suffering placed us on the road to this book. We embarked on a descriptive study of the emotional impact of miscarriage (pregnancy loss before 20 weeks gestation).

GATHERING THE DATA

With the goal of eliciting the in-depth emotional experience of women from the time of their miscarriages to the present, we conducted interviews with 100 women ranging in age from 20 to 62 years whose miscarriages occurred 9 days to 39 years prior to their interviews. The miscarriages ranged from 4 weeks to 20 weeks (4½ months) gestation and included blighted ova, ectopic (or "tubal") pregnancies, miscarriages that occurred when women were not yet aware that they had even been pregnant, when one twin survivied, when elective abortion already had been scheduled, and others.

There was a wide range in the study group in terms of cultural, religious, and educational background, and socioeconomic status, age, and race.

About half the women came to us from word-of-mouth referrals. Whereas there is a range in women's emotional responses to miscarriage, these self-referred women who stepped forward to participate in a study on the emotional experience of miscarriage may have been more aware of their grief than the general population of women who have miscarried and/or may have been from the end of the spectrum in which grief was more profound. Also, the fact that they wanted to talk about their losses suggests the possibilities of insufficient attention received at the time of their losses or afterward, that they wanted to help other women, or both.

The same applies to another approximated quarter of the women who were referred to the study by support groups for pregnancy loss in San Diego and Los Angeles. Also, perhaps the women referred by support groups were more aware of their need for social support or of the option of social support than the general population of women who have miscarried. These can be seen as limitations of the study.

Another quarter of those interviewed were women we knew directly or indirectly and whom we asked to participate. In all but a couple of these cases, their miscarriages had occurred prior to our knowing them and had not been discussed with us prior to their interviews, so we had no inkling how they would respond to the questions. This was of particular interest to us in that we had known them over a period of time only in social or career contexts. It is unclear what effect, if any, this method of acquiring participants may have had on our findings.

Although each woman was told that interviews would take approximately an hour and would involve personal and probing questions, we found women highly motivated to participate. Many expressed a desire to be interviewed not only to help other women but also to contribute to a book that they themselves would find helpful.

The interviews averaged 80 minutes and consisted of 85 questions soliciting the range of each woman's feelings about her miscarriage. Because some women had experienced multiple miscarriages, some questions solicited separate responses for each of their miscarriages. Most questions required anecdotal as opposed to single-word responses (e.g., "What happened in you spiritually in the time to follow?"). Descriptions or explanations were requested following positive responses to yes/no questions (e.g., "Did your sex drive change following the loss? *If so, how?*").

All the interviews were tape recorded as well as transcribed by hand at the time of the conversations. Some of the interviews were conducted in person and some by telephone. The latter method had the advantage of efficiency and provided women maximum privacy and anonymity. Actually, we found it both significant and fascinating that many women who granted their interviews over the telephone mentioned that they were in their beds with their bedroom doors closed as we spoke—some with a cup of coffee in hand—well reflecting the incredible intimacy associated with discussing the matter of their miscarriages with another woman who had had a miscarriage, who wanted to listen, and who probably would be accepting of their feelings.

FINDINGS

Over the course of the interviews, we realized that although each woman was unique, the women were also, in many ways, echoes of one another. Prevalent among them were expressions of profound grief over what many experienced as the death of their babies.

We also found in the women's stories that their grief was compounded with overwhelming feelings of loneliness, confusion, and anxiety. Their struggle in grieving and their difficulty in healing this special kind of loss were extraordinary. There were two underlying sources of the problem.

The first source was intrinsic and fundamental to the nature of miscarriage itself. The women's babies died without their or anyone's ever having had an opportunity to experience the babies directly through sight, sound, smell, or touch, as the real, whole, and unrepeatable human beings they were. It is important that, without a trace of firsthand, tangible experience of who their children uniquely were, miscarriage was and continues to be an exceedingly difficult loss for mothers and others to validate. Quite logically, miscarriage is commonly experienced as insignificant, or even as a nonloss, because we do not literally "experience" miscarried babies. In response, the feelings of loss run an increased risk of going underground. The "perpetrator" is the nebulous, hazy nature of miscarriage itself. Miscarriage is an event tailor-made for minimizing, by *all* of us—society in general and women who miscarry.

The second source of the problem was society's pervasive lack of awareness about the emotional impact of miscarriage. Communities were most often unaware that bereavement usually follows miscarriage and did not offer the needed support. The women's miscarriages were treated as small disappointments or as nonlosses.

The women did not realize that their secret and seemingly bizarre thoughts and feelings were not only normal but actually shared among them. They felt painfully alone as well as confused and frightened about what was happening in and around them.

OUR VISION

We were struck by the needlessness of this. We knew that if information about the emotional impact of miscarriage was disseminated into society, the exacerbation of women's grief would be soothed and sometimes even prevented.

Our vision was born: to free mothers to grieve the death of their miscarried children in a more enlightened and compassionate world.

This book is an outgrowth of our own miscarriages, our research, and our vision. It is written for and about you if you have ever felt a sense of loss over miscarriage. Our fervent desire is to reach you who are grieving, you who suspect you may need to grieve, you who are looking for permission to grieve, and you who have been without ally. We want this book to be an affirmation of your feelings and a confirmation of your right to those feelings.

THINGS TO KNOW

Although this book is primarily written for you, it is also for the families, friends, and professionals who care for you—both those who care about your hurt and those who personally feel the hurt with you.* Appendix A ("Taking Care") contains specific ideas for you, and for those around you, about how to get through this experience of loss.

Through much of the book we speak as researchers, yet sometimes we speak as women once personally shattered by miscarriage. We speak to you from both the intellect and the heart.

For the sake of simplicity, when we relay personal anecdotes we merge ourselves into a unified "I" regardless of which author is relaying the story. In a few instances, our anecdotes involve both authors. In these, we refer to ourselves as Shelly and Marie.

In several chapters (4, 6, 7, 9, 10, 12, 14, 15, and 16), we step back and give voice to the 100 women interviewed and allow them to speak directly to you. We provide their answers without analysis, speculation, or hypotheses.

The responses in these chapters reflect what the women recognized in themselves, not our interpretations of what they said. For example, when a woman expressed what felt to us like anger in a part of her interview but told us that she did not *feel* angry when she was specifically questioned if she felt anger, we recorded her response to that question, not our interpretation of her response.

We categorized responses to each question to give you a feel for the types of answers given. The sequencing of these categories does not indicate the prevalence of particular types of answers. In addition, some categories contain more quotes than others, not necessarily because responses

*We suggest that *fathers* read this chapter; Chapters 2, 12, and 13; and Appendix A. For *families and friends* we recommend this chapter; Chapters 2, 15, and 23; and Appendix A. *Medical and mental health professionals* are directed to this chapter; Chapters 2 and 16; and Appendix A.

in those categories were more prevalent than in categories with fewer quotes, but because those categories contained a greater array of descriptive responses. Actual statistics can be found in Appendix C. Some topics arose in the interviews without any prompting. We identify these by saying, "women spontaneously talked about ——."

Some of you may feel better reading text that objectively tells about the women's experiences and is one step removed, whereas others may prefer to read the women's actual words. This book is written in three styles: complete personal stories, text interwoven with clusters of quotes on specific subjects, and straight text. From these you can pick and choose according to what will comfort you most. Portions of the book may be helpful now, and portions may be helpful at another time down the road.

THE SECRET

Many mothers we interviewed had never talked about their feelings about their losses, even immediately following their miscarriages, often because they did not want to be critically viewed as "silly" or "dwelling on it." Yet when provided the safety to talk, they were eager to do so. So, in many instances, we were the first and only people these women had spoken with about their miscarriages and the feelings they harbored about them.

It is our feeling that they revealed so much of themselves because they were starving for the opportunity to do so. They also seemed to feel a sense of safety with two researchers who had "heard it all" and were obviously concerned about the emotional impact of miscarriage by virtue of the fact that we chose to conduct this kind of research. They seemed to feel safe knowing that we would maintain their anonymity and that they probably would not encounter us again. As one woman stated:

> *I can talk about that with you. I haven't said it to anyone else because most people don't see it that way. I had this tiny little boy who was ours and he died.*

In many cases it was not evident from individual answers whether the women's losses had occurred days or decades prior to their interviews because most women did not have personal or societal permission to grieve, and had not evolved through the process of grieving to a sense of healing. On one hand, women who said they felt embarrassed to talk about their miscarriages to friends and families because their losses had occurred "so long ago" were commonly talking about losses that had occurred as recently as 10 weeks earlier. On the other hand, some women who talked about the pain of seeing a pregnant woman walking down the street had miscarried 10 or more years earlier!

The women also vividly remembered and re-experienced the details and emotions of their miscarriages years and even decades after their losses. Regardless of the time that had passed since their miscarriages, many of the interviews were tearful and filled with strong emotions:

> *My miscarriage was 21 years ago. Yet I have absolute recall of the devastation and the sadness.*

We want you to know that your experience is shared by countless others. The scores of quotes throughout this book are from the 100 women in our study. All these unidentified quotes have been taken directly from their interviews. (Names and identifying information have been changed to respect their privacy.) It is our hope that you find yourself within the pages of this book and that you feel you are in the company of other women who understand you and hold you in their hearts.

One in every four women has had a miscarriage. Among them may be your friend, your neighbor, your coworker, your sister-in-law, your doctor, or the cashier at your grocery store. They are women you see and talk with every day.

Many of them have not let on that they felt a sense of loss over their miscarriages or even that they had miscarriages. They keep their feelings about their losses tucked inside. They live their lives and go about their daily work and play, and they carry their secret within:

> *I would smile for the outside world to see. But inside, I was dying.*

GRIEVING, GROWING, AND HEALING

At the foundation of our philosophy is the belief that we, as individuals, naturally seek to flourish and do so when embraced in a nurturing world—a world that allows us to have and express our feelings.

We extend an invitation to you to explore without judgment and with acceptance the diverse emotions you feel. Sometimes we need to respect our need to hold together, and sometimes we need to respect our need to fall apart. Here it is okay to grieve or not, to be silent or to scream, to discuss, cry, pray, or rage.

Of course everybody who feels grief does not need to fall down and sob, have a funeral, and write poetry! Yet, *if* a sense of conflict or confusion, a weight or a depression, exists within our hearts, then that fog may dissipate or that weight may lift as we acknowledge that we carried babies, that our babies died, that we may have some feelings of loss, and as we express any feelings of loss that may be there.

Some women may not feel grief over their miscarriages. We are not suggesting to them that they have grief buried inside. We distinguish this from what we address in this book: expressed grief and inhibited grief.

Although the women in our study felt grief, and while we discuss the usefulness of expressing and working through grief, we realize the potential for inverting the overall problem we have described. Women who don't or didn't grieve their miscarriages may begin to feel guilty, abnormal, or alone. We are not implying that to grieve is smarter, better, more sensitive or aware, or in vogue. Whether we feel our miscarriages are deaths or blessings, both, or something else altogether, our feelings are okay.

Our feelings—whatever they may be—are messages of wisdom from within, calling to us. They are telling us what we need to do to feel better. When we feel sad, we need to say so, cry, sigh, or receive a hug, for instance. When we feel angry, we need to vent our anger or alter the situation about which we feel angry. When we feel lonely, we need to reach out and connect. Our feelings lay out a path for us that, when followed, naturally and efficiently leads us to feeling better eventually. When we let our emotions guide the way, they become the stepping-stones to healing.

In the process of bringing our feelings to the surface and releasing them, the feeling of depression or the "emotional overcast" lifts. Through expressing our emotions, something from within is awakened, and an inner vitality is restored.

In contrast, we sometimes try to brush our losses aside with pat phrases like "It'll all work out" or "I guess it was for the best." While it *may* all work out or it possibly may *be* for the best, the trouble is, if we say those things and we don't genuinely feel at peace or free inside, we may need to go back and work through our feelings about our miscarriages so they don't live on inside and keep hold of us.

All our lives, we receive powerful messages to be happy. Yet sometimes we have to hurt more before we can hurt less. Sometimes the way to feel good is to take the time and the opportunity to feel bad. There is no shortcut around grief. Fritz Perls, the father of Gestalt therapy, said that the only way out of painful feelings is through them. As Ann Kaiser Stearns wrote in *Living Through Personal Crisis,* "Although we will not always believe that our lives are permanently ruined, we do need the freedom to feel our feelings of ruin fully."

This book contains expressions of no-holds-barred grief, the human response to loss. You may experience many feelings in response to some of the text, including pain and sorrow, compassion and hope. We naturally respond to emotion with emotion.

Before completion of our book, we asked some women who had had miscarriages to read drafts of the manuscript. One woman's husband looked on as she cried her way through the book. "Why are you *doing* this to yourself?" he asked in frustration. His question was a good one. Why write or read such a sad book?

Although doing so may seem senseless or self-torturing, there *is* sense in our gravitation toward sad things. Reading a book about pain and grief does not create new pain and grief in us. Rather, it may evoke in us an awareness and expression of grief that is already there. We may identify with such books or find pieces of ourselves in them. They are useful as they put us in touch with our own pain (whether or not we are consciously focused on it). The sad elements in them parallel and tap the pain deep inside all of us, and our own pain is accessed. They mirror the grief in us all, and provide an avenue for releasing our grief. They bring us to tears and help us get our sadness out. That crying is healing.

In the long run, squelching grief is more painful than facing grief. "Griefwork" means thinking about our losses, feeling them, expressing them in some way, crying over them, learning about them, or growing because of them—all increments in the healing process. Grieving is accomplished piece by piece and over time, at safe times and places, and sometimes with compassionate others. Healing takes time. It does not take forever.

Sometimes during bereavement, we see only darkness ahead. That darkness becomes bearable when we realize that the story does not end here. This is a book filled not only with death, but with life. It is about people in motion: struggling, reaching, and working. The stories of the women in this book are far from over. They are unfolding, growing, and emerging.

It is our hope that this book will be a key for moving beyond your own confusion and self-doubt, through your own process of grief and unfolding, and toward the place of peace within you.

CHAPTER TWO

The Mother Who Has Miscarried

We want you to see your complex experience outlined, including the obstacles that may complicate and interfere with the healing and resolution of your grief. We want you to discover that your feelings make sense and are not only normal but also typical reactions to the actual happenings within and around you. And we want you to understand why you feel as you do and that circumstances warrant your emotions.

While each woman we interviewed expressed a unique degree and style of grief, specific themes and problems were echoed again and again among them. This chapter is a gathering of these recurring problems and themes faced by so many of them. Common facets of the miscarriage experience are described in this chapter in the form of a composite woman.

A woman who miscarries is emotionally set up by multiple events that have an accumulative, or stacking, effect. The experiences surrounding her miscarriage intertwine like the threads of a web in which she often becomes caught. Too many traumas suffered in succession result in the breakdown of her coping mechanisms and an obstructed emotional future. The relationship between these occurrences and feelings is tangled. (For instance, event A leads to feelings B and D, event C leads to feelings B and G, and feeling G sets up event C.) The following are some of the parts and pieces of a woman's experience that interweave and form the web.

A woman gets the message all her life that babies in the early stages of pregnancy are perhaps not really babies yet. They are not even "fetuses." They are "embryos." Certainly, the loss of a full-term baby is acknowledged as a more substantial loss than the loss of an embryo. One is viewed as a real baby; the other is not. A woman is told from early on that miscarriage is "no big deal" in a culture that discards and incinerates miscarried babies. When her miscarriage occurs, the reality of her baby and the legitimacy of her loss and her grief are already invalidated by her prior learning.

On a personal level, once pregnant, the mother feels quite different. Research on maternal attachment has indicated that bonding often begins well before conception. We start to bond with our future children when we begin even thinking of ourselves as mothers, and that feeling of attachment to our future children grows and develops in stages throughout our lives (for instance, when marrying, planning for children, or trying to conceive). So by the time a woman knows she is pregnant, she may already be deeply emotionally linked with her baby. She maintains constant awareness of her baby when making decisions throughout each day about what she will eat, what she might take for a headache, and how she will put on her seat belt. In everything she does, she holds her baby in her heart and in her mind. To her, the being she carries inside of her is already her very *real and whole* baby, and powerful maternal love is long under way:

> *I wrote to my baby, "I wanted so badly to love and nurture you, to see your smile, to let you grasp my finger with your perfect little hands. I wanted to hug and hold you, to let you feed from my breast, to raise you in a way that you would know you were deeply loved. I had all this love prepared for you, and now it has nowhere to go. It's turned instead into a deep and lonely ache."*

When a mother miscarries, she is hit with full-blown, human grief. She feels the profound loss of her real and whole baby, for whom she aches with longing and loneliness:

> *It was the most devastating experience ever in my whole life. All the slats were knocked out from under me. I lost my faith. That baby was real for me even though he did not make it. I felt profound grief. I'd set out for the grocery store and end up not knowing where I was. Once I got there, I'd sob in the corner.*

> *Having a miscarriage is not "like" anything! It is the death of your child!*

> *This was as difficult as losing my father. That was surprising to me. Lots of people think that it's not that important.*

A woman who is pregnant exists in a deep and intimate state of symbiosis with the baby in her womb. They are fused. Her baby is, quite literally, a part of her mentally, physically, and emotionally. This point is crucial toward understanding a woman who miscarries.

A woman's experience of her baby moving within her womb marks the origin of a very long process of separating their identities. When the mother first becomes aware of her baby moving within her, she begins the process of realizing that her baby is a separate human being. Miscarriage usually occurs before 12 weeks. Since the average woman does not consciously feel movement before 16 to 20 weeks, miscarriage nearly always occurs before the lengthy emotional separation process has even begun. So the woman experiences the death of her own flesh and blood, a part of her own self. This phenomenon, which feels bizarre to her, is impossible for many to understand, isolating her further:

That baby had been a part of me. We were still a package. When it was taken from me at the D&C, I felt that I was taken with it.

Her physical experience of miscarriage is usually bloody and often necessitates a D&C. She experiences it as jarring, traumatic, and scary. She undergoes medical procedures that, to her, feel invasive, humiliating, and painful:

I felt like I had been vandalized, like someone had broken in and ransacked me. It's like having something ripped from you. When it's done by D&C, it feels brutal and violent, like a vacuum cleaner sucking the life out of you. A very special, loved part of my own body was torn out of me.

I felt exposed. It's so humiliating. Parts of your body are coming out of you.

Standard medical terminology feels confusing to her and sometimes in her mind translates into her failure: *miscarried* as in "mis-carried" or "carried wrong", *missed abortion* as in "failed to expel", *incompetent cervix* as in "inept body part", and *blighted ovum* as in "impeded egg" (by her body):

I hate that term "miscarriage." It's like a football that's being tossed to you and you don't quite catch it.

Fetus? Tissue? What is tissue? I didn't know what was tissue—or what was happening!

Typically when someone dies, there is a known cause of death. But in the event of a miscarriage, a woman usually has no such answers. She is often told that the miscarriage occurred because of "fetal abnormality." Yet, chromosomal abnormalities account for only about half of all miscarriages.* She will never know how or why her baby died. She is left hanging with the unanswerable. How does she resolve the reason and meaning of a death without ever understanding how or why it occurred?

Guilt over the death of a loved one is a normal grief phenomenon. In miscarriage, the death actually occurs within the mother's body, so she turns to herself as the only available cause of the death. She worries that she did something wrong that resulted in the death of her baby, and she goes over every detail of her pregnancy in search of her fatal error:

*Margaret W. Thompson, Ph.D., Roderick R. McInnes, M.D., Ph.D., and Huntington F. Willard, Ph.D., *Genetics in Medicine* (Philadelphia: W. B. Saunders Co., 1991).

Was it the one aspirin I took, when I lifted groceries once, the one time I stepped on a ladder and slid down one rung? Did I turn over too many times in bed?

Maybe I was under too much stress.

At the same time, she feels a sense of betrayal by her body. She trusted it to house and nurture her child. She feels that it failed to protect and keep her own baby:

My husband was putting babies inside me and my body was destroying them.

I wanted to miscarry naturally but I couldn't even do that. The D&C felt like the final failure.

Her sense of trust is broken in another way. On some level, she expects someday to bury her parents. And she expects someday to be buried by her children. But it is never her expectation that she will bury her children. It feels so shocking, so backward, and so very, very wrong. When her life's plan is abruptly altered, her security is shattered. She asks herself the frightening question, "My God, if *this* could happen, what *else* could happen?!" She fears for what is next, for the further loss of herself or of her loved ones. She feels a new vulnerability to anything that might come along:

I became terrified my two-year-old was going to die. Somebody would take her. I would check her breathing every 20 minutes at night. I wouldn't leave the heat on for fear it would blow up. I knew it was not rational, but I would hug her 'til she cried.

I was sure I had a brain tumor, AIDS, or some disease as long as it was fatal. I kept going to the doctor for tests and I was sure he was missing something.

To complicate matters further, she had no evidence of the reality of her baby—a kick, a visibly pregnant belly, knowledge of the sex or identity of her baby, or a corpse to show for her loss. She cannot validate that there ever was a baby at all. She can't even prove it to herself. She has no concrete memories and no acknowledgment of loss. But she continues to feel loss. So she secretly wonders if she has gone crazy:

I didn't want to wash my panties of the blood from the loss.

I don't want this interview to end. Talking about it makes me know it really was real. I really did *go through this!*

Maybe this really didn't happen.

This lack of evidence of any baby aids her denial of the loss as well as her confusion. The baby is nebulous. The loss is nebulous. Her ability to grieve, which has been defined as the slow realization of loss, is seriously impaired. She has first to validate that there was a baby before she can mourn and then say good-bye to him or her. It's difficult to grieve what is no more visible than air:

I was grieving this abstract thing. I had nothing to grieve, so how could I grieve? How could I feel bad about something there was no proof ever existed?

She can't see, feel, or describe her baby. She wonders, "Who was he? I never met my baby!" She must live with the loss of ever meeting face to face or knowing her own child:

Those children are my children and I'll never see them take their first step, grow up, or see who they'd have been.

Would he have had hair? Would he have looked like the others? You created life and it's gone forever and you never got to see it or experience it. I wanted him to know me. I wanted to connect with him and for the baby to know that I loved him.

She faces another loss as well. Leave-taking rituals for grieving loved ones, such as memorial services and formal burials, are crucial to healing. They afford a needed and formal tribute to the deceased. Those who loved that person may rest assured that a grave marker will stand in honor of their loved one forever. This woman experiences quite the opposite. In the event of a miscarriage, there is no burial or memorial service, and the mother lives on with no mementos of a life at all. It is the mother herself who must stand as the marker. Without opportunity for closure, she cannot begin the process of resolving her loss. In fact, her child is incinerated and unspeakably dishonored:

I wanted to bury the babies. I felt they weren't safe and cared for. They were sort of just "out there." I had a dream that resolved where they are. There is a beautiful, old cemetery near where we vacation. In the dream, they were buried in it. My inner life resolved where they are. Once I finally had that dream, I felt much more at peace. That's where they are [softly reassuring herself]. I go to and walk around that cemetery. My husband doesn't know. This is so private for me.

Miscarriage most often occurs before the father has had any firsthand, tangible experience of his baby. Even an ultrasound is one step removed. Seeing one's baby on an ultrasound screen is quite different from feeling the physiological changes of pregnancy within oneself or from sensing the presence of a son or daughter in one's own body. Therefore, the baby often isn't yet experienced as very real by the father. Although he may feel a sense of loss, he usually does not feel the loss as the death of his real baby in the same way that the mother does, because each had an entirely different experience of their baby.

The mother doesn't understand why the father doesn't share the same depth of grief, nor does he understand why she feels as she does. She feels hurt, thinking that, if he loved and valued their baby, he too would be devastated by their baby's death. She wonders, "Didn't our baby mean anything to him?" In addition, our society overwhelmingly urges the suppression of men's feelings especially, which feeds the problem and widens the gap between them. Their relationship is threatened, and serious problems frequently develop within it:

I felt abandoned by him in my hour of need.

My husband called me repeatedly and asked, "Why did you abandon me?"

In order for me to feel better, I needed to talk about it. In order for him to feel better, he needed to not hear it.

When a woman has a miscarriage, her sense of loss is exacerbated by the innocent blunders of an unaware medical community, family, friends, and even strangers. Without information about what women normally feel inside when they have miscarriages, people in her life inadvertently bring about greater suffering for her through their well-meaning words and actions.

Whereas she feels a deep and painful loss of her baby and of herself, others around her usually do not think of her loss as legitimate. Friends and family members are uncomfortable to hear her talk about her miscarriage as a real death. It radically conflicts with their perception of miscarriage. They are sure she is making a mountain out of a molehill, and they try to smooth it over with statements that minimize, to "snap her back to reality." She is told that her miscarriage was a good thing, that she is lucky it happened when it did, and that there was probably something wrong with her baby. She may even be told how much fun she can now have trying to get pregnant again. They belittle her loss, or negate it as even being a loss all, and then turn away:

What else would I like people to do? Not act like it was a bowel movement! Like you're supposed to flush the toilet and wash your hands and walk away. You're not supposed to be emotional. They'd be much more sympathetic if you told them you had run over your cat.

With the disparity between the depth of what she feels, and others' indications to her that she has simply experienced a little disappointment, she feels an abyss between herself and those she felt supported by and close to just yesterday. Everyone wanted to share her joy when she was pregnant, and then . . . silence. They all went home. She feels abandoned, and, ironically, she feels a loss of those she loves. Her loneliness is greater than ever:

> *The loneliness was cellular, in every cell of me. The grief happened in me. No one else understood. I felt like an alien.*
>
> *I was totally alone on the planet.*

Interestingly, the fact that there is a range in emotional responses to miscarriage presents a problem for the mother. Because some women may not grieve after miscarriage, she can't turn to another woman who has miscarried and safely know that she will be understood and that her experience is shared. In contrast, if her baby had been stillborn, she could safely turn to another mother who had had a stillborn and be certain of many similarities in their thoughts and feelings. But she may express some of her feelings to another woman who has miscarried who may respond, "I don't feel that at *all,*" echoing everybody else in her life. So she swallows and concludes, "God, it must be me! I've gone crazy!"

> *When my friend was nonchalant about her miscarriage, I thought, "Then I'm obviously psycho."*

In general, people in our society don't say things like "I feel so grief-stricken and lonely." It does not feel safe. We don't often hear about deeply personal or painful things, especially what it feels like to have a miscarriage. Mothers grieving miscarriage are particularly frightened to expose their feelings, so they don't. Without documented and available information on normal and actual emotional reaction to miscarriage, the woman who has miscarried is literally stunned by her feelings. They seem bizarre to her, and she is frightened by them. She wonders in fear, "What is happening in me?!" She feels a tremendous loss of confidence in her perception of what is real, a conviction that something is wrong with her, and she suffers a severe loss of self-worth:

> *When I was at my lowest, I felt frightened I'd never come back again. It was so unknown.*
>
> *I felt lost, ashamed, embarrassed. I failed. I am broken.*

Starving for acknowledgment, support, and care, the woman grieving miscarriage believes that she is alone in her feelings. She concludes, "I am the only person in the whole world who feels this":

> *I felt so isolated and alone and not understanding what was going on or how to express what was happening and how I was feeling. It was so difficult to express how I was feeling. I lost my voice. I wasn't sick. I just lost my voice.*

With no one to take her seriously or offer her compassion, she has no outlet. She has no one with whom to safely express her feelings of grief. It stays bottled inside her, where it circles and festers and cannot heal. She will eventually and consciously go on about the business of living. She will tell the grocery clerk who inquires how she is doing, that she is "fine." But behind her veil she is still injured, and she bleeds in secret:

> *I think it's more tragic now because of my age. One is missing. There is a finality. It's truly over and done.* [20 years after]

> *It was half my life ago and it still hurts. It's not going away.* [19 years after]

> *It's a lifelong loss, something you think about through your whole life. You see a child that age and you think about it. You never get over it.* [15 years after]

Caught in the middle of so many simultaneous insults added to injury, she sinks into despair:

> *I could no longer bear to listen to music which was once very important in my life. I became limp. I no longer had the energy nor the mental capacity to even feel, dream, or think of a child in my life. It was a very, very sad time, the saddest I've ever known.*

> *I felt I was falling into a black hole. There was no way out. I still feel a dark cloud over me. I will never be as happy.*

Through the years of her life, the mother who has miscarried remains the lone guardian of her baby's memory, which she retains in astonishing detail. She, herself, stands in permanent commemoration of the life of her dead child. She carries her sorrow within her, along with a need to hold on to that sorrow, as the sole remnants of her baby's existence. If she lets go, her baby will have gone unnoticed, lost, and forever forgotten:

> *I think about it a lot still. It's still a loss. It's still not forgotten.* [11 years after]

> [At the end of the interview] *I feel drained and sad. But it's good that those babies haven't been forgotten. There's a special place in my heart for them, like I'm communicating with them. Their spirit is here with me. I'm able to tell those babies, "I haven't forgotten you."* [18 and 20 years after]

THE WEB

Events . . . **Can lead to . . .** **Feelings**

End of dream
Death of baby
Death of part of self
Traumatic expulsion
Medical terms = failure
Lack of answers why
Lack of information about grief
No leavetaking rituals
Loss of control
No evidence of baby
Father's incongruous grieving
Others belittle loss
Feelings don't match other women's
Need to guard memory
Grouped with other losses
Too many traumas at once

Anger
Guilt
Loneliness
Humiliation
Loss of self-worth
Betrayal
Shattered security
Unjustified
Crazy
Despair
Fear
Injured/hurt
Confusion
Frustration
Sorrow
Shock/denial

CHAPTER THREE

Shelly's Story

It has been over three years since my miscarriage. I have lived with it, talked about it, written about it, and volunteered with an organization which helps women who have experienced it. Marie and I have interviewed a hundred women who have had miscarriages and talked to countless more about their experiences. I thought I would be desensitized by now. But as I reread my journal from the time I found out I was pregnant to the present, I could not read without a film of tears and an ache in my chest. My shoulders felt so heavy and burdened with the responsibility of sharing the story of my loss so that others may find support and solace.

In thinking back about my emotional response to my miscarriage, I realize that the depth of my despair following my miscarriage was in direct contrast to the height of my joy over being pregnant.

For me, pregnancy was all-encompassing. Before I found out I was pregnant and even while I was trying to get pregnant, I talked to my future child, aloud or in my mind. Once I knew I was pregnant, I visualized and imagined my baby in my arms or nursing at my breasts. In my mind, I saw my baby's features and heard my baby's cries. My mind and my body were no longer my own. I shared them with the tiny baby growing inside me. I ate for the baby. I exercised for the baby. I rested for the baby. All my senses were acute. Smells and tastes were exaggerated. Sights and emotions screamed where they once whispered. To me, pregnancy meant life intensified.

When I found out I was pregnant in August of 1987, I was ecstatic. It was my first child with my husband, Gary. I remember going to my general practice physician for the pregnancy test. I sat in a waiting room filled with sick people who had colds and flus, and I remember thinking that I didn't belong with them. I was not there for illness. I was there for life.

After what seemed like an interminable amount of time, the nurse took my specimen and disappeared into the back office. I spend the next 15 minutes pacing the waiting room floor while people stared at me. When she returned, the nurse told me that the test was positive. In fact, she said it was the strongest positive result she had ever seen. I started crying and shaking. I was happy, nervous, and scared and I was finding it hard to believe. I made her show me the paper with the test results.

I hadn't told Gary about the doctor's appointment so I could surprise him with the news. He was so happy when I told him. I have a daughter, Lorien, from a previous marriage and her father and I share joint custody, an arrangement that is painful for me. I feel a great loss every other week when I have to give her up. So when I got pregnant, I thought, "No one is going to take this child away from me." This was going to be a baby I could be with and nurture all the time and not have to give up every other week. This child I would not have to lose.

Those first weeks of being pregnant were both exciting and nerve-wracking. I had a book which showed pictures of fetuses at various stages of development. I looked at those pictures every night before I went to sleep. I knew what our baby looked like at each stage of development and I felt she was a girl. I could feel her beside me on the bed.

But because I did not experience the morning sickness and fatigue commonly associated with pregnancy, my journal entries were laced with doubts and worries:

4 weeks—It's still hard to believe I'm pregnant. I remember feeling the same way when I first found I was pregnant with Lorien. Just like with my pregnancy with her, before I went to my obstetrician for an examination and confirmation that the internal changes of pregnancy were taking place, all I had to go on was the written report on a chemical test I didn't even see performed. I don't have any symptoms. My breasts feel a little tender and seem a little fuller. But other than that, I'd never know I am pregnant. This is a hard time. I want to be big and to see and feel my baby kick. That was my favorite part of my pregnancy with Lorien—feeling her move inside my body. No wonder mothers feel so close to their babies so immediately. The baby is so close (literally next to my heart) for so long, and is literally a part of me. I so very much enjoyed being pregnant with Lorien. I hope this pregnancy goes like that one.

5 weeks—I want this baby so much. I think about her constantly. I talk to my baby aloud and in my head. But it's hard. I still check to see if I got my period when I go to the bathroom. I wish it were time for the appointment with my obstetrician. It's silly but I need lots of small confirmations that it is real. My mind tells me to trust God. That makes me feel better, more at peace. My baby is a fighter, a survivor, perfect, complete and whole. Thank you God. I love you little one.

6 weeks—Although I am tired, I do not yet have the overwhelming fatigue I had during the first three months of my pregnancy with Lorien. I no longer fear miscarriage. And I really believe it is real. I no longer check every time I go to the bathroom. Now I take care of myself and wait for all the wonderful miraculous happenings of pregnancy—hearing the heartbeat for the first time, feeling movement, seeing and feeling a kick. I love you little one.

10 weeks—I finally saw my obstetrician for the first time yesterday. I love this baby. I anxiously await my baby's first felt movement. Even thinking

about hearing the heartbeat soon brings tears of joy to my eyes. I pray my baby is normal, healthy, and happy.

Gary has been so sweet. It must seem unreal for him. Last weekend he impulsively bought me a gorgeous amethyst ring. When I thanked him, he said, "Thank you for the baby."

Sometimes he asks how big the baby is or what the baby looks like at this stage (he knows how I gaze at the book), and sometimes he asks if I am really pregnant. I think it must be hard for him. When I try to reassure him, he asks, "How do you know you're really pregnant?" And all I can say is, "You don't really 'know' until you feel the baby moving. Until then, it's all a gigantic act of faith." I love you little one.

At 14 weeks, Gary went with me to my obstetrician's office so we could both hear the heartbeat for the first time. I remember lying on the examining table. The doctor was joking, we were all laughing, and Gary was kidding around like he always does. Somewhere in the middle of it all, I realized that the doctor quit joking. He kept moving the amplifier around on my belly trying to find a heartbeat but he wasn't finding one. At some point everybody got really quiet, and I got really scared. He tried to reassure us that everything was fine and even made us schedule the next routine appointment with him. But he also sent us to get an ultrasound to check things out.

We couldn't get an appointment for the ultrasound for three hours. Part of me was nervous. But I never thought the baby might be dead. I never ever ever ever thought that in my wildest dreams. Part of me thought something was wrong with the baby. I remember calling a friend of mine at work and asking her to pray. But I remember also being excited during those three hours because I was going to see the baby.

The ultrasound technician had the monitor facing me so I could watch, and as he kept trying to find the baby, all I saw on the screen was blackness. All we saw was a black hole, which was my uterus. There were little scraps of something in there but that's all. No baby. I asked him what that meant. I thought maybe the baby was too little to see. He said that either I had miscalculated when I conceived (which I knew I hadn't) or—I remember him saying—"there was no pregnancy." My world crashed down around me. My first words after that to Gary were, "This is not all in my head."

They sent us back to my doctor who started using terms like "missed abortion" and that's when I realized what was happening. It was so hard to believe. I could see and hear the words as if they were shrieking to me, as if they were all lit up in front of me on a huge marquee. I couldn't utter the words myself. If I did, everything in my world would shatter all around me and I would be crushed.

I thought I was going crazy. I thought I had caused it even though I knew that I had been so careful. I thought I was being punished because of what I had said when I got pregnant about no one taking this baby from me. It was like the universe was shouting back to me, "Oh Yeah!?!"

A D&C was scheduled for two days later. Those two days were so hard. I didn't want them to do it. I found myself crossing my arms over my belly as if to protect the baby while in my head I knew that the baby was gone. I woke up early the day before the D&C and played music loudly over and over again while I sobbed. I wore headphones so I wouldn't wake Gary or my visiting in-laws. I didn't realize until later that I hadn't turned off the speakers, so everyone in my house had had to listen to that loud and repetitive music for almost three hours.

On the day of the D&C, the doctor asked if I had any questions. I had only one: "What did I do to cause this?" He said, "I already told you that you didn't do anything. I already told you that this was not your fault." All I could say was, "I don't believe you," and I started crying. From that point, I have no memory of the D&C except being on the table and getting the anesthesia and feeling like I was falling.

Four days later, I drove to my favorite meditation spot at the beach. I wanted to be alone, to hear the ocean pounding at the cove. I felt a need to communicate or to feel a connection in some way with my baby. I wrote my baby a series of three letters there:

Dear Little One, I love you. I miss you. I was going to say I miss having you inside my body but I guess I really should say I miss thinking you were in my body since you weren't really there very long. I'm so sorry I won't have you to hold in my arms in April. When you're ready, find yourself a fine strong body and a beautiful mind and come to us. My body will be ready to carry you and nurture you and hold you next to my heart. And we'll all be ready to love you and teach you and learn from you. You're going to love your sister Lorien. She's waiting rather impatiently for you. She's been around in this world before, and she'll be a good guide and a loving teacher for you. And your Daddy . . . you've chosen such a special man for a father. He has so much love to give. He has many gifts to give you including a love and talent for speaking to the world through his music. I'm convinced he has already communicated with you that way. So prepare yourself my love. Touch God and gather strength and health and wisdom, and come back to us. I love you.

Dear Little One, I'm very confused. I don't know whether to want you or to let you go. Should I be saying I'm waiting for you to come back to me or should I be saying good-bye? Other people tell me it's better that I'm not having you because something was wrong with you. But I want children so much. Why has this happened? What is my lesson? I feel like I am a good mother to Lorien. And I feel it would be good for her to have siblings. And I feel it would be a blessing for Gary to have his own children. What is my lesson to be learned from this?

> *Dear Little One, Part of my lesson from you is to learn when to let go. Part is to cherish each of my children for the treasured individual souls you are. You are not a soul who needs a new body to come to me. You have already come. You have done your work for this time by your very existence. You are a beautiful little soul who came to me, made me feel loved, and left. And by leaving when you did, you brought me and your Daddy closer than we've probably ever been. I will always love you and cherish your memory as my unborn child. And when I get past the tears, I will remember you with a smile for your love and your lesson and for giving me your short life. I love you with all my heart, little one.*

Those letters sound so "together" for so soon after the loss. But for the next few months, I went through my "hell period." I felt like I was in it, and I'm sure others around me thought I acted like I was from it. I felt betrayed and out of control. Things would have been so much easier if I had known why the miscarriage happened. Then I could feel that there was something I could do differently the next time to prevent it from happening again. I hated the feeling through the whole experience that I was out of control, that my love and desire and nurturing of my baby did not matter, that it didn't do anything to protect or keep her but that the universe took matters into its own hands and decided that I would have this experience. I hated the world and God and whoever or whatever was responsible for this loss.

That black hole I had seen on the ultrasound monitor symbolized my ultimate fears about life. I had feared that I would somehow end up in a black void all alone and unable to find my way back to reality. My life had been up to that time a conscious effort to control my reality so as not to fall into that blackness. And yet, here I was, confronted with that black empty nothingness right inside my own body.

It felt like my life was shattered in little pieces all around me. It was like I was watching a movie of my life. As I watched, all the pictures exploded in slow motion, and I couldn't put them back together again because they were in so many scattered pieces. All I could do was watch in horror and then in rage.

I was powerfully, incredibly angry at everything—at God, at my body, at the baby. I wanted to get back at whoever or whatever did this to me. I felt like destroying something fragile that couldn't be put back together again, something that would shatter into a million zillion pieces and be so minutely scattered all around and so jagged that it couldn't possibly be put back together again. And then I wanted to just walk away. That's how I felt—shattered and abandoned.

It's not that there weren't people around who supported me. Gary was very supportive. Even though there were things I think he didn't understand, I always felt he was supportive of my grieving. And I always felt he was there for me. He was a strength to me. Any time I wanted to talk, he was a good listener. If I wanted to talk to Marie, he was supportive of that. If I had wanted to stay home from work longer, it would have been fine. He supported whatever I wanted or needed to do.

Six weeks after my miscarriage, I hit a real low point in my grief. We were supposed to go to San Francisco for a short vacation. An hour out of town, I got an incredible wave of depression and anxiety and made Gary turn the car around. I needed the security of my house. I needed some sense of being in control of something. Being in my own environment gave me that. I felt awful because it had been six weeks since the miscarriage and I felt I should have been past it but there I was in a pit again. Gary felt okay about turning back. He took care of me. I felt supported, safe, and loved.

The only time I had a problem with him was a few months after the loss. We were with some friends when Gary said something about being 37 years old and not having any kids of his own yet. I wanted to scream and tear at him and yell into his face and eyes and ears, "Yes, you have a child! Your child died! The fact that she was never born is irrelevant. She lived inside me and she was yours and ours and she died! You are a father!"

My miscarriage taught me a lot about other people too. I had relationships that were affected positively. Some people sent sympathy cards that acknowledged my loss as a death. I met Marie through a support group immediately after the miscarriage. I felt so understood by her. She knew what I was feeling and accepted my feelings, and what was best was that she had had the same experience and had felt the same feelings. I felt like I had been holding my breath and here was someone with whom I could breathe.

There were people who stayed away or didn't call. I found their avoidance painful, and I remember it still.

I wish it had been socially acceptable to grieve longer, that it was okay after weeks or even months to still express sadness about a miscarriage. I was still feeling sad. If people conveyed that my sadness was acceptable, I wouldn't have had to pretend I was okay.

I wondered why there is a word for a person whose spouse died but not for a parent whose child died. Maybe we all want to forget about it, to pretend it never happened.

After my miscarriage, I had one dream that I remember about the baby. In the dream she was about a year old. I can still see an image of her with her head cradled in my neck and her arms around me, saying "mamma." I remember feeling her too. Some dreams are vivid visually, others are auditorally clear. In this dream, I felt the baby. I could actually feel her warm skin against my neck.

At a support group meeting about six weeks after my miscarriage, I heard a woman describe a little angel she got for her Christmas tree in memory of her baby, and I really liked that idea. Gary and I went shopping for angels. We would see beautiful angels, and Gary found some he liked. But I kept saying no. Finally when I heard myself saying, "We can't get this angel; it doesn't look like us," I realized I had actually been searching for my baby in this angel. Later I found two little white porcelain angels. I bought them both because I couldn't decide between them. My journal entry in March, five months after my miscarriage, reads:

> When it was time to put the Christmas things away I couldn't bring myself to pack away the angels. It was like parting with my baby again, like "burying" them. I hardly ever looked at them any more, but I couldn't put them away until a couple of days ago. I saw them standing on the shelf, and it finally felt okay to wrap them up and put them away until next Christmas. I thought it was okay until just this second. As I write about it I can't help but cry again for my lost baby. The emotions sneak up on me. Just when I think I am fine, it hits me all over again, and the waves of grief flood over me and pound at the shore of my heart, which has to be rock solid for everyone else. I can't let people know I am still as grief-stricken as I am. It is not acceptable, not yet, not still. My baby, my little one, I love you still, and I am afraid I will love you forever.

I collected and saved things like the angels, the candle from a support group memorial service, and the doctor's appointment cards from before the loss. They give me something tangible in a situation in which there is nothing tangible. For a long time, the amethyst ring Gary had given me when I got pregnant was my symbol for our baby, the only thing I had to look at that was a part of the baby in a sense. For a long time I was unable to take the ring off. It was as though by doing so, I would be abandoning my baby. It took months before I could leave the house without it and longer than that for it to lose some of that significance. When that happened, I felt a bit guilty but also a bit more at peace. I was finally getting over the all-consumingness of the miscarriage.

I went through a spiritual crisis as a result of my miscarriage. Up to that time, I had believed in God as a powerful being who could do anything. But where was His power if my baby was dead? After the miscarriage I searched for spiritual answers. I read When Bad Things Happen to Good People *by Harold S. Kushner. The author said that while God can't control who lives or dies, He is there to help you through. I remember thinking, "What good is that?" It took me a long time to feel at peace about what I thought God was. My journal entry six months after my miscarriage reads:*

> I rather doubt that God has too much to do with it anyway. I went to the last support group meeting and met a warm, wonderful, loving couple who had experienced a neonatal loss and a miscarriage. They had been married for many years, conceived and lost a baby two years ago, miscarried a baby,

and had been trying unsuccessfully to have another baby since then. I have thought about them a lot. They are my case for why God, if He is a loving God, can't have anything to do with this. Why would He do that to this couple? They are a gentle pair who radiate love and kindness, understanding and acceptance, and for whom I immediately felt love. Surely they would make "good" parents. Surely God must want people like them to raise His children. What kind of sin could they be paying for, to keep them childless?

No, God just sort of has to be there and not in on the decision part of this baby stuff. Maybe He is just the string we hold onto to keep from plummeting into hell. Maybe sometimes He is a thread and sometimes a twine and sometimes a cord or maybe He's the same all the time and just feels different depending on our circumstances.

But if He does play with the cards or make the decisions, it feels so unjust. Perhaps there is not supposed to be justice. Or maybe we just can't see it. I keep remembering Richard Bach's book *Illusions* and the quote about the caterpillar: "The mark of your ignorance is the depth of your belief in injustice and tragedy. What the caterpillar calls the end of the world, the master calls a butterfly." Okay, so maybe I am so caught up in the cocoon that I can't see the wings blooming and all the colors developing.

What can we do but wait and have faith? When little children in Sunday school are taught about faith in God, the lesson is often illustrated by the planting of a seed with the faith that it will become a plant. But what they don't tell you is that some of the seeds don't make it, that sometimes the plant never reaches sunlight. The odds are that it will sprout and grow and blossom and flourish. But sometimes the seed never opens; sometimes it just plain dies; sometimes it gets eaten by the birds. I'd like to think that in this case the baby got carried in the winds and taken to a gentler place. My wish is that my baby knows I love her, wherever she is.

Writing this is cleansing for me. It gets the feelings out and away from me so they don't cut up my insides with their jagged points and edges. I have bled enough from them. I write them down so I can see what stabs within me. The writing becomes my cleansing cloth to soak up all the blood and pain so it doesn't kill me.

My journal entry from the day after my due date:

I helped a friend with her daughter's birthday party today. How ironic. Working on a birthday party on a day that felt so un-birthing for me. When I got home, I felt so drained from physical fatigue and from keeping my feelings locked up inside all day, that all I could do was lie on my bed and stare at the ceiling and cry. My body ached, my heart ached, and my arms very literally ached from the emptiness of what I did not and could not have. I remember when I was pregnant and I wanted to make it feel more real, I would lie in bed and visualize the baby lying next to me and nursing. Last night, I couldn't even lie on that side of the bed. It was too close and too real. My breasts hurt like a woman's engorged with milk. Gary asked why, and I just told him the date and he understood. I guess he hadn't realized what day it was. He must really be past this. I envy that in a way, and yet in a way I feel sad for him perhaps because he didn't have the same depth of feeling for this baby. It is that depth, that amount of love in me, that overwhelming, all-encompassing, every-cell-and-fiber-of-being-filled-with-love, that I am grateful for.

I thought about what would have been helpful to me at the time just following my miscarriage. What I needed was someone to give me a book that said, "This is what you've been through emotionally, this is what you're going to go through, this is what other women experienced, we understand, you're not crazy, you're not going to die, it's going to be horrible and awful and painful but it will get better, and it's okay to feel the pain."

When Marie and I interviewed each other to try out our questionnaire, I found that in the process of talking about my loss, I re-experienced all the emotions. In a way, it was comforting to know that the pain was still there. It had been almost two years since my miscarriage. I no longer consciously thought much about my miscarriage on a real emotional level. I could talk about the book and talk about miscarriage and support other people as a volunteer and not feel my own emotions. As I began my interview, I almost feared that I didn't have the pain anymore. In a way, the pain I felt during the interview was a relief. I didn't have anything else connected with my baby. All I had was what was in my heart. I felt that it was necessary for me to have the sadness because the pain was all I had of her. If I lost the sadness, I lost her.

At this point I don't know what I grieved for more—the baby I lost or the fact that I had to go through the hell of it. I have come to believe that my baby, whom we have since named Jamie, is with me. I don't mean she is with me bodily. But I do feel her presence. It feels very peaceful. I feel very loved by her and connected to her. I "talk" to her and she "talks" to me sometimes in my mind. I feel that she is with my deceased Grandma whom I loved so dearly. Together they watch over me and come around from time to time to see how I am doing and to let me know they are with me. I wonder if they are really there or if I have made myself believe it to feel better. No matter. I feel better just thinking they are present and connected still. In a funny way I feel more connected to her than if she had lived. Our living children come into our lives and then go on about their lives. Sometimes they are with us and sometimes they are off doing their own things and living their own lives separately from us. But with Jamie, I feel I can "call" her at any time and she will be there. I can be connected with her 24 hours a day.

I see that I am still sometimes quite emotional about my miscarriage, but I am much more at peace about it too. Marie gave me a note about a Buddhist belief in "bodhisattvas"—souls that manifest for someone else's life and lessons rather than for their own spiritual growth. That made me feel so good. It helped explain the loving gift I had received from Jamie's life. With this in mind, I re-read a part of my journal in which I said I would give back everything in order to have my baby. I think a part of me still feels that way.

Certainly no earthly thing could replace a child. However, I also now feel that Jamie gave an ultimate gift of love. She gave me her whole life. It was like she said, "I am only going to manifest for a short time and I will be yours and yours alone. No one else will know me as you do. I will come into your life, have an impact, leave a gift, and then I will go." It would seem unfair to Jamie to want more. Asking more of her is impossible.

PART TWO

MATERNAL LOVE AND ATTACHMENT

CHAPTER FOUR

Our Pregnancies, Our Babies

From the time we are young girls, we learn about and practice nurturing by playing house, taking care of pets, babysitting, and more. Over the years we watch our models—our mothers and grandmothers—nurture us by cooking, singing, caressing us, and so on. We identify with them and learn who we are from them. We are our mothers' daughters. Nurturing and motherhood remain parts of our pictures of ourselves as females as we grow from childhood into adulthood. Seeing ourselves as nurturers and probably as future mothers, we begin to bond with our future children when we are children, and those bonds strengthen as our pictures of ourselves become actualized. When we marry, the first questions we are asked often are when we will have children or how many children we are planning to have. Even at bridal showers, a common practice is counting the number of broken ribbons from opened presents to predict the number of children the bride will have.

Yet the source of our feelings about motherhood and babies goes beyond conditioning. We have an instinctive sexual drive to reproduce, and that drive insures the survival of our species. It is basic and powerful. Through reproduction we become a part of the making of generations, a part of the cycle of life. Through bearing children we leave a legacy; we often feel a sense of fulfillment and completion within the cycle of life. Life's purpose and meaning are often broadened. We make a contribution toward the future and the continuation of life.

When we become pregnant, the feelings that have grown over the years become uniquely and lovingly attached to the very real being within us. The deep emotional drive to bond now has a concrete, tangible, real focus and recipient. And years of dreaming and pretending gel into fulfillment.

Now our pictures of ourselves as nurturers move from the future, or "what will be," to the present, to now. We experience ourselves as mothers to the real babies within our wombs. In our hearts, our spirits and our minds, when we become pregnant, we are mothers. Jacquelyn Mitchard wrote in *Mother Less Child, the Love Story of a Family:*

My baby. This is what thinking got you. My Joey-or-Lucia. My brown-eyed child who, if I let it, would tug at my breast, and cry for fear of the thunder, and make noises like a big, fierce lion, and learn what the Stop sign said, and win the spelling bee, and fall in love, and cling to me the night before the wedding—who would assume form and presence in the space of an eye blink and tear my heart in two.

In this chapter, mothers share their feelings about their pregnancies and their concepts of the realities of their babies.

FEELINGS ABOUT BEING PREGNANT

There was no correlation between women's feelings about being pregnant and their feelings of loss when their pregnancies ended. Women grieved following their miscarriages whether or not their pregnancies were planned, whether or not their pregnancies were wanted, whether or not they knew they were pregnant prior to miscarrying, and, in a few cases, when their babies' twins survived, and when elective abortions had already been scheduled.*

I was surprised by the intensity of my grief when I miscarried one of my twins. I mean, I still had the other twin. But of course one human being can never compensate for another.

I felt awful about being pregnant. I didn't want more kids. I wanted an abortion. After I miscarried it took about three weeks for the emotions—the mental part—to kick in. I felt very, very sad. It took me about six months to realize the loss.

Some mothers who felt unhappy about being pregnant clearly differentiated feelings about *being pregnant* from feelings about *their babies.* Although the timing of their pregnancies, their financial or marital status, the number of children they already had, and so on, may have led them to feel burdened or anxious about attempting to raise more children, sooner or later they still bonded with and felt love for their babies. When their pregnancies ended in miscarriage, they felt grief over the loss of their babies:

I had children already and was ambivalent about the pregnancy, but by the time I had the miscarriage, I knew I did want the baby. I bled for a few weeks before I miscarried. During those weeks I would hope and pray and bargain.

*This is in keeping with the research findings of Magda Denes as reported in her book *In Necessity and Sorrow.* Through her interviews at an abortion hospital, she concluded that women who undergo elective abortion do so because they feel it is necessary, and at the same time they experience sadness.

We didn't want more children. There wasn't enough money. I was shocked by the pregnancy. It was a very emotional time. Then the sonogram showed there was no baby. I knew there had been a living being in there. I knew I had lost a life. I felt very empty.

HOW THEY CONCEPTUALIZED THEIR BABIES

In almost three-quarters of the miscarriages represented in the study, women experienced their babies in their hearts and minds as whole and living human beings:

We knew this person was real. He had his own soul right at conception. He felt loved.

More than three out of five of the women consciously visualized their babies during their pregnancies. Some of them conceived of their babies as unique, specific, and unrepeatable individuals with whole and distinctive identities. They experienced their babies in precise detail including specific characteristics like hair or eye color and personality traits. Their hopes and dreams for their babies' futures were also specific, such as how their babies would interact with particular family members or which colleges their babies would attend. These women were more likely than not to have named their babies (either before or after their losses) and were likely to have had a sense of the sex of their babies:

I saw her as a teeny, tiny newborn. I could see her face. She was a little red in the face, and grumpy. I knew who she was. She looked just like my husband. She had my eyes and my husband's hair. I would daydream about her baptism, playing with her, her looking really feminine, and changing her into pretty dresses I bought for her over a period of years before I became pregnant.

He has the biggest soul I've ever seen. He is very gentle and loving and beautiful. He has big blue eyes and soft curly blonde hair and little pink hands. He would've been independent and would've had a funny sense of humor and a lust for life. I sensed it was a boy. I knew.

Others, especially those who had had previous miscarriages, deliberately viewed their babies as "potential" rather than "real" babies in order to protect themselves emotionally in case of further miscarriages:

I didn't envision it as a real baby. It was more of a "possibility." It didn't appear real yet. I knew I was pregnant but I stayed distant. Being in the medical field, I am cynical. I knew many women have miscarriages, and because of my age, I stayed realistic.

Other women experienced their babies as anonymous and without detail. The hopes and dreams these women held for their babies were more general and nonspecific, the most common of these being wishes for their babies' health and happiness:

I visualized a generic little baby—a little bundle, cuddly and sweet and very young.

Of those who did not consciously visualize their babies, some had not realized they were pregnant until they miscarried. Others had known only a short time, and to them their babies were a part of their bodies and not yet distinct and separate entities. Some, especially those with previous losses, had deliberately chosen not to focus on, and therefore emotionally connect with, their babies while they were pregnant, to protect themselves in case their babies did not survive:

I've never let myself visualize my baby. I removed myself from that option. If I had seen it as viable in the universe, it would have been incredibly devastating when it died.

I think I only had courage to be hopeful and to dream about the first baby I lost. He was clear in my mind; the second baby was blurry; the third was very blurry. I tried not to pay too much attention to the third baby and that made the grieving much more difficult. It was amorphous. It was vague.

As the years following the women's miscarriages passed, the babies did not age in the women's conceptions of them. Instead, the babies forever remained babies in their minds:

About four years later we were kneeling in the pew at Mass. There was a three-month-old baby screaming on his mother's shoulder in the pew in front of us. James reached over and stroked its cheek and the baby stopped crying. Seeing him interact with that baby, I realized that's what our baby would have been like. I have never projected what it would look like today. In my mind it was and always is a tiny baby.

SIXTH SENSE ABOUT THEIR BABIES

There was no doubt about the presence of a sixth sense in many of the mothers. Some relayed stories spontaneously, revealing their intuitive sense of things about which they had no physical evidence or prior medical verification:

I had a dream. There was some big bomb blast—a huge explosion with heat and fire. The next morning I woke up and I was bleeding streaks of blood.

I knew something was wrong, but the doctor kept telling me nothing was wrong; he kept giving me statistics, that 25% of all pregnancies end in miscarriage. Every time I miscarried, I was treated like a distraught mother who didn't know what I was talking about. I felt such anger because I was right that something was wrong, yet no one believed me.

I felt like I was miscarrying. But then they found a heartbeat. It was confusing. I had twins in the back of my mind. I dreamed of a miscarried twin repeatedly. Later when Luke was five months old, he became very ill. They ran tests and collected records, and I found out that remnants of a twin had been found in the afterbirth. Since Luke's twin was confirmed, I haven't had the dream anymore. The twin is named Jonathon. He was named in my dream.

KNOWING THEIR BABIES' SEXES

Although almost none of the women had physical evidence or medical verification of their babies' sexes, half of them "had a feeling" about the sex of their babies. Some described a knowingness about it, whereas others felt a suspicion and were less certain:

I feel it was a boy in the image of his father. I had that feeling all along. Yet there is this game I play. Part of me really knows *it was a boy. My critical side says, "You don't know anything." My intuitive side says, "It's a boy, and it was healthy." My practical side says, "I really don't know, and I just got a bum deal."*

Some women did not have a feeling about their babies' sexes. Some of them did not feel a need to know, and others needed not to know:

It didn't change the feelings of loss I felt. It doesn't matter. It was a baby. I would have been happy either way.

Not knowing made it easier. That way it didn't seem so much like an individual yet. Not knowing kept it from being a baby.

Some women who did not have a feeling about the sex of their babies felt pained that a piece of the puzzle was missing. For them, that missing piece of information left them with profound feelings of loss from never having known their children:

Not knowing the sex enhanced the feeling of unfairness. I felt very cheated. I feel empty. There's a void there. I didn't know my baby. If I knew what sex it was, it might be easier to grieve the loss. Not knowing is a gap that never gets filled.

NAMING THEIR BABIES

About a third of the mothers named their babies, some before they were pregnant, some during their pregnancies, and some after their miscarriages:

After the miscarriage, we decided to name him Robin. And then a robin flew down the fireplace into our house.

It felt really good to name her Katherine Rose, my mother's name. It lets me know she was alive and a part of me. It's like accepting her as mine and accepting myself as her Mother.

I named her Angel. Afterwards I felt more settled. Naming her actualized her, like I was honoring her. She existed. She had a beginning and an end, with substance inbetween. But it leaves a hollow spot just the same.

Other women did not name their babies:

I needed to not do that at that point. I felt afraid to bond, to know the sex. Not naming the baby allowed me to distance myself.

It didn't occur to me to do so.

THINKING OF THEMSELVES AS MOTHERS

During almost two-thirds of the pregnancies, the women thought of themselves as mothers to their babies:

When people ask, I say, "I had two children, but the first one lived to only three-and-a-half-months' gestation." Saying that, was very healing to do—to accept my Motherhood.

I wrote in my journal, "Mother's Day was to be forgotten in 1979 and 1980. I remembered you, Tyler, and cried myself to sleep on these 'should be forgotten days.' I knew I was a mother, and I knew YOU remembered Mother's Day. On Mother's Day 1983, I was pregnant with you, Justin. I thought maybe Daddy would get me a card from you, but he said I wasn't a mom yet. I'm sure he was afraid to acknowledge that I was. Mother's Day 1984 was again full of despair and sadness. Both my sons were gone and the future looked bleak. Daddy shared my emptiness, and he said he was sure my little boys were smiling at me from heaven. That helped so much. He finally acknowledged my invisible motherhood."

While they were pregnant, these women clearly knew that they were mothers. After their miscarriages, however, many of them felt very doubtful about being mothers anymore:

I had become a mother. Then all of a sudden the motherhood part of me, so excited about the creating, had to stop imagining and totally reevaluate. This little voice inside says, "You're probably not really a mother." Now suddenly I'm "Margaret, the whatever."

Twenty-four hours before, I was a mother. I was pregnant and had a child inside of me. Then my child was gone. With a stroke, I wasn't a mother anymore. My whole life changed. I had a terrible, empty feeling. There was this emptiness I wasn't able to shake.

With each loss, it's the loss of Motherhood. The concept of me as a mother dies. I'm just myself. I don't feel I'm a mother because I haven't given birth. I failed at Motherhood without actually being a real mother. I may never be one.

A few women who did not feel this doubt at the time of their miscarriages, did so in response to later life events.

CHAPTER FIVE

Julianna's Story

My miscarriage was 10 months ago, and I was 3 months pregnant. Eight months before my miscarriage, I also lost my 15-month-old son.

I was elated about the pregnancy. I was spotting and scared, but the doctor thought nothing was wrong. I saw him several times over a period of 10 days. A blood test showed my hormone level kept lowering.

The doctor didn't say, "Your baby is dead." He said, "Your pregnancy hasn't progressed the way it should've progressed. You're not at the stage you should be." That's not telling me! *I thought, "If I wait a little longer, maybe I'll* get *to that stage." I kept saying, "Are you* sure*?" Then he advised me to have a D&C done. I had assumed that if I ever miscarried, I would expel the baby naturally. They told me to sign a paper that called the procedure an abortion. The word "abortion"* really *bothered me. I said, "I'm not going to sign for it!" My doctor had to almost sign a paper promising me the baby was already dead.*

The D&C was terrifying. I'd never had surgery before. I woke up screaming. My blood pressure was rising. I said to the doctor, "Are you sure *this was the right thing to do?" I still had my doubts. I still couldn't believe it.*

Later that day I began blocking it out. I had to put up this facade. I was trying to rationalize with myself and others.

I had nightmares about the surgery. It scared me; it seemed so cold—even though they were so nice to me. The anesthesiologist was holding my hand, but the fact is I'm going to come in and I'm going to have my surgery and I'm going to go. It wasn't anything like being in labor where, after the pain and everything you're going through, you're going to have this reward, this ultimate prize. After I left there I didn't have anything. *They took it away.*

I was under anesthesia, and all of a sudden they came in and did what they had to do. That was the final thing—cut and dried. My *doctor said, "This is the best way." I was devastated. I was just so sad and still in disbelief even though they told me and I had the surgery. I still couldn't accept the fact that my baby was dead and gone. At my six-week checkup, I still questioned whether the baby had really been dead when I had had the D&C, and I had regrets about not passing my baby by myself naturally. It was hard on me because I didn't actually* see *my baby.*

I experienced the death of a child with that baby. I had to grieve that baby. I didn't carry it long enough to bury it. But even though I didn't carry it that far, it still bothers me that here I had a D&C done, and I don't know what happened to the remains. It bothered me. Even though they say it was just tissue and this-and-that and it was just like you had a period, well it's not *like you just had a period.*

This loss is harder than the loss of my little boy in the sense of what everybody expects of you. They don't understand the pregnancy was hope of another baby. The miscarriage is more of a silent grieving. You go through the bereavement and the guilt. It's hard to believe it was not my fault. I feel responsible. I felt I grieved my miscarriage as I did my son, just not in the same way. With my son, I missed his smell and his touch and his sounds, whereas with the miscarriage, I didn't have that! But I still missed that! I missed knowing what the baby would've looked like. With the miscarriage I missed not being able to see the baby, touch the baby, and smell the baby. It's an unknown thing.

Was it an embryo? Was it a fetus? I don't know what it was! I don't know what week-stage it was in. I didn't visualize it. I felt conflict over the reality of the baby. The sex doesn't really matter to me, although I had a feeling it was a girl, but we didn't name her. It was a combination of not knowing anything *about the baby. Would it have had hair on its head? All the things you wonder about when you're pregnant.*

I was already planning for that child. I still have this desire to buy baby clothes. In the stores, I'd think, "Should I go sneak over to the baby department?" and I would! I'd go look at the baby things and would just think. Then I would wonder, "What am I doing?" But I was like a magnet to the baby departments. I'd go shopping with my sisters, and we'd be in a totally different area of the store, and sometimes I would even sneak away from them and go there.

But I didn't belong in the children's department. A little neighbor girl and I went there to buy a gift. I kept feeling like someone would come up to me and say, "What are you doing here? Your baby is dead," like I had no right to be there. I'd think, "Did I come to this store when I was pregnant? Because if I did, I'm not going to go in now because I don't want people to say to me, 'Did you have your baby yet?'" You start getting paranoid.

My spiritual beliefs got stronger. The thought that I'll see the baby when I die keeps me going. That's kind of confusing too. Was it tissue like they said it was? Or was it actually a form of a being? Sometimes I question myself, "Am I going to see this baby that I lost, or was it even a baby?" The doctor said it was just like a period; you pass tissue. Well when you have a period and you pass tissue, that tissue isn't going to go up to heaven where you're going to reunite with it. Will I see the baby when I die? It's jumbled because I didn't have a grown baby.

My husband is very concerned with my well-being. He doesn't try to compare his position with mine, but it is hard to talk with him. We kind of put up this big facade. My relationship with him was kind of rough. We had the same dreams of a happy, healthy baby. He would fill the car up with gas, for instance, so I didn't have to inhale the fumes, because he has the same concern that I do for the welfare of the baby. But he also understands that the baby wasn't inside of him and that he doesn't know what it was like for me when I had to have the surgery and everything else.

I had a lot of support. (I wonder if people think I'm bad luck.) Knowing that people were there and that they cared felt good—just calling me and saying, "Can I come by?"

But I felt bad when they said, "You're young. You can always have others. You were lucky it happened when it did. You didn't carry full term." I know they aren't sitting at home saying, "What can I say to hurt Julianna's feelings?" But I went into a shell. I kind of avoided people.

In June, I started seeing a doctor for stress. He said I was holding the miscarriage inside, which I had already known. But that's what I thought was expected of me. I mean, people just took it as, "Oh well, you've had a surgery and you're recovering." But that's not the way it was. I held it all in. I wasn't getting better up here in my head. Emotionally I wasn't healing because I didn't have anybody to talk to. My friends shrugged it off, like, "It's over now." I saw a therapist because I could say what I wanted to because I'm paying her.

I worried that I caused it, but I don't know how. As the woman, I took a lot of self-blame. My husband never points his finger at me; he never even hints it, but sometimes, well, it's just like with me; he must wonder and think too. Sometimes I get this uncomfortable feeling that people think I did something. I feel like they're looking at me and thinking, "She had a miscarriage, so she must have done something wrong." I feel like the whole world knows. My doctor says it wasn't anything I did, but what does he know? It's hard for me to accept that! I can't pinpoint it to anything.

Everything is totally unknown to me—the reason why it happened, what the baby would've looked like, where I would be now in my life, had the baby lived . . . everything. Knowing the reasons why would have helped. A lot of the depression has been over the unknown.

I felt concerns about my sanity. It's hard to get a grip on your emotions. Your mind has so many things going on; you can't control it! I felt out of control mostly because of the anger. I also had panic attacks. I had never had panic attacks before. Not after my son died either.

Somebody took a piece of my heart. A part of me did die. There's so much love in the expectancy of a child. And you know what they say; it comes from the heart. I don't know why it feels that way. But that's how it felt, like somebody came in and grabbed a chunk of my heart when they did the surgery. I went home, and part of it was missing—that part of my heart that was for that child.

I would describe my loneliness as an emptiness. A part of you growing inside of you that you thought was going to be a baby you would have a future with is taken away. This was supposed to be your family. The real loneliness came around my due date. I thought, "Here it is my due date; I have my flat tummy."

I was at my lowest when I came to accept that it was over. I didn't think about it at first. I shut it out and did other things around the house. Then I had to face the reality after a certain period of time, that it was true. I've got this paper in my hand saying I've got a check-up from a D&C I had.

This miscarriage has made me believe more strongly that life is precious. I realized, "Life's not a guarantee!" It was another harsh reality that I had to face. When you're younger it's like a fantasy life. You never see a baby doll with a disease. Every baby doll is perfect. Nobody told me something could happen. Even after my son died, I still trusted I wouldn't lose another one. I thought, "I'm going to have a baby!"

I don't anticipate the pain will ever totally go away, although I did feel remarkably better six months after the due date. It was not that I put the miscarriage in the past then, but it was almost like then I could accept it and go on. Because I thought, "Here it is September, and I don't have this baby; I'm not pregnant; I'm not showing—nothing; I don't even have the final stages of pregnancy." It's almost like I convinced myself at that time: "Do you see, now? You're not having a baby." Even though for the whole nine months I wasn't growing! Now this date came, and I could believe it.

I have a hard time conceiving. It took a year to conceive my son, and another year for the second pregnancy. They make it sound so easy. It's been a year since I miscarried, and I still haven't conceived yet. I'm grasping at straws. Here I am a year later, and I am still childless.

It wasn't like my doctor could tell me, "We finally found out there's something wrong with you." I'm at the fork in the road, and he's not telling me to go this other way, to try to adopt. It's almost like I'm hoping he could say that because after this miscarriage, it was devastating to the point that I was almost hoping he would say there was something wrong with me so I wouldn't have the hope that I have. Then I could take other options and start my family in a different way. The part of me that's protecting me is telling me, "Hopefully he may tell me one day that I can't have kids." I've thought about adopting. But I would like to conceive and have my and my husband's own child. To this day I still have hopes.

I think of myself as mother to my baby. I still feel her spirit is with me. That's the part that's sad: I wasn't able to physically see her, smell her, or touch her, but I still have that bond with her because I carried her and cared for her for three months.

I want to help others, through this interview. After miscarriage there aren't a lot of places you can turn to. A lot of people don't understand. They believe that since you didn't actually see that baby, you didn't look forward to it. Your child is cut off from you. The loss of a child is a devastating loss because there is no alternative for you. You can get pregnant 10 times after, but you can't replace someone you lost! If you lose a child, you can't say, "Well I'm going to have another one and replace it." You can't replace a baby.

PART THREE

ECHOES OF MOURNING

CHAPTER SIX

A Death

When we miscarried, the babies who were a part of us, physically and in our hearts and souls, were gone. With the loss of our pregnancies went the human beings who were the focus of our mothering, our nurturing, and our love. Our babies, those unique human beings who lived within us, have died and are gone from us, now and forever. Sometimes with the loss went our concepts of ourselves, our realities, and even our worlds. Those parts of our physical and emotional selves that created, carried, and nurtured life—those parts of us that were so touched by the miracle of life—experience a loss often so profound that many of us are shaken to our cores. Our miscarriages mean the death of our babies, of the future with our babies, and of those parts of us that connected with both the concept and the beings of our pregnancies.

Picture the face of a mother of a two-year-old child as she hears a screech in front of her home. Imagine the pounding in her heart and the sensation of blood filling her head as she races out her door. Fathom her utter devastation as she realizes it is her lifeless child laid out in the street.

It is easy to understand her pain because it is easy to see the source of her pain. It may seem that her pain is very different from that of a woman who has just been told her pregnancy is no longer viable. Yet, more often than not, the grief of the two women is essentially the same. The loss of a child is the loss of a child, regardless of the cause.

THE DEATH OF A CHILD

Over two-thirds of the miscarriages were experienced by mothers as "the death of their children":

> *It is the death of a child. You have a more intimate closeness with a baby than you do with any other being. This was my child, and it died. I tell people now, "I lost my only child." It is the death of hopes and dreams and of a collective future. It's the same thing as losing a living child fully grown and developed. A lot of people look at miscarriage and say there was no personality there, no physical child that cooed and talked back and smiled and cried. But for you these things are very real.*

It's losing a baby.

Some mothers also spontaneously brought up sorrow and worry about how their babies might have physically suffered at the time of their miscarriages:

> *Emotionally I put myself in the position of the fetus. What did this little fetus experience as it was dying? It must have felt pain dying. I cried that he went through the pain.*
>
> *This poor little baby! I felt he was suffering, experiencing a slow death. I felt a tremendous sense of loss. I wish I could see him. I have not resolved it because of how it was handled. I feel sad.*

They wondered with worry, fear, and concern about what happened to their babies after their miscarriages:

> *I wish I hadn't flushed the toilet. It didn't dawn on me to go into a bedpan because I wasn't expecting to lose the baby. I felt so badly afterwards that the baby went down into the sewer. I wish I had buried him. I wish I had evidence: "This was my child."*
>
> *I used to have dreams about trying to bury these babies, and I couldn't find a place and I was very worried about where they were. After I lost the second baby, I thought, "Wherever they are, at least they are together; they have each other." That somewhere they're together, comforts me.*
>
> *I wanted to see him afterwards. The idea seemed bizarre then. But not sending him off, and doing something more dignified. . . .*

Some women thought of their miscarriages as "the loss of their pregnancies" rather than "the death of their children":

> *I felt not so much a death, but the loss of a dream, the loss of an ideal, the loss of what the future would have meant. It was the death of a wish and a fantasy and a hope. I put the loss of a child out of my mind. I told myself something was the matter; it was for the best. I haven't let myself experience it as a death.*

There were women who did not experience the death of their babies immediately following their miscarriages but who subsequently came to view their miscarriages as such:

> *I had two ectopic pregnancies. I really do think of them as the deaths of my children, but at the time I didn't acknowledge them as that. The first time I was sick; the second time I was scared. It was all I could do to heal physically.*
>
> *I didn't think of it as the death of a child at the time. But I did many years later when my kids verbalized it as the loss of a child and I learned that my feelings were okay.*

GRIEVING DOWN THE ROAD

When *other* losses or traumas occurred at some point in time following their miscarriages, deep feelings of grief over their miscarriages were sometimes activated for the first time or were reactivated on a deeper level.* Later events jarred realizations about "what might have been" and made women focus on or become more aware of the impact of their losses. (For example, some women had planned moves or college or work leaves around their babies' births. When the planned college semesters or the time for maternity leave arrived, their awareness of the depth of their grief grew or their feelings of grief intensified.) Sometimes a later death of some other loved one elicited feelings of grief for the previously miscarried babies:

> *I didn't deal with the grief until about five years later when both my parents died. At my mother's funeral, I realized that I don't have a mother and I'm never going to be a mother. I began grieving my mother and the baby who never got to be.*

> *I suppressed it. I didn't get into the emotion because no one was there to support me. Years later when there was another death in the family, I experienced emotion about it, that at one time I was carrying life and it was a loss.*

Women's awareness of the depth of their losses was also sometimes triggered when they received validation of their losses from others after time had passed:

> *I don't remember any great emotionality about the loss of the baby until 15 years later when it came up in conversation with my teenage son. He said, "You mean I could've had a big brother?" It was then that it became clear to me, and for the first time I felt a great amount of loss. Over the next year I went through full grieving. I had put it in a corner until I could deal with it. It had been too overwhelming back then.*

For some women who did not have children prior to their miscarriages, the birth of later children sometimes triggered grief over their miscarried babies. It was at the time of the subsequent births that they comprehended on a deeper level the reality of what had been lost:

> *When I had my daughter two years later, the loss became very real to me because I realized how amazing it is to have a baby. Now that I've had a child, I feel the miracle of life, and I feel the loss much greater.*

> *When I saw that my second subsequent baby was a different person from the prior subsequent baby, I felt the loss of my miscarried baby. I realized each one was*

*According to a number of medical sources, delayed grief reactions have been noted up to 21 years after miscarriage.

different, and I wondered for the first time, "Who was the one I lost?" I took it worse then. It was a greater reality then. It hurt more then. I had put it away.

Sometimes when grief was repressed, it found ways to manifest in the form of physical symptoms, dreams, or behaviors that seemed uncharacteristic of the women prior to their losses. When the connection between those manifestations and their grief was eventually recognized and the women allowed themselves to grieve their losses, the manifestations disappeared:

I had the miscarriage in September. Between September and January, I never mourned, grieved, or cried. I was so glad it was over. But I had physical symptoms—dizziness, fainting, temporary blindness. I was checked for a brain tumor. The night before the next school semester was to begin, I began crying. I cried for hours. I realized the baby had been due in March, and if I were still pregnant, I wouldn't be going back to school the next day. That's when my awareness hit me. Then all the physical symptoms disappeared.

Eighteen years later, I started freaking out. I went into an anxiety mode. I started thinking about babies. I had a series of dreams over a period of about a year. In each dream I was more and more pregnant, and in the last dream I had a baby girl in my arms and we had this intense love for each other. When I woke up it was like she died because she was gone from me. I realized I hadn't thought of my miscarriages as babies. I then gave each a sex and a name and visualized each in relation to my living son. I saw them as my five children. Once I did that, I stopped having the dreams and the anxiety.

THE DEATH OF A PART OF THEMSELVES

Following over three-fourths of the miscarriages, women felt that a part of them had died. Some felt that a physical part of them had died:

I carried somebody who would be part of our family. It was a part of me! It was my egg. It always will be a part of me. My heart and soul went into that baby. Then it died. It's gone, and it is never coming back. I feel an incredible sense of loss. It feels like my heart has been ripped out of my body.

You had something, and you aren't going to have it anymore. It's like losing the use of your hand. It was like I lost a limb. There was this death within me. Part of me was gone, and I couldn't get it back. I felt a physical sense of missing, like a leg was removed.

Yet most mothers who talked about feeling that a part of them had died, did so in terms of the death of a part of their own spirits:

I felt shot down by life. The child within me, the part that is able to be spontaneous and trusting, is gone. My optimism toward life died.

When I was bleeding, something was going out of my body, like a part of me was going.

The part of me that was strong, competent, nurturing, and "Woman" died.

My heart went with them to the grave.

There was a death within my body, of an unfinished life that just hangs there in suspension forever in an ongoing hell.

CHAPTER SEVEN

Grieving

Our pregnancies are over, our babies have died, and many of us have tumbled into the awfulness of grief. It is so complex, confusing, and lonely. We question ourselves, our worlds, our relationships. Our sense of time and reality come apart, and we are tossed about by questions, sorrow, and despair. To many of us, the grief feels arduous and never-ending. We wanted so desperately to bring forth and protect the life within us. Yet that life ended; we feel we failed. We feel guilty. We anguish over our losses, and for a time we look at our lives through a film of sorrow. In their interviews, women described their soul-destroying experiences of grief.

Although a range in degree and intensity of grief was reflected in the findings, all 100 women felt at least some degree of grief. To be clear about what we are identifying as grief, at one end of the sampling, in depth and intensity of grief, was a woman who told us in a comfortable tone of voice that she was glad she miscarried, she never made any emotional attachment to her baby, she didn't think of it as a baby, her miscarriage was "meant to be," and it had no impact on her life at the time of her interview. This woman also said,

> *I cried. It didn't really hit me for a week. Then I felt sad and upset. . . . I always feel I have to be in control. I don't think I knew how to feel. I felt confused about why this happened. It was an act of love between two people. . . . I felt a part of me had died.*

We acknowledge this woman's experience as grief.

We have grouped their responses according to the feelings or other experiences they expressed, and we have captioned them accordingly as follows.

LONELINESS

An interview question about loneliness received the greatest number of yes responses among all 85 interview questions. After 83 percent of the reported miscarriages, mothers felt loneliness.

Some described their loneliness in terms of feeling misunderstood by others, without empathy, and therefore emotionally isolated:

I felt very empty and alone, like there was a hole in my stomach that couldn't be filled. I loved the baby even though it didn't have a name or a shape. But no one was able to understand or relate to me, and I wasn't able to relate to them. I had nothing in common with anyone. It was like I landed on a planet and everyone knew each other, but they didn't know me and I didn't know them.

People didn't see that I was hurting. They saw the surface and didn't see below. I could be with people yet feel so alone.

Six months afterwards, I felt the worst pain. No one understood. I felt so alone. I had no one to let know I was hurting. There was nobody who could help me. Who cared? They were so busy. I felt betrayed and unloved. I felt sorrow.

I've never been a lonely person. But I'm very lonely now. I feel a sort of "world" loneliness. I feel isolated and cut off from the world. I feel like I have a terrible, deep, dark secret in a foreign language.

Some women described loneliness for their babies. They missed the relationships they had shared with the little beings inside them:

I had this life inside of me. It was the closest person in the world to me. It was a really warm feeling. Then all of a sudden, it was taken from me. I felt so empty and lonely. Nothing could take its place. I needed something to hold. I deeply felt that baby's absence. My body was all by itself again. I felt a great yearning. There was this great hole in my life. I was empty and gaping.

A SENSE OF CLOSENESS WITH THEIR BABIES AFTERWARD

Half the women felt a sense of closeness or contact with their babies after their miscarriages. For some this was comforting. The feeling of closeness brought with it a relief from the loneliness and bridged the painful distance they felt from their lost babies. For others, the sense that their babies were near was distressing, as if their babies were so close but forever unreachable. The majority of mothers who did not feel a closeness with their babies afterward felt that such a feeling would have been painful:

The closeness is still my special secret, even after 39 years. It makes me feel good even though there is sadness there.

I felt like I was still carrying the baby. It was haunting. I felt confusion.

CONFUSION

More than three-quarters of the women talked about feeling confused about emotional *and* physical experiences during and after their miscarriages. As their miscarriages were occurring, they felt confusion about what was happening, what to do with the babies or tissue, whether to call their doctors or go to hospitals, and about medical procedures they were facing. After their miscarriages, they were unprepared for what they went through physically, about what happened to their babies' remains, and about how they could have been so unaware of what was happening in their own bodies. Their miscarriages shattered many of their life assumptions and led to unanswered questions about their ability to bear children, about why the losses had occurred, and why they had occurred *to them*:

> *Your body is doing strange things. To have feelings going on in your system, like still having swollen breasts, catches you off guard. Sometimes you forget you're not pregnant. You think, "I'd better eat my vegetables or take my prenatal vitamins for the baby," and it catches you short.*

> *I thought I could have all the children I wanted. We were trying to accomplish this feat that was defeating us! My body was rejecting this baby I really wanted. It wasn't gonna let me be a mother.*

> *I was trying to make sense out of something that had happened that made no sense.*

> *Where do I fit in between a baby dying and a tonsillectomy? There is this vagueness!*

> *Why, and why me? I've never really been a bad person. This shouldn't have happened to a good person like me, having her taken away from me.*

Regarding about a third of the miscarriages, women said they experienced conflict about the reality of their babies. Some women's miscarriages were diagnosed as blighted ovums. These diagnoses posed a conflict, in part, because medical opinion on the meaning of the term is ambivalent. Some medical sources say the pregnancies resulted in the formation of placentas but not fetuses, whereas more recent medical opinion says that the fetuses existed but died "early" (another ambiguous term) in the pregnancies. Some women felt very confused by the term "missed abortion". They did not know that the medical community uses the term "abortion" to mean elective abortion as well as miscarriage. Some saw ultrasound pictures in which the fetuses were not visible. Even though their pregnancy tests had been positive, these women experienced great conflict over whether they had actually been pregnant:

> *When the doctor said there wasn't a fetus, I thought, "What does he mean? Where did it go?" He said it was a blighted ovum. I thought, "Was I pregnant? Was this a joke?" The radiologist explained to me that I had been pregnant.*

> *I am a nurse. I saw that there was no baby on the ultrasound screen, yet when I miscarried, I saw the baby, the sac, the cord, and the placenta in my hand.*

Still another cause of confusion was that most women had no concrete experience of their babies before or after their miscarriages:

I had a D&C. It was so fast. I had such an empty feeling. I didn't get to see, hold, or touch my child. He didn't even seem real. I thought, "Maybe I imagined this."

I never felt pregnant, so I didn't absorb the reality of the baby. I had no signs of pregnancy and no drag on my system, so I didn't have much of a sense that it was a child. It didn't sink in. It seems like just a heavy period. So it surprised me when I felt a tremendous sense of loss.

For some women who saw their babies or placentas by ultrasound prior to their miscarriages, what they saw confirmed the existence of their babies:

I saw it on the sonogram. There is no question there was something living in there. I saw the body. The sonogram validated the baby.

A few mothers actually saw, touched, or held their babies' remains. For almost all of them, there was no question about the reality of their babies:

I was alone with my kids when my water broke and the baby came out. It was three inches long with sort of webbed fingers and toes and not-well-formed genitals. I think it was a boy. Even though I had seen pictures of fetuses, it was so strange. *It was* amazing. *I was in shock. I wanted to look him over. I felt a scientific curiosity. I went through bouts of crying for 6 to 12 months afterwards. I was very grief-stricken.*

The doctor was extremely sympathetic. He left the embryo in the room and let my husband in with me for a half hour. I handed my husband the baby in a paper tissue. We had a chance to grieve over it.

I got to hold him, to touch and see him. That let me know he was an actual human being. That comforted me. I didn't want to give him back. It didn't matter that he was dead. Had I not miscarried, he would be calling me "Mommy."

What others saw, either by ultrasound or firsthand, meant to them that their babies were *not* real babies:

I saw tissue coming out. It was a mass of gook. It looked nothing like a baby. I felt fortunate that it in no way looked like a baby. It wasn't a baby.

Many women did not have factual verification of real babies, yet they still felt certain of the reality of their babies:

It's a child I don't know anything about. I had a very hard time with the whole notion that there is no name, no face, no ceremony, and very little acknowledgment. So you have to invent your own, and you try different ways. Yet I'm very clear about the reality of these babies. Conception is conception.

Conflict also arose from society's continued undermining of their miscarriages as deaths or even as losses at all. Most women talked about confusion in response to the reactions of others. Without success, the women tried to fit their perceptions and feelings about their miscarriages with the perceptions and reactions of those around them. With no one to validate the legitimacy of their losses, most women therefore struggled with terrific confusion about whether they had a right to grieve:

Others were afraid to say anything to me. I sensed that I was being watched. They would look down if our eyes met. Yet I needed them to acknowledge my loss. I felt so hurt. I was exploding with no right to my pain.

The doctor said, "There was no baby there." That's denial. I also became conflicted after hearing from others. They said maybe I wasn't really pregnant.

There is this person you knew, but no one else knew. To others, it didn't exist. To you, it was very real.

I was confused about what I was feeling and from not knowing what the appropriate feelings were. I wondered, "Is this a real, warranted, and normal reaction to what I've experienced? Am I overreacting? Why do I still feel this way? Why is no one concerned about learning why it happened?" I had strong feelings, but the world at large was trivializing this.

Almost three-quarters of the women felt a sense of "internal chaos or disorder." Many of these women still went about their everyday routines, all the while feeling disoriented and out of sync with the world:

Everything was out of order. The world was out of whack. I couldn't put it together. I had a sense of things not being nailed down. I couldn't relate to the flow of the regular world. My whole world had been turned topsy-turvey. I was feeling conflicting feelings, feeling alone, and feeling like I couldn't handle things. My routine broke down; I babbled; I was late for work. I made all kinds of mistakes there. I was forgetful and indecisive. My brain went haywire.

I felt very tired, dull, very confused, and disoriented. I was afraid to go downtown. When I would try, I would get lost. I almost ran a red light on my way to the doctor's office. I was a space case. I nearly hit a car. I felt like I wasn't on the earth. I felt alone. My life had been on a track up to that point. I felt derailed, knocked off course. I lost my direction. I had nothing to hold on to.

I lost my mental sharpness. I couldn't problem solve. I didn't know what day it was. I didn't care. I was completely out of sync. I felt a sense of loss and of being lost. I had been a superefficient person who always completed things, yet I now have a very hard time completing anything. I think that everything is sort of open-ended now, and I don't bring things to completion. I can't read, study, or do all the things I used to do. I don't want to travel. These are new phenomena in my life.

Motherhood is generally considered a highly valued and primary role for women. After their miscarriages, some women went through a crisis of identity or suddenly felt lost in terms of their purpose in life. Without their babies, some felt that a huge part of their womanhood was missing:

Something is wrong. I am soul searching. The reason I am here at this point in time is to be a mother. Now what is my purpose? I am trying to clarify my identity.

I went to the bathroom and cut off all my hair. I thought, "If I can't have a baby, I might as well be a man."

Because the emotions that accompanied their miscarriages were often intense, overwhelming, and grossly out of proportion with the expectations and responses of other people, nearly half the women felt concern about their own sanity:

I felt I had lost my child, and people couldn't understand that because my child was not tangible. I wondered, "Am I making more out of this than I should be?" It was no big deal? Then what's wrong with me?

Almost two-thirds of the women described thoughts that seemed illogical or strange to them:

Nothing made sense. All my thoughts were illogical. I wanted my husband to go and to stay at the same time. I'd ask him to go and get me something at the store and then not want him to be gone. I'd have fantasies of him being smashed up on the freeway.

The most illogical thought I had was that I had no right to try to get pregnant again because I would just be "killing another baby."

Seemingly illogical thoughts were often directed toward pregnant women, mothers of young children, and "women who don't have miscarriages":

I didn't want anyone else to get pregnant. I didn't want to ever have to look at them or their babies. I was angry at women who have kids easily and take it for granted. I wanted to kill them. I was so hateful. I wished miscarriages on women, and then I would feel guilty about feeling that way.

I wanted to steal babies! It was the oddest thing!

I became jealous and afraid because others who bled had babies, but whenever I bled, my babies died. I felt a desire to tell pregnant women what could happen, to take away their joy. That scared me.

Most mothers did not concretely experience their babies' deaths. After ultrasound or an inability to locate heartbeats, they were only *told* that their babies were no longer living. Without any evidence of death, they privately questioned whether their babies were, in fact, dead. Some wondered whether their babies had miraculously survived their miscarriages:

One month after the miscarriage, I had these thoughts. "What if the doctor was wrong? What if the ultrasound just didn't show what was really there?" To not see the baby, to not touch it and feel it cold—to help you know it's dead . . . you can't know. Maybe the baby would have made it.

I thought, "Are you sure this baby has expired?" When it came time for the D&C, I put myself in a catatonic state. I was in shock. . . . I'm afraid it was still alive. [sobs] I let them take it!

Sometimes I think they were wrong. I think, "Maybe the baby's still in there. The pregnancy was too strong and too perfect to have anything touch it. Their machines didn't work that day. Maybe he survived" - like he's a superman baby.

They kept telling me to push, but I wouldn't do it. I thought it would be fine. It fell into my vagina, but I still thought, "It will be alive. They'll put it back in. It will be okay. Its eyes will open and it will start crying."

Some of the women felt personally rejected or abandoned by their babies:

I kept thinking that the baby deliberately left.

I felt like he was avoiding me. It was his decision. He died. I felt rejected by him. How could he do that to me?

In many cases, the babies were diagnosed as dead before they were delivered. In some of these cases, many women felt protective of the babies and did not want the babies abruptly removed from their bodies through D&C. They needed time to labor and deliver their babies without intervention. In other cases, women needed to have quickly removed from them what they perceived as death within their bodies:

Before I passed the baby, I felt really, really scared knowing it was dead in there. All I could see in my mind was a real cadaver of a dead baby in my stomach. I got panicky like you would having a bee on your shirt, like, "Oh my God! Get away!"

Many of the women said they felt desires or yearnings to do things that seemed odd or irrational to them:

I wanted to move back to Texas even though I was mad at everyone there.

I wanted to dig a hole and bury myself. I wanted to pack up everything and drive and never stop. I wanted to scream and rant and rage.

Two months after, I chose to fly home to London in a split second on Christmas Eve without my husband. It was very hurtful of me.

I would be in so much grief that I wanted to get the pain out in any way that I could. I would slam myself into a wall, bang my head into the wall; I pulled my hair; I screamed and yelled at God. I was empty. There was no relief.

I didn't have desires to do irrational things. When you're grieving, there is nothing irrational.

ANGER

Many women described feelings of anger at themselves, God, their partners, medical professionals, friends, or their families:

Nobody understood. I eventually became fed up with being a wimp about it. I felt sheer rage. I wanted to kill my husband. I said, "Get me help!"

I feel hurt and angry. I feel an incredible sense of loss and an unfairness and anger. Anger is the biggest feeling. Anger at everyone for being able to have children, at God for doing this to me, at my body for not doing what it was supposed to do, and at other people for not being there. There is a foundation of anger in me. I pulled up all the plants in my garden.

I am so frigging angry at all those people who treated me like it was nothing! I wanted my husband (who's a physician) to go back to that hospital and tell them, "You fucked up in treating my wife!"—*to stand up for me! My rights were jeopardized! Human rights were not respected! I want to say to that hospital, "You fucking assholes! You treated me so badly! You've made it so hard for me to heal!"*

GUILT

Nearly three-quarters of the women worried that they had somehow inadvertently caused the demise of their babies. They cited a host of ways in which they thought they may have caused their miscarriages:

My cerebral part says, "No, I didn't cause it." But I'm really confused. I have real denial. I think I'm lying to myself if I say I didn't cause it. If I pushed myself, I'd say, "Yes, I did." Part of me does think there must be something I did. I'd be lying either way.

I was ambivalent about the pregnancy. I thought that by wishing for a miscarriage, I caused it to happen.

I had been traveling and had carried two big bags for two hours. When I found out I miscarried, I thought, "That's what caused it."

I keep wondering if I hurt him from stress or took his life away somehow. I found myself asking forgiveness. I didn't mean to hurt him. I'm sorry.

My body was inadequate. Maybe I just have some sort of general weakness.

I had had a drink or two before I knew I was pregnant.

I thought I had caused it by having sex too many times.

I should have eaten better; I didn't eat enough.

Should I not have had the D&C? Maybe it would have lived.

Did jogging affect my hormones?

Maybe I'm too old.

I had taken a pretty hot bath.

I spent time with my mother-in-law, who makes me tense.

I was doing too much—skiing and swimming.

I should've exercised more.

I went to Mexico. I wonder, "What did I eat, breathe, walk by? Was it something on the plane, or the aspirin I took when I had the flu before I knew I was pregnant?" I have a list 20 miles long!

I had an argument with my husband. We shouldn't have fought.

I may have done it pushing the trundle bed in.

I was not careful enough.

I put a flea collar on my dog. There were toxins.

I painted on my hand.

I danced too much. I jumped in a Hannukah game.

After the second miscarriage, I got very thin. I wondered if that caused the third miscarriage.

I didn't put my feet up when the doctor said to.

I had bodysurfed in Hawaii. A wave dragged me under. I got hit by a rock on my hip. I miscarried four weeks later.

We went on a two-and-a-half-mile hike at high altitude to the falls in the mountains. I could feel blood pulsing in my abdomen. I was breathing hard. I had to take breaks.

I got pregnant too soon after the pill.

I fell in the tub the day before I found out I was pregnant.

Our neighbor had started to construct a garage. I helped clean it up. I was carrying bricks.

Pollutants? Caffeine? Nutrasweet? Something I ate?

Maybe there is something genetically wrong with me.

While the loss of their babies through miscarriage was repeatedly belittled, many women felt guilty about "grieving too much":

I thought, "This was not a real *tragedy. I have no right to be so upset. I shouldn't be feeling so emotional."* Now *I see that* that *was strange to think.*

I was carrying all the feeling. But nobody seemed to understand the intensity, so I thought, "I shouldn't be feeling this bad. I should be able to deal with this." It's been six months. I should be over this. I should be more stiff upper lip. I feel evil, foolish, and self-indulgent.

A few women felt guilty for "not grieving enough":

I realize now that I felt guilty I didn't look at them as babies at the time. I rejected that. It would have hurt too much. They were babies, and I didn't grieve for them as I should have.

ANXIETY

Although less than a tenth of the women experienced what they labeled as panic attacks prior to their miscarriages, over a third of the women said they experienced panic attacks after their miscarriages:

I had panic attacks for a whole year afterwards, about what might be wrong with me. I felt like I was going to die. I was shaking and sweating and my heart was pounding. I felt like I had just seen someone get run over. I felt gut wrenching, searing torment. It came out in primal screaming and sobbing.

Over a third of the women said their losses triggered thoughts about their own mortality:

D&C's and general anesthesia scare me. It makes me think I won't wake up again.

I had thought I'd never grow old. Life is on such a thin thread. You never know when it will break. It's a really scary feeling. Time runs out. I feel desperate. There are things I haven't done yet. I no longer have the illusion of control. I am no longer protected from profound fear.

I almost bled to death. When it was all over and I was physically healed, I realized how close I came to death, that the babies had died, and how fleeting life is.

Sometimes women were frightened by the depth and intensity of emotions that felt too big to handle. They felt they could not cope and would not be able to endure or survive their feelings of grief:

My sadness is so big that I don't dare cry. It's so big; it's scary and my throat hurts. I can hardly breathe sometimes. I could never empty my tears.

I felt dead inside. I felt frightened I'd never come back to life and the world again; I'd never feel again. It was so frightening. It was so unknown.

I am a gestapo with petticoats now. I am a strong woman outside and a scared girl inside.

LOSS OF CONTROL

At the time of or after their miscarriages, three-quarters of the women felt out of control emotionally, physically, or both. Some women described feeling out of control in the face of their inability to stop their miscarriages from occurring:

I felt paralyzed—I couldn't make decisions or think intelligently. I felt frightened of my own self. I felt out of control and vulnerable, overwhelmed and scared. I felt so close to death.

I tried to be light and cheerful, but I couldn't control my emotions. I fell apart at the seams. I would get one seam sewed up, and another would fall apart. Others would bring my miscarriage up and I'd start bawling. The crying didn't stop. One night my cries turned to screams.

There was nothing I could do to stop the miscarriage. I had no control. It was not my choice. My free agency was taken away. I work for abortion rights, but all my *controls and rights were taken from me.*

I was a superorganized, high-control superwoman. I was real concerned about getting everything in order, in control. But things went out of control. I was treading water, and everything was washing over the top of me and I couldn't get out from under it. If I went out of control, I would just go crazy and they'd put me away.

A SENSE OF SEARCHING FOR THEIR BABIES

Over a third of the women recognized in themselves a sense of searching for their lost babies. They searched for them in the faces of other babies, through mental questioning, through probing for facts about their babies or their losses, or through accessing their medical or pathology lab records and in many other ways:

I was so aware of his presence, his soul. He was so there. When he died, it went away. I have searched and longed for that again. I miss him. It's difficult to describe. It's almost dreamlike. It's a hopeless longing.

I had nightmares that I was crawling inside my body around my female organs, screaming, "WHERE'S MY BABY?!" I couldn't find it anywhere.

I have been tempted to go to the sewage plant and retrieve and bury the tissue.

I went on a search-and-destroy mission with doctors. I accessed my records. I pursued medical reports with a passion. I needed to know everything. I read books with a vengeance. I was drawn to stories and poetry about lost children. There was a lot of searching going on. If I could find them . . .

We had buried the remnants. Then one day I dug them up.

HAVING DREAMS ABOUT THEIR BABIES

Over half the women remembered dreaming about their babies after their miscarriages. Often, their dreams had to do with future experiences with their babies that would now never happen, such as holding or nursing their babies or going on family outings together. For some of these women the dreams were positive. They felt a closeness to their babies that was otherwise denied them and had the opportunity to share those experiences with their babies in their dreams:

They are usually whispy (not tangible) dreams. There is someone there, but I can't see. They are hiding. The dreams are usually comforting as if I have contact with my child.

I dreamed a full-term girl was born dead, but then she came back to life. She was still alive. I was still pregnant in other dreams or I was giving birth, like the miscarriage never happened.

I dreamed about being a mother and having the baby, and sometimes I would wake up and have this chilling feeling like, "Wait a minute. I don't have a baby." It was like "The Twilight Zone."

NIGHTMARES

Almost half the women recalled having nightmares, that were usually about the expulsion of their babies from their bodies, the loss of blood, their feelings of loss, or about catastrophic events such as wars, disease, or natural disasters:

I kept having a dream. In it, somebody would be telling me the miscarriage happened to them, and I would be sad for them and then I would realize it happened to me.

I dreamed that the D&C would hurt. I would never wake up from it. I had no control. I was about to die. Someone was trying to hurt the baby and I couldn't intervene.

I had nightmares: big animals and violence, loss of body parts, blood, terrible accidents, and about the blood all over the sheets.

(I feel guilty; I had carried bricks right before my miscarriage.) In the dream I kept seeing myself carrying bricks, and then I'd wake up.

I dreamed I had the baby and I was pushing it in a carriage and I lost it and couldn't find it. I would see the baby far away, but I couldn't get to it.

I dreamed of them crying. I would panic and awaken. I'd bolt up and listen.

I dreamed about a baby with no face.

I dreamed I had just given birth. The baby was in a blanket. I would get just ready to pull back the blanket to find out what sex it was, and I'd wake up.

LOSS OF SELF-WORTH

Many women talked about feeling publicly exposed as incompetent or as reproductive failures and felt uncomfortable, guilty, or deeply ashamed around others:

> *I had an inner feeling that I was not a competent grown-up woman who could do this.* My *self-esteem was shot. I felt like I could do everything career-wise but I couldn't have a baby—the one thing that most women without brains could do. I feel so unfinished. What good am I?*

> *It felt so public. I felt so exposed. Everything private and personal had been laid out and displayed: what I am, how I performed, how I failed. I thought, "Who am I? I'm a mother and I can't take care of my babies." I felt inadequate. I couldn't even control my body. I was horrendously embarrassed. It was an important public failure. They all knew and could see that I couldn't perform.*

> *I felt really embarrassed, and then they felt embarrassed. It was awkward. I made light of it to put them at ease. A friend of my sister didn't know and said, "It's so wonderful. When are you due?"* I hated *to tell people. I let some still assume; I hid from others.*

> *It was hard to look anyone in the eye for a long time. I could tell when someone didn't know how to deal with me. They looked at me funny. I interpreted it to mean there must be something wrong with me.*

> *I stuck out like a sore thumb because I've had so many miscarriages. I scare people that they will have many too, and they think they have no right to grieve their single miscarriages next to me.*

Because they believed that perhaps they should see their losses as nothing, some women felt undeserving of others' compassion and comfort and that they burdened others with their grief. In addition, many felt guilty, embarrassed, or undeserving when others demonstrated compassion for or "made a fuss" over them, and they pretended to feel fine. Some even tried to console and emotionally attend to those they felt they had hurt or failed:

> *They were feeling sorry for me. I spent energy trying to make them feel okay. As much as I wanted people to be sympathetic, I wouldn't allow them to be. I would say, "I'm fine."*

> *I'm too uncomfortable to cry in front of others. I hate to put them through it. It was easier to make myself feel better than to try to make them feel better. I have a tendency to try to help people feel better about my loss.* My *husband took it especially hard. I had to take care of him and myself and my parents and everybody.*

SPIRITUALITY

Over the course of grieving their losses, some women drew quiet strength and comfort from their spiritual or religious beliefs:

I could not fathom the reason why it happened, but in my faith I always knew there was a reason. I may not accept it or understand it, and I may never find out the reason, but I believe it was a good reason. God is taking care of my babies. I'll have them later on. It's a really good feeling.

I felt much more connected to my spiritual self. That's where my healing took place. I prayed and found it a comfort. I say "The Serenity Prayer" all the time. I don't believe it was for a reason or God did it. It was just nature. He didn't cause it, and it's not the result of sin. God is here to support and comfort me. God loved my babies too.

Several said they became more spiritual or religious:

I became very spiritual (consciously, anyway). I became closer to God. My miscarriage strengthened my belief in a God that cares about the fall of a sparrow. He will be there in all things, in whatever I have to walk through. That doesn't mean it will be easy. Our way of valuing life is superficial.

The baby brought me to Christ. It was really healing.

I had had two ectopic pregnancies. The hospital priest came and asked, "Have you prayed to Mary?" I'm not Catholic, but I said I had prayed to everybody. I hadn't. In my heart I knew that if I could get the baby into my uterus, I could carry and deliver it. At that point, I did start praying. The next year, I had my son.

For a large number of women, the time following miscarriage was one of intense questioning and spiritual crisis. Their miscarriages rocked the foundations of their faith. For a few, the crisis irreparably shattered their previous spiritual belief systems:

When I was pregnant I thought God had blessed me. It was a miracle. Then I couldn't imagine why God took my baby away. I felt betrayed by Him. The miscarriage shook my spiritual beliefs.

I keep praying to God to give me another child. I have made a novena to St. Jude. Nobody's been answering my prayers. I'm kind of doubting them. I'm beginning to wonder if they're going to help me.

I felt like the Lord pulled the rug out from under me. It's been an adventure in faith! I still even struggle with my faith today.

People put spiritual band-aids on me. It was bullshit. It made me so angry.

Some women wondered whether their miscarriages had occurred as some sort of spiritual punishment:

> *I had seven years of infertility. Why did I get pregnant if I couldn't have a baby? Why give me this and take it away? Why me? What have I ever done to deserve this?*
>
> *I had had an abortion when I was very young, and I never stopped feeling guilty. I would think, "How many more times before I've paid my debt? How many more before it's even?"*
>
> *I thought I was being punished. I thought it was payback time. Then I read* When Bad Things Happen to Good People, *and I realized I was not being punished.*

Many women expressed their anger at God:

> *I got down on God! I had a lot of doubting, anger, and bitterness. I thought, "How can You do this to me?!" I didn't want to have anything to do with Him. He gave me this gift, and then He took it away. He could have prevented that. Why was He letting this happen when we had so much to give? I felt very sorry for myself. I was the supreme martyr. I didn't blame myself as much as dear old God. Then I would feel guilty. I was up and down the roller coaster.*
>
> *After six losses, I thought, "What's the point of serving a God who can't control this?"*
>
> *After the miscarriage, I had the feeling there is no God. All these years I've kind of thought that, but now I'm sure. I was angry. It was beyond anger. It was rage.*

As a result of allowing themselves to feel and express these feelings and thereby working through their spiritual crises, some women developed a broader level of spiritual understanding and a more peaceful relationship with God:

> *I always had such strong faith. But I just did not understand why God took my baby. I had to grow a lot. It was so painful. I finally realized my spirituality was very naive. Just because I was a good girl didn't mean it would go alright. There is suffering in the world. I am not immune. And God is not immune from grief. He lost His own son. All of that is part of life, and we can't ignore or control or explain it. It just is.*
>
> *I turned to God, and I felt I got an answer in the second baby. When I lost that baby, life didn't make sense. I didn't understand why. I didn't see God's purpose. I read* The Road Less Traveled. *I was soul searching. I needed to let go of things a bit. I wanted to live life as honestly as possible. You can renounce religion, or explore what life means and learn and grow and take a philosophical approach.*
>
> *I had a very interesting spiritual experience. I don't know how you feel about this, but I spoke with a psychic. She accurately described my stillborn son, and she said, "He did whatever he needed to do in this life." Well, I applied that to my miscarried baby, too.*
>
> *I had felt I understood my religion. But I went into spiritual chaos. I had to reidentify my whole sense about God. My spirituality matured. I thought God took care of children—and where did God go? Now I feel I don't want that kind of God, puppeteering and controlling all. God was sad and didn't want my babies to die.*

Jessi's Story

Three and a half years ago I became pregnant. I was unhappy about it. It was our sixth pregnancy. Our finances were bad. It was not a wonderful time.

When I was three months pregnant, I began spotting. Then reality hit. I realized, "It's my BABY!" I didn't want to lose my baby! Then "it" happened; I miscarried. When I went in to my doctor's office, I was in a daze. He did a D&C, and he said I might feel sad the next day. I hadn't realized before that a woman might feel sad after a miscarriage.

One day I was pregnant; the next day I was not. I felt strange, sad, empty, and lonely. Nobody had forewarned me about the lonely, empty feeling. I had been pregnant. I had this life inside of me. I knew I had a baby. But the next day—there was no baby. My child had died. I knew I lost a whole child. After that I had my tubes tied. I thought, "No way! I won't do this again!"

I saw my baby as a little red-haired girl. She was my blessing. She would be my husband's girl. She would be a wonderful little pleasant addition who would draw us all closer. She would complete our family. It makes me cry! I see a little red-haired girl in the street and I cry. I cry in celebration of her.

I didn't name her. That's another incomplete part of that puzzle that I wanted finished.

The miscarriage had a devastating effect on my relationship with my husband. It almost broke us up. I thought, "Here is this baby's father, and we should be feeling the same thing." I felt real pain. He had no response. He never cried, never felt pain, never discussed it, never said anything! Nothing! Nothing! I felt so bitter and so angry, so cold and hurt. I wanted to get even with him in the worst way. I didn't want him to touch me sexually. I couldn't experience orgasm for a long time. I was so angry!

I have a sister who had had two miscarriages and no children. She phoned and—there were no words; she just cried with me. She felt so bad and so terrible. She understood.

My aunt said, "It was probably for the best." I turned cold. I had loved her to death. But that was so cruel. Other people said, "It would have been retarded," "It was Mother Nature's way," and "Be glad you were only in the third month." Well I didn't care what stage she was in. I lost a whole entire child! It was as big a loss as if she had been born. But nobody acknowledged that. There was no validity to my pain.

I felt very lonely, like I was the only person in the world who knew what I was feeling. I was in my own little world. It was like a dream. The outside world was going on, but it was so different for me. I was in the world, and life went on but I was in a plastic bubble. I was living, but I wasn't alive. A part of me had died. I was going through the motions. I was seeing myself performing the motions. It was like an out of body experience. I was elevated above myself and observing.

I got cold. I got on a real destructive thing. I only brought on more pain. Oh God I had panic attacks! I felt out of control. I thought about suicide. I doubted I'd ever get through the grief. I was so depressed! Very very depressed! I imagined that my husband didn't want me. I wondered, "What good is my life?"

I felt confused because I had been sad about being pregnant. I thought I had gone crazy! I wondered, "Am I turning into a nut?"

I wanted people to say they understood it was such a sad thing. And it would have helped if someone had told me, "You're not crazy," and if I could've talked to someone who shared the same pain and who could say to me, "It's okay to feel grief. It will get better."

I found myself searching for my baby all the time. I'd think, "Where did she go?" "Does someone else have her?" I dream about her still. I dream that I am with her and that I finally have a chance to hold her and to experience love from her. I get to know her and love her. The circle is complete. Sometimes I feel close to her, and that feels wonderful.

I felt a lot better two-and-a-half years after the miscarriage. I have come to terms with the loss. I grew in my spirituality. My mother had died. I decided to do spiritual work and to meditate and to be constructive. I realized how lucky I was to have my other five children and how wonderful they are. I appreciate life more.

I am more compassionate to all types of pain now. I take time to look at people. I stop the world for people who need it stopped—and I listen. I am a good listener now.

I still have all these questions. I still feel sad sometimes; I still cry. It's like losing the closest person to you, whom you loved, through death. It's always sad. I will always be able to cry about it.

[Authors' note: When asked at the end of her interview if she had any heartfelt message to express personally to another mother who had had a miscarriage, Jessi burst into sobs for the first time in her interview and cried, "I'm so sorry! I'm so very sorry! That's all I can say! That's all I can say!"]

CHAPTER NINE

The Hardest Part

Sometimes we talk about our emotional pains with people we trust. But sometimes we shy away from uncloaking our worst emotional pains, even to these trusted few, because we are afraid our emotions are too crazy, too miserable, or too deep to reveal. It is in these very areas that we are most injured and in need of healing. That healing comes, in part, through identification with others—learning that we are not abnormal or alone—and receiving acceptance and compassion from others. Toward the goal of providing this to you, we asked women about the very worst of their grief. This is what they told us.

DEVASTATION

Following nearly two-thirds of the miscarriages, women said they felt devastated:

> *I went through a weird depression, but I wouldn't admit it. I was sick, sleeping, and lethargic all the time. That was not like me. I was irritable. I couldn't handle anyone with problems. Emotionally, I became a wrecking house. I stopped going to church because I would bawl my eyes out. I was a spectacle. It's one year later now, and I'm still devastated. I'm really sad most of the time. I feel I have to hide that. I can't show anybody. I feel distant from anyone who hasn't had a miscarriage because they think miscarriage is nothing.*

> *I was walking around like an open wound. I felt nonstop pain. I was feeling like things were never going to get better, like everything had been taken from me.*

REALIZING THE LOSS

Women described overwhelming feelings of loss when they realized that their babies were gone. This grief was pegged by many as the most difficult aspect of their miscarriages:

> *I started thinking about what the baby would have looked like, what our lives would have been like, and about our loss. The most difficult aspect was knowing that this person we had all these hopes and dreams for, wasn't going to exist.*

always wanted to have a baby. The worst was losing something I'd waited years for. I had it, and then all of a sudden it was gone. The baby was a gift from God that was just snatched away from me. It was knowing that I lost my baby. I had related to that child immediately. I was bonded with it.

When miscarriages came about abruptly and without prior signs (for example, when women went to their doctors for routine pregnancy appointments only to find that their babies had died), the utter shock of the news was sometimes described as the most difficult aspect of their losses:

There was a clear emotional storm inside me. It was difficult to shift so quickly with no transition. One minute I was pregnant and planning, and one minute later it was all gone. Everything stopped dead in its tracks. The worst was the abruptness, the deep sadness that something that was alive in me and that I saw as precious, was suddenly gone.

Some women who had several losses grieved those that occurred earliest in their pregnancies in special ways. They felt cheated of the chance to experience their pregnancies or cheated by society because those losses received no recognition at all and the women received no allowance for grieving.

Of my seven miscarriages [including one at four months], *the miscarriage that had the most extreme impact on me was the one that occurred at the earliest stage because I had just found out I was pregnant on a Thursday and didn't have time to digest the fact before I lost the baby on Monday. The pregnancy was so fast. It hadn't had time to sink in. I hadn't had time to assimilate it. That loss was particularly hard. I was really off balance.*

I wrote an article that appeared in Shattered Dreams' newsletter. As I wrote in it, "Watching my nearly ten pound baby son die in my brother's arms was one of the most painful experiences I have had. Yet, I have always felt more cheated with a miscarriage—cheated out of carrying the baby, of feeling him move, of getting to know his personality, and the special acknowledgment of pregnancy. I didn't even know if I had a boy or a girl."

So some women had no time for transition and to adapt before being struck with the finality of their losses. Other mothers, however, had more time because their miscarriages took several days or even weeks to diagnose or come to completion. But they could not use that time to adjust to their losses because they did not know for sure whether they *were* making the transition from motherhood to loss. They felt hung in suspension and did not know "where to go" emotionally. Were they having babies or losing babies? Was it a time for joy or sorrow? For these women, the *uncertainty* during that period of time wreaked havoc on their emotions and was most difficult for them to deal with. They could not aim themselves emotionally in any particular direction. They felt torn in two:

> *The hardest part was the waiting. I had to wait and wait and wait. The waiting to find out wore me down to a frayed thread. I became like a robot as time went on without answers, because I was controlling myself from becoming hysterical. It was so crazy to not know day after day after day whether I was* having *a baby or facing the* death *of my baby. I just couldn't stand the not knowing any longer.*

> *I thought I was losing the baby. Eventually, at 4:00 in the morning, it came out while I was in the bathroom. It looked like a little baby bird. It had been dead for a long time. Talk about relieved! I thought, "Thank God the miscarriage is finally over." I smiled. Yet I was mad at myself for three weeks because I had smiled. But I smiled because the pain of not knowing was over.*

Most women whose miscarriages occurred in their first pregnancies feared that their miscarriages signaled their inability ever to bear children. Those who already had children feared that their miscarriages meant they could never have more children. For some women, these fears were the most difficult aspects of their losses:

> *The worst thing was feeling like we were never going to have a family. No matter what we tried, it didn't work out. I threw my prenatal vitamins away. I thought, "I'll never need these."*

> *Being pregnant, we thought of our lives in a completely different way. It means the loss of Motherhood. Now I feel I shouldn't put off anything because I may never have children. It's this kind of yo-yo: pregnant, not, pregnant, not, pregnant, not.*

One of a mother's basic instincts is to protect her children, but women found themselves helpless and unable to do so. The worst was happening to their babies, and there was nothing they could do to stop it. Some described this as the most difficult aspect:

> *I lost control of my pregnancy. The worst was the fact that I was entrusted with these special gifts and I blew it. They depended on me, and somehow I violated their trust.*

The greatest difficulty described by many women was the lack of empathy from those around them and the loneliness that resulted from it:

> *I didn't get* any *sympathy. I had* no *one to say, "I'm really sorry." I didn't matter to anyone. People didn't care—not even my family. It was no big deal to them. It was nothing. It was like it was null and void, and life continued to go on. There was not enough pause. I started building that wall around me.*

> *I was not supported. It was all dealt with so matter-of-factly, like a surgery, not like I had really lost babies. It was treated more like an appendectomy. The most difficult aspect of it all was the loneliness. The real, real loneliness.*

PINPOINTING EMOTIONAL LOW POINTS

The women pinpointed their emotional low points, which ranged from the time of their miscarriages to two-and-a-half years after their losses. The average time was nearly six weeks after their miscarriages, though most clustered throughout the first 30 days. (One woman said that her low point was 15 years after her miscarriage. We omitted her response, the "I don't remember" responses, and one "not yet" response from the average.)

We spoke with a significant number of the women soon after their miscarriages. Their responses could reflect only their low points up to the time of their interviews. Because little time had passed since their miscarriages, they could not yet view their evolution through grief from a grand vantage point, nor could they peg their low points from that broader viewpoint of their experiences. Yet their responses *were* calculated into the statistical average. So the average would very likely be later if all 100 women were able to respond after more time had passed because it is likely that some had not yet reached their lowest point in their overall grieving process by the time of their interviews.

Descriptions of the women's feelings when they were at their emotional lows were diverse and included rage, hopelessness, sorrow, despair, confusion, and loneliness:

I was in a very, very deep depression. I didn't want to get up. I felt an utter emptiness which I feared would never go away. I felt a hopelessness and a deep, indescribable sorrow. Now I understand how people can commit suicide. I was so, so low. I was on the bottom.

Many times I thought, "My husband would be better off if I was not still here. Why am I alive?" I wished I had a terminal disease so I wouldn't have to live.

When I was at my lowest, I did not *like myself. I didn't want to try anymore. I didn't care. I just gave up. I thought, "What's left to live for? Why am I going through this hell? Why me? Why my baby? Is it because I'm a bad person?" I felt real, real empty.*

Following nearly half the miscarriages, women at some point in time doubted they would ever get through their grief:

It's been two-and-a-half years, and I still wonder if I will ever feel better.

I would think, "Is this ever going to end? Will I ever be able to go to a baby shower without a lump in my throat or a knot in my stomach? Will I ever be able to join in conversations about children?"

The worst part was feeling like I wasn't going to survive this. The physical stuff was nothing. The emotional stuff is: realizing that life goes on, but how am I gonna do it? I'm going to have to live with this every day, and I can't get through it right this second.

It's been six months, and I still doubt I will get through it. I know how comforting it is to have things like memories of feeling the baby moving. I don't have that kind of thing. I see others' grief as an ascending staircase. They're going to get to the top someday. But I'm going on a flat surface like ice. I'm never going to get to ascend.

Almost a third of the women interviewed said that, after their miscarriages, they had thoughts about suicide. (Although a couple of these women actually considered killing themselves, most of them only *thought* about it.) In light of the fact that miscarriage is considered by many people to be merely a disappointing yet routine fact of life, this statistic is staggering:

I thought a lot about (but didn't consider actually doing it) shooting my children and me so we could all be together with the baby as we should be. And I could be out of the pain. It was more than I could bear. But I couldn't leave my other three.

I didn't care any more. I didn't care about anything. Nothing else mattered; nothing could make me happy. If I got hit by a car, it wouldn't matter. It would take the pain away. I wanted to die. I wish I had the guts to commit suicide.

I feel suicidal when I get my period because it means I didn't conceive again.

My life flashed before my eyes. My life ended. For a brief moment, I just wanted to die so I wouldn't have to feel anymore. I just wanted everything to stop.

Some women described a sense or feeling of blackness, and some described feeling so disconnected from life that it felt like they were on a strange planet or lost out in space somewhere:

It was like sinking into and then living in a black hole, lost out in the cosmos. You can scream your lungs out . . . but nobody hears.

I could actually, literally feel a dark bag coming over me, moving from my head down. Moment by moment I could see it coming down.

I had a couple of black months after the miscarriage.

Having a miscarriage is like having all the air sucked out of you and everything fades to black.

Nothing else mattered; nothing could make me happy. I felt like I was falling into a black hole with no way out. I was trying to grab on to something, but I couldn't. There is still a dark cloud over me. I could never again be as happy.

"MISCARRIAGE IS LIKE . . ."

When women were asked to complete the sentence, "Having a miscarriage is like . . . ," their responses were dramatic. Miscarriage is like

. . . losing family. The child within you is an extension of you.

. . . losing a part of your soul, having it taken away from you and never being able to get it back.

. . . losing your best friend. Losing that person is like having no place to go home.

. . . having your insides hollowed out all the way down through the floor and there's a well underneath you. It's this bottomless pit of emptiness in you.

. . . having your heart torn out, everything you can imagine being ripped from your gut, and trying to hang on to it when you can't. It is terrible pain, like a physical pain. Nobody can make you feel better.

. . . having a very important promise broken without explanation, like a betrayal. It's not the way we were told it would be.

. . . being in a bad car accident. (I was in one.) You know you'll live, but you're spinning out.

. . . I can't relate it to anything. It's like falling through the air and your parachute doesn't open.

. . . having your body torn in two. It's a pain you don't think you'll live through.

. . . there is nothing else to compare it to. It's losing a child.

. . . I can't focus. It's too painful. I'm drawing a blank. It's like looking at it out of the corner of my eye. It hurts. . . . It's like going to hell. That's exactly *what it is!*

. . . losing a part of yourself. It's losing something alive and made out of love that was growing inside of you.

. . . nothing I've ever known before. It's a very lonely feeling. It's like giving death. When you give life, everyone is there to cheer you on. But when you give death, you do it alone.

CHAPTER TEN

Insights and Reflections

Looking back after the passage of time at our beliefs and activities following our miscarriages, we can sometimes see the impact these things had on our process of healing. Some of our ideas and behaviors proved helpful and withstood the test of time and experience, whereas some of our ideas and behaviors hampered the process of our healing and required revision. Some of our actions were more effective than others in helping us cope, and some weren't effective at all. We can look at the ways in which we tried to cope and sometimes we can distinguish what helped and what hindered our efforts at healing.

In addition, we can often identify in retrospect what information, words, actions, or attitudes others might have lent us, that helped us heal the pain and move through the grief more easily.

The following are some reflections from the women we interviewed. Hindsight affords insight.

METHODS OF COPING

Many women's attempts at coping with their miscarriages left them feeling even worse. For the most part, these efforts involved what they did emotionally rather than physically, such as isolating themselves, blaming themselves, or not allowing themselves to grieve:

> *I'd say, "This isn't happening to me." I acted nonchalant. I held it all inside. I put a wall around me. I blocked everybody out. My husband didn't know what I was going through. I felt embarrassed and stupid. I just told people the facts, not the emotions. I had a very good mask. I wanted them to think I was so strong and handling it so well.*

> *I went back to work and I got involved. I was a human dynamo. I would not allow myself the feelings. I worked hard to feel really tired in order to forget. I thought that if I grieved or pampered myself, it would have been "coddling myself." I was hard on myself. I keep thinking I should be over this. I have put on 50 pounds from depression.*

> *I drank all that stupid alcohol that made me sick as a dog. That stuff's like poison!*

I blamed myself for killing the baby. I ran myself through the guilt wringer, racking my brains out.

I pigged out on ice cream.

I walked away from everything in my life to start clean. I couldn't stand the grief in my husband's eyes. It was a reflection of my own.

To try to comfort themselves, the women more often pursued physical activities or remedies for their emotional pain. In fact, the most common response by far to a question about what they did for themselves that felt good was that they ate ice cream!

I went shopping. I got out and walked. (It's a haze.)

I started redecorating my house. I got to hammer walls down. I put energy into work. I scrubbed the floors! When I'm angry, I work.

I enjoyed soaking in the tub and pampering myself.

I got thin.

I had hot fudge sundaes.

Some learned to both respect and care more for their emotional needs:

What felt good was finally allowing myself more freedom to be truly human. Only now do I explore my emotions.

I let myself cry. I read sad books and watched sad movies. I allowed myself to wallow in self-pity for a long time. I played soft music, and I let my feelings out. I wrote a lot. I learned why I was acting and feeling as I was. I let myself love the baby.

I splurged and bought books. I gave myself permission to take three days off work and sit in bed and read. I reminded myself of the limits of my ability. I gave myself permission to be a baby and to be babied, to be selfish and take care of my needs. We also had a memorial service. That helped more than anything. Eventually my husband and I went away for a weekend. I gave myself permission to have fun without feeling guilty and to realize that that would not be erasing my baby's existence. My baby is still in my mind every day as I go on with life, and will always be there.

I decided to not focus on a subsequent pregnancy. I had good therapy. It helped to talk about it with someone who would listen. Eventually I talked to my mom a lot. We got closer.

There was nothing to do but go through the grief. Anything that would've taken away from the grief would've diminished the baby. I didn't play games about that. If I was feeling bad, I let myself. I needed to grieve.

Most of the women could remember nothing they did that helped them feel better. Some women said that what made them feel good also made them feel bad:

I drank wine nightly, and I started smoking again. I nearly became an alcoholic. I needed it. It made me feel mellow. In the short term, it was good. In the long term, it was bad.

I ate and spent money.

I kept busy at work.

INFORMATION THAT WOULD HAVE BEEN COMFORTING OR REASSURING

Many women wished they had been given explicit information at the time of their miscarriages about what to expect. Women had felt frightened about what was happening to them physically, medically, and emotionally:

I wish that I had known about the emotional feelings I would go through, that I had known what to expect. I wish I had known that other women went through it and didn't die from it or go crazy; it didn't kill them; they came out of it.

Statistics would have helped—a "guilt-free" handbook. It would've been nice to have information about medical procedures, what to expect beforehand, and physical symptomology you go through (because your body is screaming, "YOU WERE PREGNANT!"). It would've helped to have a book that told me that maybe I would survive this and that contained a list of all available resources.

Later I had the courage to talk to my OB. I said, "My life has been on hold for three years. My husband and I haven't made love; I can't go back to work. Why didn't you tell me, 'Here is a group of people who will sit down and talk about this with you. Here is a list of books'?" He's a wonderful, tender, sensitive guy. He's a lovely man who personally knows about children and loss. He put his eyes downward, and he said, "I know that's something I have never been very good at, and I'm sorry." He said, "We don't do a very good job with this." They see so many miscarriages; there are so many women who fall through the cracks! Somebody's gotta talk to these people! By gosh, somebody's gotta lay on a hand and say something helpful and not whistle a tune.

They also wanted to see and touch their babies and to be included in medical decision making over matters such as what would be done with their babies, when D&C's would be performed, whether or what kind of anesthesia would be used, and whether they wanted testing performed on the remains:

If I could have kept what came out of me . . .

I wish I had some kind of knowledge about my baby like why he died. I wish I had been told of the option to see him and to have tests done, and to be told it's normal to want to see your baby.

I wish I had been given footprints, respect, and a right to grieve.

WHAT THEY MIGHT HAVE DONE DIFFERENTLY TO BETTER PROMOTE THEIR HEALING

Following their miscarriages, most women were limited in their ability to tend to themselves emotionally because they were so burdened with pain and grief. Yet in retrospect, they could see what they might have done differently to heal more efficiently. Most spoke in terms of granting themselves permission to feel and express their grief:

> *I wish I had felt the feelings instead of burying them, cried, and tried to understand my emotions sooner instead of hiding them and letting them build up inside.*
>
> *I wish I had found a support group and shared this very quickly after the miscarriage. I never should have waited as long as I did. It would have been better if I had sought information that would bring my feelings out, to get my husband and me into counseling, to have asked for help, and to seek communication and validation which would get me to take the lid off my grief and deal with it.*
>
> *I could've gone ahead and let my job go to hell. (I went back in three days.) I could've let myself take care of me longer. I could've taken more breaks. "Getting on with life" didn't work! It would've been helpful to allow myself to feel bad when I felt bad. Because I didn't, I have to go back and do it now.*
>
> *I could've not blamed myself, even if my husband* was *mad at me.*
>
> *What I would do differently is this: If I become pregnant again, I would ask a hospital or an OB in advance, like you shop insurance or anything else, "What will you do for me if I miscarry?" If I miscarried again, I would have the strength to make choices, like not throwing my baby away, and I would see and touch my baby.*
>
> *I would've been better off had I not crawled into a shell, had I gone to a support group and heard some of the goofy things they've done, too. I could've reached out and explained my feelings better to my mom. I could've not worried about burdening people, called, and said, "I need you."*
>
> *I might've taken more time to be introspective, time for reading and walking on the beaches. I could've gotten out more, walked in the park, fed the ducks, swam. I could've developed other areas of my life.*
>
> *I could've paused, taken time off work, and let people do things for me. To not force myself to make life normal. To succumb. To take a weekend or a week and go away and relax. To take care of myself more physically.*

THE IMPACT ON THEIR LIVES TODAY

In response to the lack of firsthand experience of their babies as real human beings and in response to societal misconceptions about miscarriage and about grief, many women never grieved to a point of resolution and healing.

Women's miscarriages continued to color their daily lives. Most women still thought about what life would have been like had their babies lived. Some, especially those whose miscarriages occurred many years before, still questioned many aspects of their losses. They continued to ponder, question, and dream and feel the impact of their losses at some level throughout their lives:

After 11 years, I think about it a lot still. It is still a loss. It's not forgotten. I'll never be the same again. I wonder about women who never talk about it.

This has enabled me to comfort other mothers who have miscarried.

I think it's more tragic now because of my age. There will be no more children. I can't compensate for the baby anymore with another baby. It is truly over and done. There is a finality now. I have an empty nest. One is missing.

I have so many feelings about Nathaniel—the joy of him, the pain of losing him, how much I miss him now, how scared I am that I'm not ever going to have children, and cheated.

My miscarriage was 15 years ago. It's a lifelong loss, something you think about through your whole life. You see a child that age and you think about it. You never get over it.

Even though it's been 19 years, every time I see a pregnant woman or a child, it always triggers something. I say, "Oh, that's what I lost." My baby will always have a place in my gut and in my heart.

With respect to over two-thirds of the miscarriages in our study, women felt that the emotional pain, although somewhat eased over the course of time, would always be with them in some way and on some level:

You never get over it. You just put it in the back of your mind. Yet the pain isn't so raw anymore. It's a lingering sadness but it is clearly not on the surface. It is deep and it is there. My soul is marked.

I've had two children since my loss. The loss is still there, but it's not the same as it used to be. But the memory of that baby will always be there.

I still need to grieve.

I have worked through a lot. The stabbing, acute pain is resolved. But they'll always be losses. Those children are my children, and I'll never see them take their first step, grow up, or see who they would have become. I still feel a gentle sadness. There is a place in my heart for each one. I will never forget them.

Whereas many women were surprised and/or glad to still be able to feel sadness about their babies and their losses, some felt upset that they no longer felt it:

Although you try to put a lot of things out of your mind, there is still more hurt there than I thought there was. Even after 40 years! There are more memories there than I thought there were!

I thought I had forgotten. She is still really close to my heart. It still bothers me a lot. I haven't put it to rest yet.

The pain has not gone away, and I hope it doesn't *ever go away because I wouldn't want to forget her. Even though she never made it all the way, she was still my baby, and I wouldn't want to forget her. If the pain ever went away, it would be like forgetting her. The idea of forgetting is horrendous. I would never pretend that she never was. But I think there's a terrible conflict, too, about keeping the pain going.*

I'm sad that it doesn't hurt as much anymore. It's scary because I'm forgetting a bit. The hurt is all I have left. As it decreases, I'm doing the baby an injustice. I feel guilty.

CHAPTER ELEVEN

Leah's Story

My miscarriage occurred 3 1/2 months ago at 10 weeks into my pregnancy. I'm very scared right now to remember the good feelings about the pregnancy because it hurts too much.

I felt beautiful with our son or daughter inside me. Absolutely intrinsically beautiful. I could look at the world like a smiling Madonna. I felt in better health than I have most of my life. I wanted to be healthy for my baby as well as for me. I did all the right things. And I did things during the pregnancy that I have never done before. I went sailing. I went to Disneyland. The pregnancy kept me on course and centered. I had a sense of joy and peace that was all-encompassing. I was in the calm of a hurricane—the serene part. Everything else around me could go its own way in a whirlwind, but it didn't touch me.

I talked to my baby all the time. I told the baby often that I loved him or her and that we would do our best to be good parents. I felt like I had a really good relationship with my baby.

When I had the miscarriage, I felt like my universe was being ripped apart. I had no control. I couldn't believe it was going on. It was like I was in a nightmare. I hemorrhaged and almost died. I felt that if I closed my eyes and kept them closed, I would just slip away and die. At one point, I did close my eyes, and I realized I had a choice between living and dying. If I died I could be with my baby right away and be with my parents. But I realized that I couldn't be with my husband, Charles. It was Charles' world that drew me back. I love him so much. So I chose to live.

Because of the blood loss, I had to stabilize before they could do the D&C. They ended up doing it the next day. I had always thought that when I went to the hospital I would be having my baby, not losing it. You know, they didn't give us anything at the hospital. No information. Nothing. Now I can never go to that hospital without feeling that loss.

The baby is there and the baby is not there all at the same time. I never actually felt my baby kick. I never actually heard the heartbeat. I don't really know what sex the baby was. For some reason we refer to him as a boy. On an emotional, intuitive level I think he was a boy. After the miscarriage we named him Michael. It seemed the right thing to do. I am not worried about what society thinks.

I haven't been able to visualize Michael. My visual sense is not as good as my kinesthetic sense. But I have "felt" him, his shape, his touch, his feel.

The worst part of the loss was the total loneliness, the emptiness. It was more painful than words can express. I feel it even now. When I had Michael inside me, it was like I was never alone. I feel my stomach now and say, "Where are you?" I still have the shape I had when I was pregnant. It is a constant reminder. Sometimes I forget about the miscarriage. I talk to the baby as if he is still there, and I have to remember that he isn't. But I know that my baby knows I love him, and that gives me a sense of peace. I feel a closeness to him now if I allow my mind to touch him.

The miscarriage strengthened my relationship with my husband. We have always made it a priority to communicate even when it is painful. I realize that he didn't have to feel the same as me. He was there for me. He stayed with me throughout everything he could. He reassured me that it wasn't my fault and that he loved me. I felt loneliness because the baby was gone. At the same time, I never had someone stick with me through thick and thin like my husband did. Just holding hands with him gave me so much strength. But I felt like I was failing him because I was miscarrying. I lost the baby. I miscarried.

I was driven to do things just to keep myself busy. I would work 'til I dropped, doing stuff until I was absolutely exhausted. I just wanted to keep myself from remembering, from thinking.

I had nightmares. I often felt out of control. I had panic attacks. Panic attacks and I are old friends, but they are more on the increase since the miscarriage. When I was at my lowest, I kept wondering if I was crazy because my grief was so deep. I had suicidal thoughts. If my husband was late coming home, I'd say to myself, "Someone *else I love is gone."*

I went to a psychiatrist who told me I was crazy and wanted to put me in the hospital on medication. I wouldn't let him. He wanted to rip me away from any support I had. I also went to a priest. You know, he said all the wrong things but he let me cry *and I* knew he cared. *The support group helped. I talked to other women and listened to them and realized that my responses weren't out of line.*

But it was hard to be around most people. Their expectation was that the miscarriage happened and I should just recover and go on. My family expected my emotional and physical recovery within five days. That really hurt. I felt compelled to really hide a lot of my emotions from them. I had a friend whom I called three weeks later. She didn't even have a moment to say a kind word. I'll never forget that. On the other hand, I had three other girlfriends who really took time to be with me. When I needed to talk about it, they allowed me to.

I did a couple things for myself that felt good. I got angry. I got angry at the universe, at myself, and at the psychiatrist. I had so much anger. I was totally angry! What I really wanted was for people to try to help me get the emotions out and not block them in. When I allowed myself the anger, something snapped. It was good. I could look at my grief and realize it was normal.

We took my hospital bracelets and put them together and buried them during an eclipse. That gave it an ending. The eclipse was important because the moon goes away but it comes back again. That ceremony allowed us to remember our baby in happiness, not just in grief, and to know that we will be together again sometime. A weed with a beautiful white flower grew right where we buried the bracelets. I felt like the universe honored what we did.

Spiritually, this has been a journey. The miscarriage has made me feel more strongly about some kind of life after death because I want to be with my baby. I see death as a part of life. To me, the universe is like an embroidery. On our side, we see the tangles and the knots, but on the other side the pattern comes through.

PART FOUR

RELATIONSHIPS

CHAPTER TWELVE

Our Partners

We are social beings. We need and thrive on a social network that supports and upholds us, especially in times of need. When deprived of that support, we exist in a barren loneliness.

We see ourselves reflected through the mirror that others provide. As Stephen Levine wrote in *Meetings at the Edge,* "When you love someone, that feeling is not coming from them; they are just acting as a mirror for the place inside of us which is love. And when we lose that loved one, that mirror has been shattered. We have lost our connection, our contact with our original nature, which is love itself. We mourn the loss of our contact with that part of ourselves as reflected through that other being."

Because of the great discrepancy between what we experience when we miscarry and what society understands about what we experience, our social systems do not provide the compassion and support we need in order to work through our grief. Without the safety net of a support system, we feel loneliness for others on top of our loneliness for our babies; we feel the loss of our other relationships on top of the loss of our pregnancies and babies; we feel self-doubt and confusion about our feelings on top of confusion about how and why our losses occurred. Grief on top of grief; struggle on top of struggle.

In this part, "Relationships," women describe for us the pains, sorrows, anger, confusion, and yearnings they felt after their losses in response to people in their lives.

We asked the women about their relationships with their partners after the miscarriages. There were two elements about which they were particularly concerned: (1) the depth of their partners' feelings over their babies and (2) what their partners *did* with those feelings. Through sharing and expressing caring feelings together, many partners reportedly became closer emotionally following their miscarriages, later, or both. Many partners were out of sync with each other in terms of their feelings about their miscarriages, both partners felt hurt, and the issue was neither initially nor ever resolved between them. In a few relationships, the pain between partners surrounding miscarriage was too much to bear. Instead of being a bridge for emotional closeness, these miscarriages became chasms across which neither partner could cross, and these relationships ended.

WHAT FELT HELPFUL

It is important to note that the women's responses in this chapter reflect the experiences of the babies' fathers *as seen through the eyes of the women.*

When women felt that their partners accepted their feelings and provided the women safety in which to feel and express those feelings, couples drew closer and relationships were experienced as consoling and healing:

> *I just felt so sad about the whole loss. I felt so stripped. I wanted him around. I needed him. His presence made me feel reassured and warm. When I wanted to talk, he listened. I felt taken care of.*

Some fathers also felt a deep sense of loss. When they shared their feelings of loss in some way, couples drew powerfully close. The men were a safety net for the mothers. The women felt that their feelings and the lives of their babies were honored and validated by their partners. These couples felt united in their parenthood, in their love, and in their grief:

> *At the D&C, he held me and rubbed my tummy. He cried with me and said, "I love you. It's not your fault." He brought home flowers to plant in remembrance. I felt secure and comforted.*

> *The miscarriage brought us closer together. His being with me when I miscarried made it much more real for him. He delivered the baby. He held me for a long, long time afterwards, and we both cried. That way it doesn't get into a crippled thing. There was nobody else I would rather go through it with.*

> *There was grief in his face and tears in his eyes on the drive home. I saw how much of a loss it was to him. That validated that it really was a baby. In the time that followed, we went to each other with our sorrow. I leaned on him. He let me wallow. We had a memorial service, and we each wrote a goodbye letter to the baby. I didn't have to ask him to stay home from work. He did, and he held me and sincerely said, "I'm so sorry." He said, "I need to be here with you."*

WHAT FELT HURTFUL

The most hurtful aspect of the fathers' responses to their partners' miscarriages was their need or ability to move on with everyday life while the women still needed to mourn. Women were in the thrusts of their grief while their partners seemed to be well past the losses:

> *After the miscarriage he felt sad. But now he says, "It's time to march on." I don't feel any support from him. I feel abandoned.*

> *He thinks I should be over it. He says, "Please don't cry. Don't fall apart." I feel like an emotional basket case.*

Sometimes I cry during the night. One night he said, "Are you still rehashing this? Stop thinking about it and just go to sleep."

It was nice to learn that we could support each other. But then he decided I should get over it.

Many women felt hurt when their partners negated or minimized their losses or turned away, and the women's grieving processes were exacerbated. The women felt that their partners did not understand or experience their miscarriages as significant losses, and the women felt alone in their grief:

It happened at night, and he just went back to bed. He handled it like it was a bad cold, like, "If you make it through the night, we'll handle it in the morning." I didn't want to be around him after that. I wanted him to talk it out, to let me talk it out, and to let me know it was okay to feel this way. It wasn't handled. It was just forgotten, like you throw it away and forget it because you can't see it anymore. You deny it. No emotions were said. It was not even a human being to him. It was just a fact of life. You "deal with it" and you're just a statistic. To this day it is not brought up.

It hurt me when my husband said, "You focus on it too much. As a physician I see it happen all the time, and women go on to have other babies. I know better."

I quickly became aware of what seemed like my husband's lack of empathy, his not understanding the sadness. It wasn't until many years later, when we started going to support group meetings with other people who had lost babies, that I realized there was a similar pattern in how fathers respond, even cross-culturally. There were couples from so many different cultures, and the thing that struck me most was how differently the mothers' responses were from the fathers' and that the fathers seem to move through it much, much faster. It was at least helpful for me to know that, and it made me less angry at my husband. But by the third miscarriage, our marriage was dead. We had grown very, very far apart. It has never been completely repaired.

I didn't want to take the baby into the lab. I wanted to bury it and grow a plant or flowers from it. He discounted that idea, and I felt angry.

With the first miscarriage, my husband's friend was with us. They ran a half marathon while I was lying in bed. I was angry and hurt because they acted like I had just had a normal day. I had just had a miscarriage! With the second miscarriage, I had the D&C, and he met me at the doctor's office so we had both cars there. Afterwards he asked me, "Can't you drive your car home?" It hurt me deeply.

Women did not want to be cajoled into not grieving when what they felt was pain and what they needed to do was grieve:

I needed him. But it was difficult for him to tolerate my feelings. We almost lost our marriage.

He tried to just jolly me along. He tried to bury the loss. That hurt me.

I wanted him to reassure me it wasn't our fault and that we could get pregnant again—but not before we dealt with the sadness of it.

That the fathers *didn't* directly communicate, often felt painful to the women. Many women acknowledged that their partners showed concern through actions, but the women needed expressions of tenderness and loss expressly through words or tears:

I would have liked him to cry instead of being "the strong man." I would have liked him to come out and directly tell me, "I'm hurting, and we need to talk about this and help each other." He was trying to do it by his actions.

I couldn't get him to share his feelings with me. He said he cried, but I wish he shared that with me. *I was grieving* that. *It was crucial to our divorce.*

He's never, ever brought it up. He bought and installed a dishwasher for me. That was his way to show he was concerned. But I needed to hear *it. I missed the actual words. That made it even more lonely and even more "not all right" to be having those feelings. I just wanted him to be with me and talk about what it felt like. I wish I had had someone I could've vented the anger with. My grieving process got caught. It got turned inside, and I became depressed.*

It was more what he didn't say that hurt me. I would wonder if he thought about it and whether it still affected him. I wanted him to be more open instead of waiting until I brought it up. Now I know he was nervous about bringing it up because it made me sad. But I needed to be sad with him.

Some mothers felt bad that their partners had not been physically present in the doctors' offices, hospitals, or emergency rooms:

He wasn't able to get time off. He was unable to come to the hospital. But he was not insisting on being there! He could have tried harder to come be with me. I just needed somebody. I was an emotional wreck. He couldn't handle it.

The hospital encouraged me to walk around. But after walking around awhile, I started to feel sick. My husband wheeled me back to my room where painters had been painting. The fumes were really strong and I panicked, *"Get me out! I can't stand it!!" He just left me stuck in a wheelchair there to go get a nurse. Then he got mad at me for getting mad at him, and he didn't call or come for the remainder of my hospital stay.*

For some women, their partners' reassurances that they would together try for or succeed at having future babies felt helpful. For many others, fathers' suggestions to try for further pregnancies were felt as very painful and as a diminishment of the value of the miscarried babies whom the fathers could so quickly and easily replace. These women were still in the throes of grief over their babies and did not want different babies yet:

I was terrified to conceive again. But my husband wanted me to. I felt pressured to try again.

Most mothers spoke of responses from their partners that felt both helpful and hurtful. The experiences of many couples changed as time went by, during which some couples drew further apart. Other couples, whose miscarriages initially created tremendous stress and trauma, eventually discussed their feelings openly and drew closer together:

> *At first I really resented him for not seeming to grieve in the same way I did. He dismissed the miscarriage, shut down, shut it off, and went on with life. It didn't seem to affect him. But he was sympathetic to me and how I was feeling. He let me run the gamut of emotions. He acknowledged that I was hurting. But it hurt at first that we didn't talk about it. Then little by little things would come out. He had written a letter that he was going to give to me when the baby was born. He gave it to me two to three months after the miscarriage. We read it together and cried. I realized he had really mourned the loss. Up to then, I had thought of it as* my *baby and* my *pregnancy. That was a real healing point.*

WHAT WOMEN WANTED FROM THEIR PARTNERS

Given freedom to imagine more consoling responses, women expressed wishes for their partners' support of their grief in whatever form and for however long it took. They wanted acceptance of and compassion for their feelings:

> *I would have liked him to know that it was a death and that you have a right to feel it is one. I would have liked him to bring me a flower and say, "I know you're in pain." I would give anything for my husband to hold me and let me cry my eyes out, to sit down and talk about it, to allow me to grieve until I was finished, to open up more, to question me about how it felt for me.*

> *I would have loved for him to buy me flowers. It's a death to be acknowledged with some ritual to honor our baby, to mark it as the death of a person. He's a potter. I would have really loved for him to make something that came from his hands.*

> *I would have liked him to have thought about it again at different stages later on, for instance, to say to me, "You would be six months pregnant now." I would have liked him to not feel the need to be positive, to come to more support group meetings, to let people know what a difficult time it was, and to ask me, "Do we need counseling?"*

EFFECT ON THEIR SEX DRIVES

Almost two-thirds of the women said their sex drives changed following their miscarriages. For most of them, their sex drives decreased:

Sex was not as good afterwards, and even now, after three and a half years, it's different. It sometimes reminds me of all the pain. I need to not think about it. I need to push him away. Sex leads to babies.

How can I have sex? My baby is dead! It would be like having a party or singing a happy song! It feels like a betrayal or disrespectful of my baby.

I was like, "Don't touch me! I don't want to get pregnant!" I didn't want to have another baby who wouldn't replace the first. I wanted attention and affection, but not sex. I didn't want to be that in touch with my feelings. The first few times we had sex afterwards, I just cried. I was scared, and I still am.

For most whose sex drives increased, sex became little more than a means to an end. They felt driven to get pregnant again and thereby fill the void or skip over the pain:

It wasn't "sex drive"; it was "baby drive"! I became obsessed with pregnancy. I had to prove I could do it. We couldn't have joyful, silly, or fun sex, but I had a frantic desire to get pregnant. I had no energy or desire until it came time to conceive. Even then, it was clinical and mechanical. I almost used him. I feel guilty about that.

A small number of mothers needed and valued the comfort, closeness, or tenderness of sexual connection:

Initially, sexual contact brought emotional pain and discomfort. Then I wanted the reassurance, the touch, and the closeness.

CHAPTER THIRTEEN

Our Partners' Grief

There is an extremely broad range in fathers' emotional responses to the loss of their babies. This examination of fathers' reactions is based on both current research and our own findings. Necessarily we will be making generalizations that we acknowledge do not apply to all men.

Some men respond to miscarriage with profound grief. Other men feel a lesser degree of grief, and some don't seem to feel any grief. Some feel the loss of "the pregnancies" or the loss of "future possibilities" more than the loss of their actual children. Some men feel relieved when the pregnancies are over. Often fathers are more bereaved than they let on.

Yet they are usually not as bereaved over their babies as mothers are. (Perhaps fathers would feel a greater degree of grief if they were a direct part of the whole miscarriage experience, as we will outline in Appendix A: "Taking Care.") The longer pregnancies were sustained, the more time and opportunity fathers had to become attached to their babies. Generally speaking, the depth of fathers' grief is in direct proportion to the length of the pregnancies: the longer the pregnancies, the deeper their grief.

Even fathers who did not have a deep attachment to their unborn children and who do not seem deeply saddened over the loss of their babies feel an array of intense feelings and usually are in crisis.

When our mates were present during our miscarriages, they may have seen us in grave distress and perhaps in pain and bleeding. They, too, may have felt traumatized, scared, and powerless because there was nothing they could do to stop our miscarriages or to help us physically (other than to get us to our doctors or hospitals). They, too, badly needed information about what was happening, but many of their questions went unanswered. They needed to be included in decision making about our care or whether or when to have D&C's, but often they were not. Many fathers were not even allowed in the rooms when medical procedures were performed. Many felt frustrated as well as alone with their fears about our health or even our lives.

Fathers often search for the cause of these unexplainable losses but to no avail. They worry that they caused or somehow played a role in our losses, perhaps through sexual intercourse (although medical studies do not support the idea that there is any relationship between sexual intercourse and miscarriage) or because of unwelcoming feelings toward our babies during pregnancy. Sometimes fathers feel anxious during pregnancy about the potential loss of our time and attention when our babies arrive. When our babies die, our partners may then feel guilty for having felt that way, or they may believe they should have taken better care of us; for example, they shouldn't have let us carry in the groceries. Some fathers also may blame us with thoughts like "I told her to take it easy" or "There must be something wrong with her."

If our partners do not exhibit a sense of loss, we often perceive them as unfeeling or uncaring. They often, therefore, feel misunderstood. If they don't feel grief, they may feel guilty about it, yet they can't manufacture grief that is not there. They may feel the need to conceal their lack of sorrow or else face our anger or hurt.

For closeness and comfort, our partners may turn to sexual contact. But following miscarriage, our sexuality often undergoes significant changes. Self-worth, necessary to the enjoyment of intimate sex, is suffering. Also, because of the relationship between sex and procreation, sex is often a painful reminder of loss for us, and we may need to avoid it. Yet, it may seem to our partners that we are avoiding *them*. In addition, they may feel conflict about conceiving again because of the dread of more miscarriages. If we are trying to become pregnant again, they may feel pressure to perform sexually according to our fertility calendars. Sex then loses spontaneity and feels lonely and empty.

Some fathers who cannot identify with our feelings of attachment and loss cannot understand why we have changed. In the face of our own grief, our partners have lost us (as they have known us) to depression and grief. One woman in our study said, "My husband was angry at my grief. I think he felt that the loss took me away from him. And it did. It took me away from everything. I wanted to be with the baby, wherever that baby was. I didn't care much about anything else." We may no longer be available to our partners in the way that we used to be. Often they miss us, feel lonely for us, and wish that life could be as it was before. Sometimes they feel hurt, personally rejected, or abandoned by us.

They may also feel that we value them less than we do our babies toward whom all our time and emotional energy is now directed and who are now the recipients of our fervor.

We feel such sadness; it may appear that we need bottomless emotional care. Our partners want to protect us from pain and take care of us, but they may not know what to do or say to ease our pain and may feel helpless or inadequate as they attempt to do so. Sometimes they feel envious of or inferior to others to whom we turn for emotional support.

Some fathers feel deep grief over their miscarried children. They feel robbed of the chance to know and care for their sons or daughters. They may feel pain at the sight of other babies, inferiority to other fathers whose babies lived, or other physical and emotional symptoms of grief listed in Chapter 19, "Emotional and Physical Dimensions."

Grieving fathers carry an additional burden. In our culture they, even more than mothers, are encouraged to "be strong," which unfortunately translates into "be invulnerable." They may act stoically because of the extraordinarily threatening nature of what has happened. They may feel a responsibility to be rational and functional during the crisis. This functioning is their way of helping, loving, and taking care of us.

But men, too, need to talk about their losses and their feelings, and need someone to care and to listen. Often desiring not to "burden" us at a time when we are already distressed, they hold their grief inside and thereby become more depressed, fatigued, and confused. They may not know *how* to talk about it, nor that they can actually best help us by sharing their feelings with us.

Other people, unaware that fathers grieve miscarriage too, don't inquire about how they are feeling, so fathers often feel misunderstood, lonely, and unloved.

WHAT FATHERS ARE ALSO UP AGAINST

So we can better appreciate the plight of fathers, let's look at some difficulties that they in particular live with and that make life harder than might otherwise be for both them and us.

Robert Bly, the American poet and an inspirer of the current men's movement, said in a television interview with Bill Moyers,

> We [males] are taught not to feel pain and grief as children. I remember seeing one of my boys. He was maybe about nine. He was hit [by the] basketball and I saw him turn around and bend down and get control of his pain and his grief before he stood up again. Now, that same boy would be so wonderful in being open to wounds and crying and so on, when he was very small. But the culture had said to him, "You cannot give way to that. You must turn around, and when you turn around, you must have a face without pain or grief in it."

This "tough guy" role emerges from cultural and familial upbringing. Bly lectures about part of the impact of the Industrial Revolution. He notes that we grew up at our mothers' sides, learning, playing, working, and communicating with our mothers while fathers went away from the home day after day to work in isolation from their sons and the whole family. Males did not really get to know their role models.

In the absence of role models, boys did not have the opportunity to learn from their fathers about how to feel and what to do with their feelings. Without a history of male models, men sometimes don't accept, identify, or express vulnerable or tender feelings. Bly explains that while women may think men are *resisting* communicating their feelings with us, men commonly are *not aware* what their feelings are.

Women also tend to cry more openly, whereas men have been trained not to. After my miscarriage, my brother Phil said to me with deep sadness and love, "I feel your pain. But I just can't cry." Some men have few words and little or no tears. Men often deal with their feelings in other ways, for instance, by becoming more involved in work or sports.

After all, men were trained to provide and protect. They learned that a real man is aggressive. Until very recently, boys were discouraged from and even humiliated or shamed for expressing tenderness, nurturing baby dolls, playing house, or babysitting, whereas girls were encouraged to do these. The message, both blatant and implied, was that bonding with babies and nurturing them was females' work.

In addition, when those boys grew up and became expectant fathers, they had no way of directly experiencing their babies except through us. To many fathers, their expected babies did not seem real. Rather, they were more of a "projected idea." So many fathers did not develop a profound attachment to their babies and, consequently, did not feel the loss of real children.

"WHAT HAS HAPPENED BETWEEN US?"

The loss of either a miscarried baby or an older child wreaks havoc on relationships. Pain is running high and self-worth is running low. All of us are grieving, for our babies, the future, loss of quality of life, ourselves, or each other. Both we and our partners—grieving their babies or not—may be emotionally bankrupt for a time, unable to comfort each other as we otherwise could and would, and unable to be what we need each other to be now. Emotional needs are heightened, and the capacity to tend to each others' emotional needs is lowered. In our grief, we have little left in us to use toward nurturing each other through the grief.

But in the instance of miscarriage, many fathers did not yet know or deeply love their babies and do not share the extent of our grief over them, so it follows that we and our partners might be even more out of sync and alienated from each other than parents who have lost an older child.

Some fathers did bond with and do grieve for their miscarried babies, and some of them are able to share their experiences with us, allowing us to grow together in closeness. But even these fathers most often express their grief very differently than we do. We often feel a need to talk and cry for months. After a much shorter period of time, fathers usually put the losses away and get on with the rest of life.

Because of this discrepancy, we may feel farther apart than ever before. It is common for men to seek emotional space while women seek emotional closeness. It is natural that this pattern would be more amplified in an especially traumatic time such as the one that follows the loss of a child.

If fathers have a lifetime of painful feelings stored up inside, the prospect of self-disclosure feels utterly dreadful. The payoff for becoming aware of, feeling, and sharing painful feelings doesn't seem to outweigh the payoff of security and familiarity maintained by distancing.

According to Harriet Lerner, Ph.D., author of *Dance of Intimacy*, when we try to get our partners to express their feelings, they usually feel an even greater need to distance. Conversely, when men emotionally withdraw, our feelings often heighten, and our drive to try to get them to express emotion usually increases. Distancers feel more of a need to distance when they are pursued, and pursuers feel more of a need to pursue when distanced.

Sometimes we become focused on each other's "faults" or "failings" to protect ourselves from feeling our own pain. Yet, focusing on each other's "wrong" style of grieving won't lead to anybody's feeling better. When we and our partners focus on each others' "faults" or "failings," nothing changes, and our pattern becomes more deeply ingrained. When we observe ourselves concentrating on each other, we can recognize it as a signal to stay connected with and take care of the pain within ourselves by expressing it and moving toward accepting it.

All in all, we can eventually grow to appreciate each other's special predicament: what it is like to walk in each other's shoes and eventually to develop a deep compassion for and share that compassion with each other.

Perhaps we and our partners never talked about our miscarriages; perhaps we fought about them or feel deeply hurt by one anothers' responses; perhaps we talked about them at length, cried, and comforted one another. How we as couples dealt with the experience continues to affect our relationships profoundly. We may feel a deeper solidarity and are bolstered by our experiences, or the miscarriage may still hang between us as the state of disrepair lingers. If the hurt in our relationships is not recognized and worked through, it goes underground to color our futures together. The rift must be mended if our relationships are to grow or continue. Untended pain of miscarriage remains between partners throughout future years until worked through and healed. It does not "just go away."

We asked some of the fathers to tell us about their experiences.

Daniel's Story

We had three miscarriages between three and eight years ago. When I realized the first one was really happening, it was very, very emotionally trying. It was the middle of the night. I thought, "How could this happen to us? This can't really be." I just did not believe it. I felt confusion, shock, and disbelief because I had never considered miscarriage as a possibility. I was under the mistaken impression that it was a very, very rare occurrence.

Then I learned that, statistically, it was not uncommon. And we spoke with others who had miscarried. I realized I was not such a rare, rare, one-in-a-thousand. That was a comfort.

I was just going ahead with life, and things took a nasty turn. I felt cheated. We lost something we were supposed to have. I didn't feel loneliness; we looked to each other. I tried to give Jeri support, and I would like to believe I was fairly successful. It was an experience shared by both husband and wife. We had to deal with it together.

Those were emotional moments! I wondered, "What did we do wrong?" "Why?" and "Why us?" Jeri was blaming herself. I was telling her it was not her fault; it was nature's way. We leaned on each other. And she went to a support group. That helped her. She drew strength from it.

As traumatic as miscarriage may be, for me it was not the death of a child. I honestly can't tell you it was the same as if that child had been born.

The most difficult part of the miscarriage was taking her to the hospital, knowing the pregnancy was not going to work, watching someone so near and dear to me feel so terribly upset and in pain.

I remember the first miscarriage in detail. The second and third miscarriages are very vague and fuzzy. Those two were emotionally difficult to accept, but not as difficult as the first. I remember that night. I remember the great distress and disbelief. I'm not as emotionally charged about it now.

The first one was a whole baby to me. During that pregnancy I found myself imagining what the baby would look like, whether it would be a boy or a girl, what it would be like, and visualizing family life with the addition. It was the "concept" of a person.

Feeling better was kind of a slow transition. It was a matter of weeks. I felt much better after a month when I realized there was nothing wrong with us. It was better than having a child terribly out of the ordinary that maybe couldn't have lived.

Having the information in the beginning of the pregnancy that miscarriage is common would have been helpful. I've got to confess: I thought maybe I was a bit of a freak. It would have been helpful for the doctors to have told us beforehand that this could happen and was a reasonable possibility. I later drew comfort and strength from that information.

I have a five-year-old and a three-year-old now. I don't really reflect much on the miscarriage these days. I have pretty much put them behind me. Perhaps that's my way of dealing with it. I look forward. I am extremely pleased with the two children I have. Had we not had children at all, the miscarriages would be much more in the forefront of my mind.

Do I think of myself as father to the babies? That's a tough question! I did up to the point of the miscarriages. After the miscarriages, I don't know. I'm not sure. I guess I'm inclined to say I don't think of myself as their father, not now. I think of myself as the father of two children, my living children. I'm making a distinction between "up to birth" and "the time of birth."

This may sound contradictory, but I considered the first miscarriage as a death. Miscarriage is like experiencing a death in the family. That might be a bit dramatic, but nevertheless it's how I feel. It's not the same as losing one of my kids now because I have had the experience of having them and living with them. But it was not an inanimate object.

I don't want to diminish the traumatic impact, but I think the miscarriages were meant to be. My wife certainly suffered the most. There is a reason and another power. Look at the two children we have. It seems to have worked out for us.

Miscarriage is a concept. It's not quite a reality.

Chris' Story

Aspects of the miscarriage affected me very deeply in certain ways at different times, but the loss of the baby overall was no big deal for me. The coming and the going of the baby were just a couple of words. There wasn't anything else there for me to experience. I felt devastated later on in the months following because I had lost my wife. She was off in her own world.

Right before the D&C, I still had lingering doubts about whether or not the baby was really dead. My wife and I said good-bye to each other, and as I saw her walking away down the hall, I knew, "That's it." I knew that, if it was not dead already, it was going to be. I felt sad and teary. I couldn't really read in the waiting room.

I had heard the term "D&C" frequently, so I thought it was a common, easy, and quick thing with no "recovery" period. I couldn't understand why she was so upset, or anything of what she was going through. I thought she was going off the deep end with it. I thought she was throwing fuel on the fire and making it bigger. I thought she was soaking it for whatever she could get. She wanted people's sympathy, and until she got it she was just going to stay there in that same emotional state. I thought we should forget the miscarriage and go on. I would have liked her to just go on with life like before she was pregnant.

It affected the whole family life. She was laid out in bed most of the time. She didn't do anything. Life was rather miserable, I guess. I felt lonely. She was here but she wasn't here. We were in different worlds. I couldn't communicate with her. I felt confused about—what do I do?

I didn't connect her crying or lying in bed to the miscarriage. It didn't matter that she read me parts of books that showed that her reactions were normal. I didn't believe that what she was going through was from the miscarriage. I thought she was just blaming any negative feelings on it.

I felt depressed. I didn't feel that my feelings over the whole thing were okay. She wanted to talk about it. But I didn't feel she'd want to hear that I didn't think it was any big deal.

The support group meetings were difficult. I didn't feel comfortable opening up there. There were times I wanted to cry but didn't. They would have thought something was weird with me because I felt like bawling over a big, in general, "dying baby" type thing. It was all about dead babies. It stirred a lot of feelings within me.

It was like having a bomb go off in our house. We each eventually went into therapy.

About three years later, we saw the movie Born on the Fourth of July. *There was this scene in which the main character, Ron Kovic, had come home from Vietnam. He was a paraplegic, and he had totally gone through hell. He had a lot of problems because of that experience. His parents just totally did not understand. He would tell them what he felt, but they still couldn't hear it. They couldn't hear how it was for him or appreciate what he was trying to say and instead just clung to their religion.*

I saw the scene and knew it was the same as the situation between my wife and me. She had told me how it felt to have the miscarriage, and I just couldn't hear it. I clung to my beliefs that it was no big thing. At the point in time when we saw the movie, I finally had empathy for what she went through, trying to get me to understand when I just couldn't. In the car after the movie, I explained that, and we both cried, and she felt a lot better because I recognized some of her pain. And I felt a little closer to her. It was very healing. She said that for her that was the most important moment in our marriage.

I wish I had been able to be empathetic after the miscarriage. I had my own totally unrelated problems. I don't even know what I would be like if the situation arose again. Part of me would probably be the same, and part of me would be totally different. Advice to other fathers? I'd say, "Be empathetic. Listen. You can't understand probably, but be there."

We both went through a lot, her because of the loss of the baby, and me because of our relationship or lack of *relationship after the loss. It backed us each into a corner and forced struggle and growth.*

It would have been helpful to have something to read that said that what she felt was normal so I could have some empathy. Although, she did read me things, and I still didn't have much empathy because I wanted to believe she was being abnormal because it was easier for me. It would have been too hard for me to be empathetic to her because then I would have to be into my feelings. It was too hard.

It felt good after four years to say to her safely that the miscarriage wasn't a big deal for me. Finally, I felt it was okay that I felt that way. I needed to say it, and I'm glad we could talk about it.

Reed's Story

Jillian and I have a son, Justin. She was four months pregnant with our second child when she miscarried. That was 10 days ago. She had been having complications, but I didn't expect a miscarriage. The doctor said that termination was a possibility, but not so soon! I was at a business appointment when I got a call on my answering machine from her doctor saying she had miscarried and they couldn't wait for me before doing a D&C. When I heard, I was shocked. It was painful that I was not around at the time when it happened.

I hadn't pictured the baby as a living baby yet. Yet I experienced the death of a child. That moment started for me at a high scale: At the hospital they asked, "Would you like to see the baby?" At first that seemed ridiculous. But then I saw the baby. He was 16 weeks, and he was dead. I started to cry. I played with him. This was a person.

Under 20 weeks of pregnancy in California a baby is called a "lab specimen." But Jillian was treating the baby just like he was a baby, a human being. He was a human being, and we did treat him as one. We named him. Jillian wanted to have him buried. The priest came. He said a nice prayer. We buried the dead. I am so grateful she thought of that. I felt a lot of relief!

This miscarriage is the worst thing I have ever experienced. I feel confusion about why I was being lied to that the baby was just a lab specimen, that it wasn't a baby. The worst was the ignorance: The state considers a baby a lab specimen. I wish they had told us of the option to have and bury our baby. They take away from you any right and responsibility. You can have your baby's body! It's your baby no matter what its age. Go to a hospital and see one of the babies from a miscarriage! Look at the baby and face it. I can't describe the feeling I had about our whole country. I was ashamed of our system, that we would handle miscarried babies that way.

If I hadn't seen him, I'd say I didn't experience the death of a child. I definitely think I'm a father. If someone asks me if I'm a father, I'll say, "I have two children and one died."

Still, it affects Jillian differently than me. I think we're not sharing the same thoughts. It's harder for her to bury her feelings about him. I have mixed feelings. I wanted her to stop talking about it because that would have been easier for me; but I didn't want her to stop talking about it because talking about it was best for her. I don't know what to say to her and how to make her feel better. But I do feel a lot closer to her. I need to hold her close.

I needed to rely on a lot of other people to help me with my self-esteem. I felt "not whole." I couldn't figure out simple things. I needed someone's help to do everything.

We had had trouble with our pregnancy with Justin, too. I knew I should have been supportive this time, but I was getting frustrated and angry about having to go to the hospital again and again. I don't want to use this word, but it was "inconvenient." I paid the price with guilt because when I got mad and let my anger show to Jillian and then the baby died, I had to ask myself, "Are you proud of yourself now?" I knew I didn't cause the miscarriage, but I felt responsible. I felt kind of ashamed of myself. I was not as strong and supportive as I could have been. I wanted to apologize to her for my selfishness. I meant to say I was very sorry. I felt like scum.

I was very lonely. I turned to Justin for assistance. (I hope Justin is still here and not a dream!) But I wouldn't have felt lonely if I hadn't seen the baby.

There's no denying that it's ours. It's flesh, and it was ours. I have to come to that conclusion. A part of me died. He was my son. It was the equivalent of walking in now and finding Justin dead. Having a miscarriage is like losing an *already existing child to a sudden tragedy. If I hadn't seen my baby, I wouldn't have realized that.*

The pain is still here. It will linger. Sometime I'll just be standing there and the pain will hit me. When I face it, I have a good cry and I let it go. I don't feel devastated, but I think I will feel devastated on his birthday, at special times, and at other deaths.

I have more motivation for life now. It's great to be here, to smell the roses. Bills and material things aren't as important. I feel less depression from general stress, and things in general aren't that bad. I neglected my family, and I learned my lesson. Tragedies are always what made me a better person.

I'd advise other men to be more aware and to not be ignorant of the facts. Guys haven't gotten in as deep as they should. If they don't, and they have a loss, they're going to feel guilt. For their wives' sakes, if they keep up with how the baby is developing, they can share their wives' feelings if she does have a loss. It's a bigger loss for her. The baby was actually a part of her body. If fathers are more involved and more aware, they will be able to understand and grieve with their wives and have better communication. If fathers don't get involved in the beginning, they're not going to get involved in the end.

It was all women at the support group. I thought, "This isn't even for the fathers." I didn't feel like I belonged. I want to be recognized for my fatherhood and my grief, and I want the respect that goes with it. If you're a father, act like one. Make people say you are part of it and don't let them push you out of it!

We don't recognize that these babies are real people. They're not blobs with heartbeats. We're taught not to acknowledge that babies are alive from the time they're conceived. They lied to me to say the baby wasn't a live person. He was a person. He was alive, and then he died.

Joe's Story

We had three miscarriages. The last one was about five years ago. The other two were 12 and 13 years ago. They all happened between two and three months of pregnancy. We had two children inbetween.

For me the first pregnancy began and ended quickly. The miscarriage was a shock. But I thought, "Okay, we'll just try again." My attitude was, "It's happened, and there is nothing you can do about it, so go on from here." The worst of it was the disappointment.

After the second miscarriage, we were starting to feel discouraged because it seemed like it was so easy for people to have kids. Probably a lot of the discouragement I recall feeling, too, was when getting pregnant again after that became a problem. I really can't separate out my feelings about the infertility and the miscarriages. I felt confusion because I didn't know why the miscarriages happened and why we had trouble conceiving again. And I felt like I couldn't make good, viable fetuses.

I guess I would have liked Stephanie to reassure me that we would eventually succeed. But she felt pessimistic, and she wasn't really in a position to reassure me. But I needed reassuring that, if I'm going to try again, things will work out okay. But she didn't really feel it necessarily would.

I think I probably could have handled one *miscarriage. But the second one really made it seem like, "Uh-oh, something's going on here." After two miscarriages, it seemed like having miscarriages could go on and on forever. I'm sure for some people it did. But we've learned of a lot of couples who have had miscarriages and then went on to have living children. I'm not sure anything would have* really *helped, but that fact—statistics—might have. Knowledge about the chances of carrying a child to term would have made sense to me, and I don't think that was made available to us. The doctor probably said something like, "It'll be okay; it'll be fine." That's not the same thing.*

The most difficult aspect of the third miscarriage was my guilt. During the pregnancies that we had carried to term, we had abstained from sex to keep from miscarrying. But with the third baby, we figured that that probably wasn't really the reason we had carried them successfully. I wish we hadn't had that attitude with the third baby. Even though I'm not sure I wish we had that baby, I wish if we miscarried, it wasn't because of something that we—or I—was responsible for.

I think Stephanie probably felt guilty, too, in some ways, and I could have been more supportive of her regarding that. Not that there was anything she should feel guilty for, but I think she felt guilty anyway. I could have reassured her more and been more empathetic. Even though my *feeling was, "What's done is done," it was a painful process for* her. *It was painful for me, too, but not in the same way.*

My reaction to the losses was so different from Stephanie's. We really couldn't empathize a whole lot with one another. And it's not the kind of experience you really want to broadcast. So it wasn't something that was easily shared with anyone. I felt lonely.

When Stephanie was pregnant, I didn't see the babies as living people yet, but I guess I feel like a father to those babies, and I experienced the third miscarriage as the death of a child.

I knew what having kids meant by the third miscarriage. I knew what having children was like. I knew how important babies were in my life. It was all theoretical before we had a living child. If you lose a child you already have, a part of you dies. I felt a part of me died. I had the most trouble with that miscarriage. I felt lethargic, washed out, depressed, lacking energy, "blah." In retrospect, I always wonder what that child would have been like.

Having a miscarriage is like being empty or feeling like you're missing something. It's a really nebulous thing because you really had no idea what it was like. It's a really nebulous feeling.

If the first two had lived, we probably wouldn't have the children we now have. I wonder how our family constellation is affected. If we had the third child, we would now have three kids. How would the interactions be different? We lost being a different family. I think about what our lives would be like if any or all of them had gone to term.

With the first miscarriage, my emotional turning point was when we got pregnant with the subsequent baby. With the second miscarriage, I never felt real bad. It was kind of a low-level feeling. The infertility went on for a long time, and the turning point wasn't until Stephanie got pregnant with Jonathon. With the third miscarriage, there's no way to pinpoint my turning point because we haven't had more children. Ninety-five percent of the time, miscarriage is a loss, but it's a loss that will be made up for many times over when you can carry a child to term. The pain hasn't gone away 100%, but pretty close.

Stephanie has been wanting to have another baby. I'm not sure she would if we hadn't gone through that last miscarriage. I've occasionally had that feeling of wanting another baby too. I've always like babies. I miss that period in our lives.

A Poem by Gary Winters to "Little One"

We had wanted you for so very long,
Or so it must have seemed at times.
Now we know we'll have forever,
To keep you in our minds.

On that joyful day when we learned
That you were on your way,
We opened our home and hearts,
And planned for a permanent stay.

We never saw your smile.
We never held your hand.
You never had your birthday.
How can we understand?

To hear you laugh, to dry your tear
To share your life each day
To see the wonder in your eyes
As you find your rightful way.

We're told we should forget you,
"You'll have another some day."
Don't they see the pain we feel,
Is bruised by what they say?

We never saw your smile.
We never held your hand.
You never had your birthday.
Someday we'll understand.

A Letter from Tom to his Daughter

Dear Maggie,

I'd already begun to love you and talk you up to people at work. I even had your ultrasound "picture" in my wallet. I love you. I'll miss you, with a special place called "Maggie" in my heart always. Good-bye.

Your brief life has changed me. Thank you. You were a gift. I now actually feel closer to you.

But I feel hurt, angry, confused. Why did this ever have to happen? I hate seeing your mother Molly suffer like this. I feel an aching sympathy for her.

This loss ties into all my previous losses, and I sense this profound sadness. I fear it will swallow me up. But the sadness seems okay because I have lost my first opportunity to have and love a child. It's over.

Love, Daddy

CHAPTER FOURTEEN

Our Living Children

Some of us have other children born either prior to or following our miscarriages. The ramifications of miscarriage spill over into our feelings about and interactions with our prior and subsequent children. In this chapter we will relay women's feelings about their other children.

The reality of miscarriage also powerfully affects our prior and subsequent children's complicated inner emotional worlds. In this chapter, too, we will talk about what this whole thing called "miscarriage" feels like and means *to them.*

For some of the 100 women we interviewed, miscarriage was a painful lesson in the miracle and fragility of life. After their miscarriages, many women felt a deeper appreciation for their living children, both those born before and those born after their miscarriages:

> *I felt especially tender toward my other children. I saw them as particularly precious. I loved them more. You tell your children you love them right then and there because you never know.*

> *I thought that maybe he would be our only child. I realized what a precious commodity he is. The miscarriage drew us closer together. Physically I held him more; I was more affectionate than before.*

After their miscarriages, most women who had other children became fearful or overly protective of their health and safety:

> *I had felt so helpless about the baby; I couldn't keep it safe. I thought there would be no more babies. It made me that much more fearful about the children I already had. I was afraid to leave them. I felt so possessive and protective. I felt they could be taken from me in the blink of an eye. I was like a mother duck gathering her children under her wings. I was trying to keep them safe. I was just fanatical! I went crazy!*

Some women, burdened or overwhelmed by their own emotional bankruptcy immediately following their miscarriages, found it difficult to muster the energy to care for their existing children:

> *I felt drained. I just wanted to stay in bed. I couldn't get up and pay as much attention to them. I needed to just mother myself. They were bored and went stir crazy.*

I cried so much; it was unfair to them. I felt angry at them for not respecting how I felt. I had no patience. I screamed at them. I was overwhelmed with myself. I went back to work to get away. I feel bad.

I didn't want to be a mommy to anyone. I wanted to crawl off somewhere, to run away and hide for awhile. He was jumping on the bed. I resented having no time to heal. I kept looking at him like, "Your brother died and you don't know."

Some women talked about their living children's acceptance of the reality of their losses and of their sorrow and how touched the women felt by that simple acceptance:

My girls remember the baby. I've grieved more with them. *They don't judge me or change the subject. They have been supportive. We are closer and have more togetherness now.*

THOUGHTS ABOUT SUBSEQUENT PREGNANCY

Nearly all the women approached the idea of subsequent pregnancy with both joy about the prospect of future babies and fear about the survival of those babies:

Seeing the tissue, I realize we're hooked together very delicately. The process of getting here is complex. A lot of things have to go right. It takes a lot of courage or denial to want to do it again.

I wouldn't have another baby, but not definitely. But I wouldn't finalize it.

I'm going to be really frightened when I'm pregnant with another baby. I feel fear and desire. If someone told me that wearing red shoes with purple laces would prevent another miscarriage, I'd probably do it!

I want to become pregnant again, but I'm so afraid. I doubt I'll ever be able to have a child. I am distancing myself from it. Pregnancy should be a joyful experience. This is too painful! I wonder, "Should we adopt?" I really want *a child.*

Many felt "obsessed" with becoming pregnant:

I felt an overwhelming need to become pregnant again. It was an uncontrollable drive that bordered on the obsessive to replace that loss. I wanted another baby right away, in five seconds if I could. I wanted to "do it right."

For others, fear outweighed the drive to become pregnant, and they needed to avoid the risk of further losses:

My mom had three losses. I have my two dead babies, and if I have another pregnancy, I'm afraid that that third baby will die just like hers did. I couldn't go through another miscarriage again. I won't try again.

I made the decision on my own to have my tubes tied. The miscarriage was crap. It wasn't fair!

Some women could not bear the thought of attempting to replace the babies they had lost with different children. The prospect of different babies offered no relief. Although they were consoled by their subsequent children, their subsequent children never replaced their miscarried babies:

My baby was his own self. Another baby would be a different person. Another baby would not substitute. I feel apprehension. I want to remember my first.

I want to give myself healing time and not try to replace the baby. I want to let a new baby be a new baby. I need to separate their identities.

THE EFFECT OF LATER PREGNANCIES

Just as the women had anticipated, subsequent pregnancy was a time of both anxiety and excitement. Women's fears about having more miscarriages usually did not diminish until they passed the point in pregnancy at which they had previously miscarried or until their subsequent babies were born:

I'm 15 weeks pregnant now. Having had a miscarriage makes it more acute some days. Some days have been so long and so rough. It's bittersweet. Being pregnant feels real good, too. I feel tremendous joy. And it brings back tremendous awareness of the loss of my other baby.

I wait until my babies are here before I get attached to them because I never know if they're going to make it. I never thought I was out of the woods until I had the babies in my hands.

I'm pregnant right now, 18 weeks. After I was 12 weeks, I thought, "It's okay to become close now." I wouldn't accept the pregnancy until then. I'm still almost scared to go to the bathroom. I'm still checking all my symptoms.

Subsequent pregnancy had a healing effect on women who had thought of their miscarried babies in more generic, general terms, such as "sweet and little" or "healthy and happy." These women felt a healing in becoming pregnant again and in the birth of subsequent children. They had wanted babies and then *had* babies:

Holding a new baby helped heal the past. It helped heal the loss. I had a baby to fill that gap.

Subsequent pregnancy did not have the same healing effect on those who had conceptualized their babies as specific and unique individuals, never to be repeated. They had envisioned and described their babies in precise detail, such as "my blonde-haired, blue-eyed boy with whom I'd play in the park," and when they miscarried, they had felt a sense of irrevocable injury:

> *The children make me think about my miscarried babies more and about the reality of what they should have been. They make my sense of loss more poignant because I look at them and they are so real. It was very difficult when my daughter was born. I had a hard time bonding with her. She made me understand what I had lost.*

> *After the second loss, my husband and I had a terrible, terrible exchange that has done permanent damage to our marriage. I miscarried the weekend the first miscarried baby had been due. I was still grieving the first child and had avoided attaching to the second one for fear of loss. The irony that I would miscarry when I was supposed to be delivering was very, very painful—AWFUL. We had a big blowup afterwards, and he said, "It's just as well you lost the baby because you never would have loved it as much as you loved the first." That statement did something terrible to my feelings. Something else died besides unborn children. It was the most devastating thing anybody ever said to me. He couldn't get the idea that these babies weren't interchangeable. I have a very strong sense of that. They were separate. They were different. Each was a soul. Something in me just got completely crushed.*

In an effort to protect themselves emotionally in case of subsequent loss, some women chose to do things differently in later pregnancies than they had done in the pregnancies that ended in miscarriage. For instance, if they had announced the previous pregnancies right away, they waited before making the news of subsequent pregnancies public (and to avoid feeling embarrassment or like "public failures" again). Conversely, some women had kept the news to themselves during previous pregnancies and had, therefore, garnered no support when they lost those babies, in turn making grieving harder and more lonely. In subsequent pregnancies, then, they told other people right away, so that others would feel a connection with their subsequent babies and would be more likely to share their sense of loss or at least offer emotional support if they miscarried again:

> *With the first one, I hadn't told a lot of people I was pregnant. I went through this emotional upheaval and no one knew. The few people I did tell afterwards said, "Well, if I had known you were pregnant I'd have felt more for you." With the second one, I told people right away so if I miscarried again people would know how devastated I was.*

> *I've told very few people that I'm pregnant this time because I don't want to miscarry and to have to tell people again. I feel the longer I keep the pregnancy to ourselves, the chances are better and everything will be okay.*

OUR CHILDREN'S GRIEF

Angels come out of the stars
Come out Baby
And you make my day
Like you make my loving Baby
And I may miss you
And if you know I may be with you
Try to be helpful Baby

Angels in the May stars
And I wish that you will be home
Please give us a dog
And I may be in your heart
And I try not to cry
And I try not to miss you
And not to laugh

Angels in the stars
I may miss you in the stars
I wish a lucky star
Can come down and give me a dog.

Angels in the stars
Make my sister stay for my birthday
And I may love you if you make true love
I may make it so much to try
And I might get a bunch of presents
For Christmas
*Baby please come and see them**

Our living children are often profoundly affected by the loss of their unborn siblings. This is so regardless of their ages or developmental levels at the time of our losses, how much time has passed since our losses, whether or not they knew about our losses, and whether they were born before or following our losses.**

Often our children are profoundly affected whether or not they visibly display or articulate feelings about the losses. They may not yet have developed the skills necessary for identifying and verbalizing their internal experiences. Also, our children love us and want to protect us from

*Although we have confined this book to miscarriage, we make exception for this remarkable and moving poem by Carl Medina, just 5 years old, whose baby sister died during the 24th week of pregnancy.

**Many of the findings in this chapter are derived from The Davis & Macy Siblings Project as well as other current research and our own experiences.

unhappiness and may cover their feelings so we won't feel upset further. They do a lot more thinking about our miscarriages then they let on to us or others.

Our children's grief is affected by the circumstances of our miscarriages, how much they bonded with our babies prior to or following the losses, how we as parents deal with the losses and with life and loss in general, how we are changed by our losses, and by the fact that we interact differently now. Their emotional responses to miscarriage change as time goes by relative to their perceptions and knowledge at each developmental age that follows.

Children experience a variety of emotions in response to miscarriage, some of which we will discuss. They often feel sad and sometimes depressed over the permanent loss that they sense in their families.

They may also feel guilty. Young children feel they are the center of the world. When they cry, their needs are met; when they feel hungry, they are fed; and when they point to a toy, someone hands it to them. They conclude that all of life extends outward from them. By the same token, children, including older ones, feel responsible on some level for things that happen, especially following a significant loss. They might have notions in their minds that they caused our losses such as, "I didn't want the baby," "I must have upset Mom," or "I didn't want Mommy to pay attention to the baby." They may feel that the baby didn't want to be with them because they were bad. They also might think they are responsible for our or our partners' depression. They can't reassure themselves it wasn't or isn't their fault.

Children may also feel hurt. When they are not included in healing rituals such as the preparation of memorials or mementos, they may feel confused, left out, or not important enough to be included. They may feel we are the ones who lost their babies. Then we became depressed and thereby abandoned them. So they may feel mistrustful of, anxious about, or angry at us. During the time following miscarriage, our children's feelings and needs commonly go somewhat unattended while we necessarily take care of our own emotionally battered selves. Children sometimes feel neglected, rejected, or abandoned by us and lonely, too.

Children may feel as if their world has gone out of control. Although it's of little consolation, we as adults do have control over at least some aspects of our miscarriages (such as agreeing whether or when to have a D&C, asking questions of our doctors, deciding on or making mementos, going to support groups, reading about miscarriage, and discussing our losses with friends). But most options and controls are not available to our children.

They may experience fear over their sudden lack of power to make things better. They may develop a general fear of death. Children may fear that what caused their babies to die may cause them, us, or their daddies to die, too.

It is scary for our children when we are upset because they are dependent on us for protection, care, and parental love. But our world is upside down, and therefore so is theirs. They worry, "What will happen to *me?*" When their families and homes and worlds are jumbled, they are likely to feel confused, disoriented, ungrounded, insecure, unsafe, and scared.

Our children may feel angry at us, their babies, God, and the doctor or the hospital. But anger is usually not tolerated from children and therefore may be a very scary emotion for them to cope with or express constructively. In addition, their anger may mask grief and sadness.

When my son Jordan, then five years old, found out our own baby had died, he ran directly into his bedroom and returned with a boy doll (in whom he had not expressed interest before). He announced, "This is my new baby brother, and his name is Michael!" He carried Michael everywhere. It was important to him that Michael sit at the table with us, be safely buckled into the car in a place of his own, and be tucked into bed at night.

After six weeks, he threw Michael onto the floor, beat the doll, cried, and screamed at it, "You're not a real brother anyway! You're just a dumb, dumb, dumb, dumb doll!" That was the end of Michael. After Jordan released his anger through Michael, he didn't need the doll anymore and gave it up. In the meantime, he had created a way to live until he was ready. It was simple, natural, and brilliant, as children often are.

Children cannot usually identify or articulate their feelings. Instead, they communicate their troubles in a different way. They may exhibit a variety of behaviors or misbehaviors following miscarriage that were not characteristic of them before their losses. Here are some examples:

- Out of feelings of powerlessness, children may try to capture some semblance of power and control in their world through acts of aggression.

- Children may be more active than usual or unable to control their activity. Hyperactivity can be a manifestation of depression or anxiety.

- They may have a range of sleeping difficulties including nightmares, inability to fall or stay asleep, or anxiety over sleeping alone.
- Children may lose their appetites or change their eating patterns.
- Children who have been weaned from bottles may want them again.
- Young children may regress in toilet training, and older children may wet their beds for a time.
- They may cry a great deal. They may cling to us or become afraid to separate from us.
- They may act like they feel indifferent about the loss or about our grief.
- Children may withdraw from others, including those with whom they are usually close. They may shift from wanting to be around one parent more, to wanting to be around the other parent more.
- Older children may sulk and be particularly uncooperative. They may withdraw to their bedrooms.
- School grades may drop. Children's minds may be distracted or preoccupied with grief, and they may experience attention problems at school or difficulty absorbing information. They may object to going to school.

(If behavior problems are worrying you, professional help can be very helpful and improve the quality of life for them, you, and the whole family.)

Children usually pick up cues and sense when something is wrong or their parents are depressed, but if nobody will tell them what is wrong, they may feel confused, anxious, and alone. My daughter Lorien, who was four years old at the time of our loss, had not known I was pregnant. I didn't know it would help her to tell her about my loss until I attended a lecture on sibling grief four months after my miscarriage. When I did explain it to her, she told me:

> *I remember Grandma and Grandpa were here and they gave me a stuffed animal. I was asleep when you left for the hospital. Gary went with you. When you came back, you were sick and you threw up and you had to take your rings off. I thought you had the flu. When you later told me what happened, I was sad.*

Then she had lots of questions: "Why did the baby die?" "What did it look like when it died?" "What did the doctor do?" and "What happened at the hospital?"

It is helpful to be open and truthful with children, provide them with information appropriate for their ages, respect their ways of dealing with losses, and embrace them with love and affection. In an anecdote from

On Wings of Mourning, Carol and William Rowley demonstrate kind-hearted acceptance of their child's way of handling loss:

> Danny was just finishing his breakfast when we returned home from the hospital. My mother stood nearby as [my husband] Bill put his arms around Danny and told him that Devon had just died and was with Jesus in heaven. Danny looked at our faces and then down to the floor without crying. He seemed unsure of how he should respond. Bill, sensing this, said, "You know, Danny, some people cry when they are sad, like Mom. Some people feel sad in their hearts, but don't cry. Either is all right." "That's how I am," was all he said. We all hugged each other.

As time passes, children do not forget. Regardless of how long it's been, they still think about our miscarriages from time to time. Also, later events in their lives can touch off memories, questions, and emotions about our miscarriages.

My daughter Terese, then eight years old, showed few signs of grief over the loss of her little brother. I know she really felt the loss of her mother. Several years later, a very special-to-us baby whale at Sea World was still in the nursing phase when its mother very suddenly died. At that time, emotions and questions emerged from Terese.

As children's initially limited ability to understand our losses grows, they need to process those losses again in a more sophisticated way. For example, I was just pregnant again when my husband and Lorien and I went out for frozen yogurt. The two of them were having sundaes, and I was having morning sickness. It was curious to me that Lorien kept urging me to eat. Finally she pleaded, "*Please* eat, Mom. You don't want *this* baby to die." We talked, and Lorien understood for the first time that our baby didn't die because I hadn't eaten enough.

In my children's school newsletter* I published an article that demonstrates many of the points discussed in this chapter:

> *In the end of December, we found out that we had a new baby brother or sister on the way. This would be the new baby that Terese and Jordan had always wanted. We all loved our baby deeply and immediately. I had a dream which indicated the sex of our child. I knew he was a boy.*
>
> *Soon after, we learned that our baby and our dreams were in jeopardy. For five weeks we waited and hoped and loved. For five weeks I stood and chewed on my thumbnail and emotionally zigged and zagged. Intellectually, I knew that it was too early to be excited and too early to be shattered. And all the while, I felt both. I also knew that when a mom's world is chaos, so is her children's; and still I couldn't help feeling those feelings. It was a tenuous and a strenuous five weeks.*

*Mission Bay Montessori Academy's Parent-To-Parent newsletter.

On Tuesday afternoon, I went to my fourth and final sonogram, and the radiologist confirmed that our baby was dead. I went right to school to pick up my children, and my heartbreak was most apparent. I felt about five years old myself when I looked down at the floor and said to my son's teacher, "Rose, our baby's not going to make it." Rose enveloped me in her arms, whispering softly to me as I cried uncontrollably before the little children. I will never, never forget her for that.

A week after the D&C, Rose spoke to me. She said she was at her wits' end about Jordan. He had seemingly transformed into a different child. He was running across the room during circle, he wasn't doing his work, he wasn't listening, and he was getting into fights every day. She said she sat down with him and said, "Jordan, I don't understand what to do. I don't want to keep benching you. I want to help you. How can I help you?" But Jordan didn't know.

That night I put him on my lap. I said, "Rose told me you're having a very hard time at school." He very genuinely shrugged his shoulders. I said gently, "I wonder if you're feeling sad about our baby," and he opened his mouth wide, and he wailed for an hour and a half. The first words he could utter were, "I didn't even get a chance to change his diapers!"

That night, we all four sat on the bed and cried together, and we named our baby Andrew Tyler. Jordan told his little brother, who would forever be his little brother, that he loved him. And as he ran off down the hall, we heard him say, "Good-bye Andy."

After school the next day, I relayed that to Rose, and tears streamed her face. She reported that the Jordan she had known had returned, and a week later she confirmed it again. For as long as I live, I will be grateful to Rose for knowing that children feel so immeasurably deeply and that Jordan most needed love precisely when he seemed most unlovable. She communicated frankly with me, even though it would seem to make my tough situation even tougher. And with her understanding, love, warmth, and communication, she helped us to quickly diffuse a little boy's sorrow and a potentially ongoing, huge problem. I feel so blessed to have had Jordan in her care during this time. I know that what I had heard is true. . . . Rose is a rose.

CHAPTER FIFTEEN

Our Families and Friends

The women we interviewed talked about their relationships with families and friends and the way many of those relationships changed after their losses. Their relationships remained positively or negatively colored for years to come by the interactions that ensued.

WHAT FELT HELPFUL

People who invited the women to talk or who simply listened without judgment, belittlement of the loss, or pointing to "the brighter side" were helpful. When others acknowledged the women's miscarriages as losses and responded with compassion and acceptance, relationships felt healing and were remembered with deep appreciation:

> *My brother is four years younger than I am. When I dream of the babies, they look like him because he's the baby that came home when I was a little girl. I think he's sort of my idealized baby. I got to help a lot with him. There's a very strong bond between us. I didn't play with a lot of dollies. I had him. He recently gave me a wonderful compliment that saved me. He told me, "This is a shame about all this. You would've made a wonderful mother." I asked, "How do you know?" He said, "Because I remember." . . . I think that sentence saved me. And that will always help because really nobody else does know. He has no idea how that helped me. He should be told.*

> *People that I was not as close to helped me get through it more than people I was close to. One woman put her arms around me and said, "This is really hard for you. You've lost a child. When you want to talk, I'm here." It helped when other people acknowledged that a child was lost, said they were sorry, could stand it if I cried, or listened. It wasn't so much what they said; it was who wasn't afraid to hear whatever manifestation of my grief. People who were supportive then have always remained special to me.*

> *Nobody tried to take the pain away. Nobody tried to say it was okay. My sister cried with us. Our pastor announced it in the service. People at church were wonderful. They were not trying to avoid me. They would come up to me and say, "I'm so sorry." Some would tell me about their losses. That's neat.*

> *My relationships strengthened with those with whom I could let my hair down. Someone left a sympathy card stuck in my door. You'd be amazed how that*

helped. Someone else called to say they were thinking of me and they cared. And they continued calling. Someone else gave me a support group card. I held onto it for a year. It gave me comfort.

My friend understood that I was grief-stricken. He was very gentle with me and forgiving me my lack of presence and having not much to give. He let me ramble and be angry and do my thing.

The men at my work gave me two weeks off. They sent me flowers and a card that said, "We all share your sorrow."

Most women were not aware that others whom they personally knew had also had miscarriages. But some women knew or came to know of others who had and who lent them compassion and understanding. Because of their common experience, these women shared a sisterhood of heretofore unspoken grief, and a bond was solidified between them:

My mother had three miscarriages. I remember her crying and my finding her bloody nightgowns. She understood, and I felt close to her.

I had an instant rapport like a mental shorthand with women who had had losses. I always ask women when I meet them if they had a miscarriage to know if I can identify with them. You don't feel so silly or so strange.

My mother told a lot of her friends. Even her own friends were revealing their miscarriages to her after all these years. I couldn't believe how many of them had had miscarriages. It was helpful hearing it. I had felt like nothing wrong ever happens to them. I saw them in a different light. I saw their vulnerability and their willingness to share to try to take some of my pain away.

WHAT FELT HURTFUL

Most women felt deeply hurt or lonely when friends or family tried to diminish their losses:

I felt my family was critical of me for reacting as I did, like I was just being a hysterical person and how dare I act like I deserve attention and care and sympathy for this. After all, they shove down their hardships; why shouldn't I? But just because they *do without, I'm not going to do without. I deserve better than that, just like they deserve better than that, even though they don't know it.*

People pretended it didn't happen; it wasn't important. Since they never met that person, it's like that person never existed. What hurt was their pretending that the loss of my baby was no big deal. It was nothing to them. I got no sympathy, no empathy. Life went on, and I didn't matter to anyone. People didn't care. Not even my family. There was no one to say, "I'm really sorry. That really hurt."

Many found that family and friends withdrew from or said nothing to them. This increased their feelings of isolation, loneliness, and pain:

When you're in the hospital having a baby, everyone loves you. When you're losing a baby, they don't have anything to say.

Many turned away. I was angry! I'd explain to them, "I'm telling you it's painful. Why won't you believe me? Do you think I'm lying?!"

I confided in my friends, but then they never brought it up again. They didn't know what to do with me. I felt like an outcast. I went to a shower, and I knew they were whispering about me in the next room. I came in and said, "I know you guys are talking about me, so why don't you just talk in front of my face?" I became somewhat of a hermit. I had no safe place to grieve.

I worried about wearing out friends and imposing on them. They were probably tired of hearing about it. But I still needed to talk and recount the emotional experience. I would go through my phone book looking for people to call. I was looking for someone who had had the same experience.

Women gave a host of examples of hurtful things that others said:

"After three miscarriages, you should be getting used to this."

"Oh well, it's common. It will work next time."

I have a friend who has four children. She said to me, "At least you don't look at your husband and get pregnant." I keep my feelings inside to keep the relationship on an even keel.

My sister-in-law got pregnant. I was miserable. My mother-in-law told me this was her turn; mine was over. She said, "Don't spoil her pregnancy with your grief."

My friends were logical with me. Logic was useless! These feelings aren't logical at all! They said, "At least you have three kids," "At least you didn't see your baby," and "At least you were only seven weeks along."

They said, "It was God's will." But it hurt no matter what. It was a part of me. It was my child whether I lost it then or when it was 20 years old.

People said, "You're too old," "You shouldn't have counted on it anyway," "Count your blessings," "I think you're overreacting," and "You're dwelling." You're down and you get kicked.

"Oh, honey, I've lost so many. It wasn't a baby. It was just a blob."

My parents don't count him. I say to them, "You have nine grandchildren." They say, "No we don't."

People said to me, "Oh, you didn't really want those children anyhow." They gave the grandma advice, the "cure all" remedies. I yelled at them.

Several women found it hurtful when people *said* they understood, but the women felt they did not understand. The women felt misunderstood, patronized, and even more alone:

What hurt was people saying they knew how it felt when they hadn't been through it and they really didn't know. Sometimes they would relate it to something which let me know they had no idea *what it was like.*

I hated it when other people told me about their friends' stories (not their own). They don't know what they are talking about because they never lost a baby. I thought, "I've lost a child and you haven't. You can't talk to me about what it feels like to lose a baby."

Because they did not experience others as acknowledging or compassionate, many women needed to insulate themselves from people. The women withdrew or pretended not to feel hurt. But they did feel hurt, they remembered insensitivities, and the pain lingered:

I was afraid to talk too much about it. They would think I was being melodramatic. I didn't want them to think I was dwelling on it, so I just avoided them. I felt like a wimp. I haven't kept in touch with anyone. I'm just not ready to face them. I feel such depression.

The hospital was crummy; people were crummy. The world was not friendly. I had no safe place to grieve. I kept it to myself. A 20-foot wall went up around me. No one was going to invade my fortress.

I tried to give the outward appearance that I was fine. I was going through the motions. I really disconnected from myself and others. I kept on a front. I avoided personal contact. I was embarrassed. I never discussed it with anyone. It was such a private thing.

I wasn't going to go back to school the following semester because I had told so many people there that I was pregnant. I needed to crawl in my shell and stay there and not come out. I wanted to crawl into a hole. Telling people at school was painful, like when I had to tell people my father died. But I felt I had to diminish this loss and act like it was okay. I didn't want anyone to know how bad it was. I didn't want to feel it. When I am telling someone, my throat feels like it is filled with shattered glass.

Most women felt deeply pained around babies and pregnant women, both those they knew personally and strangers. The sight of these women was a searing reminder of what they had lost, and it evoked sorrow, jealousy, inferiority, anger, and guilt over some of those feelings. Some wanted to tell pregnant women of the possibility of miscarriage in order to take away their joy or to protect them in case of loss. Some wished that others would have miscarriages so they didn't have to witness their joy. Other women felt that they themselves were an embarrassing reminder to pregnant women of the possibility of death:

I did not want to look at, be around, or talk about pregnant people. I had "pregnancy-o-phobia." There was a woman at work who was pregnant and bleeding. Yet she *had a healthy baby. I feel really bad about this, but I was jealous because whenever I bled I had a miscarriage. It's still painful for me.*

I resent couples who become pregnant and tell you five days after they find out, or who are real smug. I feel they're naive to capriciously take life for granted. You have to hide your feelings about pregnant women and their babies. It's hard. Not that you don't want them to have beautiful children; you just feel so empty.

I felt jealous when my OB was doing a sonogram on another women nearby. I had to turn away. I couldn't look. It hurt so bad. He was joking with her. He said nothing to me.

WHAT THEY WANTED FROM OTHERS

Giving themselves freedom to imagine more desirable experiences with others, women wanted their miscarriages to be treated as deaths:

I wanted them to say, "I'm sorry about your loss" instead of trying to be upbeat. I wanted them to hug me more and to say to me, "I know this is tragic. It's okay to be sad and to cry." They didn't have to be sad but just respect my sadness. It would be nice if they would send flowers or cards because that's what people do when you lose someone. They would be acknowledging that we lost a child.

I want them to bring up Adam like they would any baby who died, to come to a memorial service, to weep with me. I don't want Adam to be forgotten by anyone. I don't want time *to take away the existence of this child.*

I wanted people who've gone through this to talk with me at great length and to make me feel I wasn't the only woman who didn't bounce back.

What would have helped me would have been for someone to talk about the baby *as a* baby. *I lost a BABY! To say to me, "Mrs. English, you have lost a child. You are going through grieving. Here is what to expect. Here are some guidelines. Here is a support group."*

CHAPTER SIXTEEN

Professionals

Women spontaneously brought up and described their experiences, both hurtful and healing, with medical professionals, mental health professionals, clergy, and support groups.

MEDICAL PROFESSIONALS

In telling their stories, most women spontaneously relayed their experiences with and their feelings about the medical professionals they encountered. A small number of women and their babies were treated with respect and dignity by aware and sensitive doctors and nurses who, afterward, were deeply appreciated and well remembered:

> *Sixteen years ago, the doctor held my hand and ordered me tea and toast. It was a* powerful *thing. I still remember. His doing that allowed me release from denial and the loss of a baby hit me. I was overwhelmed with his kindness. He was a wonderful doctor! That was really* important to me.
>
> *My daughter was born two years later on my miscarried baby's due date. I was having a C-section, and I was aware of the baby who was miscarried. The nurse said, "Gee, I'll bet you're excited." I said, "He would have had a sibling." She got tears in her eyes. It was a neat moment for me.*
>
> *The doctor gently said to me, "Nancy, your baby has expired. It's no longer a live pregnancy." He held our hands. He took us into his office, and he talked with us. He provided a world of comfort. My doctor had called in to the hospital ahead of me, and the nurse there was waiting for me. She knew who I was. The anesthesiologist said to me, "Nancy, my wife has had two miscarriages; I know what you're going through." I got follow-up calls from him, the nurses, and my OB. I got wonderful care!*
>
> *I began to have contractions in the middle of the night. The guy on call was the most wonderful person in the world. He laid all the facts out kindly. When we got there, he was extremely sympathetic.*

Many women expressed concern about how their babies were verbally referred to or physically handled. They wanted their babies treated with the dignity given to other human beings at death, but most often their babies were regarded as rubbish. Although some women *behaved* passively in the midst of the medical situation, they *felt* enraged and were later haunted by this treatment:

I was bleeding heavily, and I passed a lot of tissue. I called the doctor, and he said to put it in a plastic sandwich bag and bring it in. I knew it was fetal tissue. It upset me terribly that he said, "Put it in a baggy."

Trying to play down the D&C, the nurse said, "Oh, just a little dusting and cleaning!" I wanted to sock her. This was my BABY.

I miscarried in my hand. The bag was thin and gray and intact. I could see right through it. The baby barely fit in the palm of my hand. It looked like a baby, just real tiny. The nurse stared at me for a minute, and then she said, "It's not a baby; it's products of conception." She flipped my hand over and dumped it in the dish. She kept repeating it. I just wanted to kill her. I just wanted to strangle her. She put it in formaldehyde, which made genetic testing impossible. Two days later, I thought, "WHERE'S MY BABY?! WHERE'S MY BABY?!" How many times I've wanted to go back there and find her and scream and yell and holler at her.

About a month after the miscarriage, I called the doctor and asked where the baby had been sent. He gave me the name of the lab. I talked to the director of pathology. He was uncooperative and hostile and said I had to go about retrieving it through their lawyer. I called a mortuary, and the mortician called the lab for me and got the remains. I found out later that the lab had lost them.

I went to the E.R. They scooped me out and flung it like slop. The doctor gave it no respect. He didn't even say I could go home. I figured it out in awhile. I wanted them to deal with me like my mother had died.

Some women found the doctors or nurses would not communicate with them, adding to the women's feelings of isolation, confusion, and anger:

Dodging the truth sets up the unknown. They didn't tell me that the baby had died. I can deal with the truth. I can't deal with the unknown. I wish the doctor had said, "Joanne, your baby has died." Because nobody told me, I went into emotional shock. I was in a fog for weeks after that. It was not soaking in. At my six-week checkup, it dawned on me that my baby had died.

The doctor talked around me to my husband. He said nothing to me. I didn't know what was going on. I felt like an island because I couldn't get an answer from anyone.

Some women felt that the medical professionals who treated them were oblivious to and unsympathetic toward their feelings of loss. When medical professionals treated their miscarriages lightly, women felt embarrassed, angry, and confused:

The doctors were unemotional and detached—really cold. The nursing staff at the hospital looked at me like I was a basket case. I hid under the covers because all I could do was cry. I felt so embarrassed and exposed. I believe that that was part of why I had so much trouble afterwards.

The D&C was a horrendous thing to go through. Afterwards, the doctor said to me, "Well I've got to go deliver a baby now." I was devastated. I hated him.

I had the miscarriage alone in the hospital. There was blood everywhere. I had to clean myself up. They wouldn't let me call my husband until a half hour later. I thought, "You wouldn't treat me this way if I was nine months pregnant."

You have to have three miscarriages before they take you seriously, before they look into why you have miscarried.

*I was listed as a "gynecological" patient, not "obstetrical." That nullified my pregnancy and my motherhood.**

It happens every day; for them it's routine. But it's so traumatic for you. The realization came in waves. It was more than I could bear. Meanwhile, the doctor acted hassled. He said, "Oh no, not another one." I was just another task.

Specific experiences with medical professionals added further trauma to the women's already painful situations. They described some of them and relayed some of the insensitivities they encountered:

The OB said that if I had a fever over 100 degrees, I should call him. When it went over 100, I called. But then he said to me, "Don't bother me. Call me if it gets over 104."

When I told the nurses I thought something was wrong, they said, "You're paranoid."

The doctor said, "I'll clean out the uterus."

I had so many hurtful pelvic exams in the hospital. Ten in two or three days! Every single time it was a different person doing it.

They took all my clothes away and put me in a room with a bunch of other people. My husband was alone out there. I was alone in the room.

MENTAL HEALTH PROFESSIONALS

A number of women spontaneously brought up warm and healing experiences with compassionate mental health professionals both in and out of hospitals:

I used to say "fetus." My therapist said, "This was your baby." Saying "fetus" was my way to depersonalize the baby.

*This is commonly done to protect women from being placed with happy OB patients and their healthy new babies.

After my miscarriage I felt like "half a woman." I sought counseling. I focused on me and my self-esteem. I had none left. It was very helpful. I began focusing on what I want, not on what I don't want. I learned to say "No."

CLERGY

A few women spontaneously brought up helpful experiences with caring members of the clergy:

The pastor came over and treated my miscarriage like a death. He gave it the significance it deserved.

I saw a chaplain today. He said, "Know this, Maddie. The pain will always be there. It may not be as strong. But you will get closure on it. You will put it in a different perspective."

Four or five couples and a priest came to our home to do a joint service. The priest said, "Be open to learning from this. Share your experience and what you have learned from it."

SUPPORT GROUPS

Some women turned to support groups, but they were not for everyone. For some, they were too intense. For others, they were too public. The women were grouped with parents who had lost babies to stillbirth or infant death because the grief is as deep. But these women who had miscarried felt unjustified next to parents who lost "real" babies. They were not sure they had real babies and felt they had no right to be there. They saw stillborn losses as greater losses. In contrast, their own losses seemed puny, they felt embarrassed, and they plunged into an even deeper sadness. This problem existed within the very support groups designed to meet their needs. For this reason, they did not return:

My husband attended the support group meeting with me. There were people there who lost full-term babies. We didn't belong. We had no right to be there.

I didn't feel I had a right to feel as grieved as my friend who had had a stillborn baby.

Some women felt comforted by support groups in which they could share their stories and air their grief:

Fifteen years after the loss I finally went to a support group meeting. I'm so amazed by the healing power of a group. I realized I had been suppressing all of my mourning. It brought my feelings out. I felt accepted and like I could talk about it there. It took about a year then to go through the bulk of my grief, but I did a complete turnaround.

PART FIVE

FACETS OF GRIEF

CHAPTER SEVENTEEN

Understanding Grief

Grief is an emotional, intellectual, physical, behavioral, and spiritual response to loss. The depth and the complexity of grief often feel overwhelming and baffling. Unfortunately, arming ourselves with knowledge about grief does not simplify it or reduce its depth.

Yet without knowledge of the symptoms and process of grief, our confusion about what we feel adds to the inevitable pain and confusion inherent in bereavement. Many of us worry that we have gone perfectly crazy—a logical assumption in light of the fact that, often, *grief feels crazy*. The anxiety and pain that accompany this assumption are unnecessary and preventable. This distress can stand in the way of our healing. As one woman in our study said, "I needed someone to sit and explain. I thought something was wrong with me. I didn't know that what I was feeling was grief!"

Armed with information about bereavement and the natural efficiency of grieving, we can avoid *additional* pain, anxiety, and confusion, and better manage our journey through grief.

No two of us will feel precisely the same way about any one loss. And the ways in which we deal with our grief are as diverse as there are people in this world. Each of us responds to life and to loss with a unique character, temperament, and personal history, and with unique values, beliefs, and more.

Our unconscious minds are eminently wise with knowledge of what we need at each point in time. There is a unique time, place, and way for each one of us to grieve (and not to grieve), depending on factors pertinent to each unique human life.

We will relay to you a mixture of both widely accepted theory and personal perspective. Because we all see life from our own unique vantage points, some of the views expressed in this and following chapters may be in accord with yours, and others may not. Some personal philosophies and perspectives, as well as accepted theories, change and grow over time as we all encounter, learn from, and incorporate new experiences.

So be discerning. You are the final authority on you. Respect and listen to your inner voice as you read. Trust your own instincts. Choose and keep what feels helpful and right to you.

Grief is the universal response to loss. We all experience a variety of losses in life, and therefore we all experience grief. We can feel grief in response to the loss of a treasured scrapbook or a very special watch, a city from which we have moved, an ended marriage even if we wanted and chose to divorce, a job we expected to get, a neighbor whom we couldn't stand, emotional closeness with a friend, approval of a parent, or feelings of safety after a violent crime has been committed in our neighborhood. The list is endless. We can experience grief not only in response to the loss of a loved one but also in response to the loss of expectations, a quality of life, and more.

Through the remainder of this book, so that you don't have to repeatedly read "a loved one, valued thing, dream, experience, etc.," we will name only "a loved one" when we refer to the object of grief. Remember, though, that grief can be felt in response to any kind of loss.

Feelings of loss range in intensity from disappointment to wrenching, life-altering bereavement. Grief is felt in different ways. It is often experienced as a welling up of sadness. Waves of emotions can erupt in bursts—perhaps uncontrolled crying—and be interspersed with feeling "absolutely fine." Grief can also be a subtle sense of sadness that is not accompanied by tears.

Grief is characterized by feelings of depression and guilt. It does not necessarily entail sobbing, and it does not identify itself with a name tag. A woman in our study said she did not grieve her miscarriage. She went on to describe feelings of sadness and guilt. Later in the interview, she said that she didn't think she "could take anymore pregnancies" because she didn't feel she could emotionally handle another loss. She didn't recognize her feelings as those of grief, yet she was grieving.

In grief we can feel that our inner being or soul is diminished. When loss feels great and when feelings are numerous, overwhelming, or very painful, we keep some of our feelings at bay. Therefore, we can feel numb, dazed, disconnected, neutral, or even dead inside. Another woman said, "I felt heavy. I finally became aware that I wasn't alive." These are feelings of depression.

When a loved one dies, we are faced with the often excruciating task of living without them. We are social beings, and our relationships hold significance and meaning to us. We see ourselves and our worlds partly within the context of these relationships. We may ask ourselves, "Who am I without you?" or "What is life without you?" We don't just feel we *want* our loved ones in our lives; we feel we *need* them in our lives. This kind of pain is so pervasive; the sounds of sadness over the loss of a loved one dominate the radio airwaves.

When someone who means very much to us dies, the world as we have seen it changes. Loss poses philosophical challenges to our previous thinking: our beliefs, attitudes, theories and viewpoints—on life, the world, what is important, God, who we are, why we are here, and what is real. We may find ourselves asking, "Why would this happen?" "Why me?" "How can God be the loving and all-powerful God I thought He was?" "What is the point?" or "How am I to live now?" and more. We feel disoriented and confused. Grief can feel as if we are in a state of internal disarray or even as if we have been mentally looted.

Loss can necessitate the reorganization or rebuilding of our inner world, step by step and piece by piece. This grief work—searching, feeling, expressing, learning, and expanding—is accomplished in layers and over the course of time. Through the work of expression, our being feels less and less diminished and our depression becomes more and more healed.

When we are grieving, we are in transition, evolving from one phase of existence to another. Grieving is the process of constructing and adapting to a new state of being without the loved one we have lost.

CHAPTER EIGHTEEN

Respecting and Honoring Our Grief

Over the course of conversation, a new acquaintance and I discovered that we had both had miscarriages. As we talked she disclosed, "You know, I wonder why I didn't grieve. I really feel like I *should* have." I could only laugh aloud and say, "*I* wondered why I *did* grieve, and felt like I *shouldn't* have! We can't win, can we?"

We never completely learn the lesson that *all* our feelings are okay. Fear, confusion, conflict, and sadness are a part of living life and being human. We all—the bereaved and "the not bereaved"—feel some degree of each of these on some level. We feel the spectrum of human emotions. We need not criticize or condemn ourselves for what we feel. Emotions are not stupid, ridiculous, awful, or crazy. Our feelings just "are."

Each of us deserves to *know* that we are important and loveable and to treat ourselves accordingly. This does not mean buying ourselves things we really can't afford, overeating, or treating ourselves as more worthy than the next person. Treating ourselves lovingly means taking our emotions seriously and expressing them, including our feelings of grief and vulnerability. It means knowing that how we feel matters. And it means thinking, feeling, and behaving with deep compassion for ourselves.

There is a prevalent notion that we should stuff down our unpleasant feelings and suffer quietly because it is better to be mostly concerned with others, not ourselves. Yet when we live according to this belief, we often feel and act less lovingly. In the long run, stuffing feelings and suffering quietly usually lead to our feeling resentment, anger, or hostility, and the purpose in stuffing is defeated. When we are loving to ourselves, when we pay attention to our emotions and express them in some way, our ability to love others naturally and spontaneously grows.

The prospect of treating ourselves as loveable feels foreign and uncomfortable to many of us. We may feel guilty, embarrassed, or unworthy at even the thought of doing so. Yet somewhere inside us, there is also probably at least a distant sense that we are deeply special.

All of us squirm and feel apprehensive about expressing some of our feelings. But this often becomes even more so after miscarriage if we hold the notion that miscarriage is "only" the loss of "potential" babies. Let's look at this notion and assume for a moment that our babies were not real babies and, therefore, we have no right to grieve the death of real babies.

For example, when we see a movie, we feel many emotions in response to a story that is not real. In the same vein, many of us suffer the same grief that mothers of deceased infants do, regardless of whether we lost babies who lived outside our wombs. *It is in light of our whole internal experience that our feelings make sense and are anything but groundless.*

If we are suffering as if a loss was terrible, then the loss was terrible for us. If we *feel* loss, there *is* loss, and it is significant enough to deserve attention and care.

We deserve the freedom, the time, and a voice for expelling what hurts inside. We can express feelings at a time, in a place, perhaps with another person, and in a way that feels right to us. We might arrange time with a trusted friend or mate or seek out another mother who has miscarried. It is helpful to grant ourselves permission to say "dumb, crazy, or awful" things, to be "irrational," or get hysterical if we *feel* hysterical. After all, quite commonly, feelings don't seem a bit rational, and we have a right to get hysterical. A variety of ways to express ourselves are listed in "Taking Care" (Appendix A).

In the face of our suffering, we need to commit to no longer abandoning our feelings and ourselves, to return to and stand by ourselves with compassion, and to express whatever we feel. We need to respect and honor our grief and who we are.

HEARTFELT MESSAGES

The women in our study expressed themselves directly to you, the reader. Their words flowed to you with hearts outstretched. They shared with empathy and from understanding—their own hearts' pain—to yours. Their messages are of compassion and love for you who know their grief and sorrow.

Some wanted to tell you that your loss is real and deep:

I'm so sorry. Without a doubt, this is one of the most difficult times in your life. Don't underestimate it. You have lost a child. He or she was real. And he or she was a part of you. You truly are a mother.

They wanted to let you know that you are not alone and that you can reach out:

> *I care and I hear you. You are not alone. Don't wall yourself off from life as I did and try to deal with it all alone. It's the hardest thing in the world to share. But do share and do connect. Some people want to help. Let them. That's the start of healing.*

They wanted to ease your guilt and affirm your innocence:

> *Don't harbor bad feelings about having "done something wrong." You are a good person.*

They felt it important that you understand you have the right to grieve and that grieving can free you:

> *Yours was a special child. It's okay to be sad. I unconditionally invite you to feel as bad as you need to feel. Don't pretend it never happened or try to put it all behind you. It won't go away on its own. Listen to your inner feeling as a woman and allow it to come out as it wants. Put no judgments on it. Go with it. You will pass* through *the emotions, and you will learn through it all.*
>
> *I encourage you to go through the complete coming apart. It's okay to fall apart, to be a wreck. It's okay to have this time in your life to not be competent and then pick up the pieces further down the road. Let "down the road"* be down the road. *You come through a changed person. But you do come through.*

Some wanted to urge you to take care of yourself:

> *Be gentle with yourself. Be kind to yourself. Give yourself time. Protect yourself. Be selfish: deal just with your sense of loss. That's enough!*

Finally, they felt it important that you know that healing does happen:

> *You think the pain is going to kill you, but don't give up hope. There is a healing process. It does get better. The bulk of the pain, the despair, does go away. Heal in your own good time. That is okay. Sometimes it takes a long time. Somewhere down the road you will be able to deal with it better. Eventually you will come to the other side of your pain, and when you do, you will be a different person. Yet you may never "get over" the loss of your child. It will always be a part of the fabric of your life.*

CHAPTER NINETEEN

Emotional and Physical Dimensions

Without knowledge about bereavement, we don't always recognize its various manifestations. The following list of emotions and facets of bereavement is designed to help you recognize your grief as grief and to give a name or a word to what you feel. We want you to have the option of running your finger down a list and locating your feelings on it so that you will understand that they stem from your miscarriage and that you are okay.

Some items on the list are self-explanatory and readily understood. Others are less so. Because terms sometimes have more meaning when we see examples with which we can relate, fictional sample quotes are sometimes provided.

You may relate with a particular sample quote yet not identify with the emotion it is here to illustrate. Sample quotes are arguable insofar as meanings vary from person to person and from instance to instance. "I've had it" may mean "I'm sick of doing this," "I'm angry," *or* "I'm tired." All three meanings are correct. So the quotes serve only as possible examples of each feeling or experience, not as dogma.

Overlap exists among the terms because we can't compartmentalize our experiences as if they are distinct and separate entities. They are all interrelated.

It is important to know that not every grieving person experiences all the following. We may experience some at some point in our grief, others at other points in our grief, and others not at all.

Emotional experiences of grief can include the following.

CONFUSION

Shock or Disbelief: We may feel little or no emotion, numb, stunned, or suspended. Things may seem unreal. We may feel an intermittent doubt that the loss occurred:

"I think the baby is still coming." "This is all a dream." "This isn't really happening." "This can't be." "No!" "I'm fine about it." "Maybe the baby is still alive inside me."

Confusion and Disorganization: Many of us find ourselves thinking or speaking more slowly than usual, pausing more as we speak, or feeling confused or forgetful even about small matters. We may be easily distracted or have a hard time concentrating, remembering, or making decisions or good decisions. We may mistakenly identify another as the one who has died. We may feel chaotic inside, lost, shunted, disoriented, without direction, distracted, mixed up, or like we're going crazy:

"It makes no sense! She did drugs while she was pregnant and her baby lived, and I administered perfect self-care and my baby died." "I am in spiritual crisis; I don't know what to believe anymore." "Why?" "I invested my whole self in this. What do I do with all of that love now?"

Conflict: Sometimes we feel torn, divided, or troubled in response to simultaneous and clashing thoughts or feelings:

"I want to cry, but I don't want to cry." "I want to hold onto my grief, and I want to move past it." "I miss my baby, and I feel angry at her too." "I want people to leave me alone, and I want them to hold me and draw me out."

Craziness: We might perceive ourselves as absurd, silly, bizarre, loony, or irrational. We may possess a diminished ability to be rational. We may experience mood swings. It is even normal during grief to have passing hallucinations. (Just because we *feel* crazy does not mean we *are* crazy. Feelings of craziness during grief are only a part of and a stronger version of "Confusion and Disorganization.")

DEPRESSION

Depression: In times of grief we often feel low, lifeless, slowed down, immobilized, apathetic, or without enthusiasm, sparkle, or vigor. Expressions of depression can include a loss of interest in life, an inability to function or function well, having little energy for basic self-care like showering (let alone putting on makeup), being less productive, gaining or losing weight, making poor or impulsive decisions, or having recurrent thoughts of death or suicide. (Many of the experiences in this list are part of depression and come under this broad heading.)

Loss: Often we feel disappointment, a void, an emptiness, or cheated:

"I feel sad." "I miss her." "There is a hole left in me." "Part of me has died." "My baby is gone and will never be back." "My future is taken away."

Withdrawal: Some of us pull away from other people, close ourselves off, or don't open up with others emotionally:

"I want everybody to go away permanently and leave me alone."

Elevation of Mood: We might feel "hyper," feel a racing sense of enthusiasm, talk more than usual, have speeding thoughts, or feel smug, better than the next person, or grandiose (which all can be denial of depression).

Energy Disturbances: Sometimes there is a feeling of fatigue, sluggishness, weariness, boredom, struggling to do normal everyday things, or being weighted down. We may yawn repeatedly. We may be restlessly overactive, twirl or pull our hair, or pull or rub our skin, clothes, or certain objects.

Sleep Disturbances: Sleeping difficulties are a normal part of grief: frequent waking in the wee hours of the morning, having trouble falling asleep at night, early morning awakening, oversleeping in the mornings, sleeping more than usual, sleeping but not feeling rested, and drowsiness.

Appetite Disturbances: We may eat significantly less or more than usual, undergo a significant change in weight, eat without enjoyment, or experience a loss of taste.

Sexual Disturbances: We might want markedly more or less sex than usual or feel sexually lethargic or energetic compared to our usual selves.

Despair: We may feel a sense of gloom, doom, bleakness, hopelessness, or sense a "black cloud" or "veil" over the world. We may feel like we are "in a black hole":

"What is there to live for?" "I'll feel this way forever." "What's the point?" "I'll never feel like smiling or laughing again." "Life is over."

Self-destructive Thoughts and Feelings: Some of us want to do or think about doing things that will physically or emotionally, and directly, indirectly, or eventually injure or destroy ourselves. We may feel pessimistic or think a lot about death:

"I just want to be drunk all the time." "I feel like severing all of my relationships." "I feel like veering off the side of the freeway."

INADEQUACY AND LOSS OF SELF-ESTEEM

Inadequacy and Loss of Self-esteem: We might partly believe we are inferior, worthless, deserving of self-criticism, or unattractive. (Many of the other feelings listed overlap this experience.):

> *"Oh, don't worry about me; it's okay." "I know my loss wasn't as bad as hers." "I didn't want to be a bother to the doctor." "My baby died; so what's wrong with* me?"

Helplessness: Many of us feel vulnerable, unprotected, weak, powerless, or that we need someone to take care of us:

> *"There was nothing I could do to protect or save her." "I had no control." "I saw the blood, and I couldn't stop what was happening."*

Purposelessness: Sometimes we feel without aim, mission, cause, meaning, or a point in being:

> *"Accomplish something? Why? For who? For what?" "What is the point in living?" "Why are we here?"*

Failure: We may experience ourselves as a disappointment, as having functioned inadequately, or as having "blown it":

> *"I didn't perform." "I couldn't pull it off." "I screwed it up."*

Embarrassment: Sometimes we feel a more mild version of shame or humiliation when we lose the image we desire to maintain in front of others. We may feel exposed as "less" than what we want others to believe about us.

Guilt: Most of us feel some sort of self-reproach, remorse, repentance, or self-blame:

> *"I should be feeling better." "I shouldn't be feeling better." "I should be able to get through this on my own." "If only I had (or hadn't) done ——, the baby might have lived." "I shouldn't think of it as a baby." "I create all of this pain by thinking about it. In doing so, I upset others."*

TRAUMA

Devastation: Sometimes we feel shattered, in a shambles, or in ruins:

> *"I was destroyed by his death." "I don't know where to begin to pick up the pieces."*

Irrevocable Injury: Our wound may feel irreparable. (In actuality, we are never beyond the possibility of significant emotional healing.):

> *"I'll never get over this." "I'll never laugh again." "Life will never be good again." "I can never, ever replace my daughter."*

Loss of Control: Sometimes we can't make things happen as we need and our worlds become out of control. Sometimes our thoughts or our emotions are out of control. Our feelings erupt when they erupt, not when we choose or expect them or when it might be more convenient for us. They seem to have a mind of their own.

HURT

Betrayal: We can feel we were insidiously sold out or led astray by life, God, our deceased loved ones, our partners, friends or families, medical staffs, or our bodies (in the event of disease or pregnancy loss).

Violation: Some of us feel we have been invaded or desecrated:

> *"During the D&C, I felt like my body was being pillaged."*

Abandonment: We may feel we have been discarded, forsaken, rejected, or deserted by our babies, partners, friends, doctors, and so on.

Self-pity: Often we feel sympathetic to or sorry for ourselves. (Many of us learned to feel critical of self-pity, yet it is natural and okay to feel sympathy for ourselves when experiencing pain.):

> *"Why me?" "Everybody's babies live but mine."*

ANGER

Anger: We can feel animosity, resentment, hostility, rage, agitation, or volatile feelings:

> *"He was such a jerk about it!" "How dare my baby die!" "I've had it with God."*

Irritability: We might feel "bugged," uptight, annoyed, abrupt, touchy, impatient, or a heightened sensitivity to noise or other stimuli.

Bitterness: Sometimes we feel cynical, reproachful, ill-willed, or pessimistic.

ANXIETY

Anxiety: We may sustain a feeling of apprehension, distress, fear, horror, or concern. We may feel unusually worried about our physical health. We may exhibit frantic searching behavior. We might feel a need to attach to someone or something that helps us feel more grounded or secure:

> *"If I start crying, I'll never stop." "My feelings are too deep. I can't let go of control of them; I won't survive." "Everything is spinning out of control." "I'm not so sure about getting pregnant again." "I didn't want the doctor to say that word: miscarriage."*

Panic Attacks: Some of us suffer occurrences of acute, extreme anxiety characterized by overwhelming feelings of being on the brink of death.

LONGING FOR CLOSENESS

Longing: Commonly we yearn, ache, and wish for our deceased loved one.

Loneliness: We experience a painful lack of companionship; we feel separated or cut off from our loved ones or from other people (because they don't understand or come around), and we feel sad about it:

> *"I'm the only one in the world who feels this." "No one understands." "I have nothing in common with anyone anymore." "I miss my baby."*

Searching: We might access records; ask questions; search out a counselor, a minister, or support group; read on the subject; or talk about the subject from every angle. We might search for, wait for, or call out to our loved ones.

Grasping: We may feel it helpful to wear, carry, treasure, or display something that symbolizes our loved ones. We hold our memories of them tightly.

Spiritual Connection: Some of us experience a nearness to or closeness with our deceased loved ones, or sense their presence close at hand:

> *"I could feel her spirit right there in the room."*

OTHER

Idealization: Sometimes we see perfection in our loved ones or in their lives or lives that would have been.

Bargaining: Some of us attempt to strike deals (often with God) or think of promises to make in exchange for what we want:

> *"I'll be a better mother if you let him live." "I'll do volunteer work if you let the next one live." "I won't be angry anymore if you let me conceive quickly again." "I'll pray more and maybe he'll make it."*

Nightmares or Unusual Dreams: Our dreams and nightmares are like parables that reveal what we feel. (If we have nightmares it is helpful to give our grief more expression during the day.)

> *"I often dreamt about natural catastrophes."*

Preoccupation: It is natural to feel fixated or obsessed, to need to tell our loved ones' stories repeatedly, or to need to play and replay our "mental recordings" of our loved ones or losses. We might be self-absorbed or emotionally unable to give to or take care of others:

> *"I just couldn't think about anyone or anything else."*

Jealousy: We may feel rivalrous with or envious of other women who are pregnant or have babies:

> *"I want to take away pregnant women's joy." "I hope she doesn't conceive." "When I see that she has what I so badly want—a baby—I feel acutely and painfully aware that I don't have mine. Even though I would never actually do it, I feel like killing her and taking her baby."*

Frustration: We may feel a tense and strained feeling in response to trying to do something we can't figure out how to do, such as delivering a living baby:

> *"I've tried different doctors, different vitamins, prayer, no prayer; WHAT ELSE CAN I TRY?!" "I keep trying and trying to make my friend understand; it makes me nuts!"*

HEALING

Relief: We may feel free or released—for instance, after surviving a D&C, after a memorial service, after the one-year anniversary, or after guilt subsides:

> *"Thank God the D&C is over!" "I've worked through so much grief. I'm so glad the worst part of the struggle is over with."*

Reorganization: Our sleeping and eating patterns eventually stabilize. We begin to pursue relationships more, take on new activities, develop new interests, and learn new ways of dealing with problems.

Recovery: We eventually develop new coping skills, regain or develop our ability to make wise decisions, feel a sense of renewal, learn to live with loss without terrific and consistent pain, feel intermittent happiness, feel a release or renewed energy, and find new purpose and meaning in death and in life.

Some avenues for working through these emotions and experiences are listed in "Taking Care" (Appendix A).

PHYSICAL EXPERIENCES OF GRIEF

Because our bodies and psyches are interrelated, there are often physical expressions of grief as well as the expected emotional expressions. These may include chronic aches and pains that we can't explain and that don't necessarily respond to medical treatment.

Because we commonly feel a heightened sense of vulnerability after loss, physical symptoms of grief can be especially worrisome or distressing. *I was sure my grief would literally kill me, but I'm still here!* If you are worrying about your health, discuss your symptoms with your doctor for the sake of your physical as well as your emotional well-being.

Here is a list you can scan and perhaps use to find your symptoms and recognize them as part of your grief. Physical feelings of grief* may include the following.

Chest pains, heaviness in the chest, tightness in the chest, or heart palpitations—exemplified in the expression "a broken heart"

Head aches, migraines, faintness, or dizziness

Throat pain, tightness, or feeling like we are smothering or choking, sometimes from held-back emotions

Back aches or tightness in the back

Stomach aches, nausea, diarrhea, indigestion, or an empty feeling in the stomach

Mouth dryness, numb and tingling lips, or the urge to yawn repeatedly

Muscle tension, aching, or weakness

*Many of the symptoms on this list are from the American Psychiatric Association, *Diagnostic and Statistical Manual of Mental Disorders (4th ed.) (Washington, DC: American Psychiatric Association).*

Sickness: colds, flu, or frequent illnesses (Resistance may be somewhat down and will get better again in time.)

Sex: decreased, increased, or no interest in sexual contact

Miscellaneous: shortness of breath, sighing, proneness to accidents, general lack of strength, altered menstrual periods, allergic reactions, panic attacks, cold and hot flashes, tingling in the fingers or feet, sweating, shaking, blurred vision, or numbness

CHAPTER TWENTY

Eve's Story

I had a miscarriage 9 months ago when I was 13 weeks pregnant.

The military hospital is the worst place to be. An ultrasound was ordered after 5:00 P.M. *and the military does not ordinarily do ultrasounds after 5:00. I felt frightened because they couldn't see the baby on the ultrasound screen. They sent me home and told me to come back in two days. I was devastated. My husband, Tom, had to physically support me to get me to the car. I was like an animal all the way home, screaming and crying.*

I remember sitting that night on the kitchen floor just wailing and pulling my hair. Those two days I couldn't think. I couldn't eat. I took care of my little girl just on automatic.

I went back for the next test, and the doctor sent me home again. Finally, on a Saturday night, I was bleeding pretty heavily, and my husband took me to the emergency room. They shuffled me back and forth. We went to the labor deck, and they sent me down to the emergency room, and then the emergency room (when they finally saw me) said they had to call someone from the labor deck. Nobody wanted to make the final decision about when, where, and if they should do a D&C. I lost control again, screaming and crying. I was just wild. My husband said the look in my eyes was that of a caged animal.

The female lieutenant commander that ran the emergency room was in there crying with me. They put me in a room and had me take off everything and put on a gown, and they left me back there, naked and bleeding and alone for over an hour. It was horrible.

Finally the nurse stuck her head in and said, "I'm going to be with you in a minute." I said, "No," and that's when I lost it. I said, "I'm leaving. I'm going to have this miscarriage at home." They checked me and sent me home again.

It was so awful because it was Christmastime and I wanted to make Christmas nice for my three-year-old daughter, Amanda, and what is this? Mommie can't stop crying!

On Wednesday I left Amanda at the sitter's to go to the doctor's appointment and be checked again. But they admitted me right then and there to do the

D&C. Everyone we knew was out of town visiting their families for Christmas, so my husband had to go and pick our daughter up. I had the D&C by myself. I could not stop crying. It was uncontrollable. I thought I would never have another baby. Everything was completely out of control. I couldn't do anything right. I mean, women are supposed to be able to have babies. And I couldn't do that. I thought, "I'm worthless. This has to be my fault. It's that one glass of champagne I had."

The next day they were going to let me go home. My husband was scheduled for duty and so I drove myself home from the hospital, still doped up on pain killers. I am still resentful that he wasn't there for me. I guess I always will be. I finally was able to tell him a few months ago that I may forgive him for that, but I will never forget it. There was something he could have done.

It was December 28th. Our Christmas tree was still up. There were presents under the tree that my mother and others had sent for the new baby.

The most difficult aspect of the loss was that I had had a baby that died and nobody seemed to understand that that's what happened. I had no one to talk to. Even my husband, God love him, did not feel as strongly as I did, or, if he did, I still don't know it. I know he was sad and upset. It would have helped me more if he had just sat down and cried.

I knew it was a real baby! That baby had a name! That baby was a girl! I thought she would have looked just like her sister with huge baby blue eyes and lots of curly dark hair. We had talked to her, and we had called her by name. She was Rebecca.

I couldn't believe Rebecca was gone, and I didn't even ever get to see her. I never got to hold her. I could not do anything but cry.

In my mind, I have two children: one that lived and one that died. But if someone asked how many children I have and I answered that way, they'd look at me like I had lost my mind. But that's the way I see it. I'm sure that if people have a child and that child dies, they don't just forget about that child. It hurts me. It makes me kind of angry, actually.

The miscarriage affected my relationship with Tom in a lot more ways than I originally thought it did. I still have some resentment. I started counting on him more, and he wasn't here. He didn't feel like he could stand up to the military and say, "Look. My wife needs me." He didn't show his emotions about it in a way that would've helped me. I wanted him to just sit down and cry. He was heartbroken. I know he was! And he's cried with me before. I thought, "For God's sakes, we've lost a baby! If you can't cry over this, what has happened to us?" I felt I had to try to bury all my depression and sadness to make things happy around here for him.

Spiritually it affected my husband more than it did me. He's not one you can easily get to church. But after our miscarriage, he wanted to be sure I took him with me every Sunday.

When he would find me sitting on the kitchen floor wailing, he would pick me up, put me on his lap, and hold me like I was a little child for hours on end. I felt taken care of.

When he was away on duty, I was trapped in this apartment and I had no one, and I was losing my mind and that made me even lonelier than I would've been otherwise because no one wanted to be around a crazy person. Nobody even called. NOTHING.

What a difference it would've made if before they ever let me out of the hospital, somebody told me, "You're going to have trouble sleeping; you're going to have problems with this; there's a support group, and here's the phone number. Don't think you're crazy. Here're the things that may happen to you, so don't think you're losing your mind."

I felt afraid that Amanda would die and I wouldn't *die and then how could I keep on living? It made me think about a lot of things. Poor Amanda, what if I die? I don't want her to grow up without a mommie. I thought, "I am going to die soon." I wasn't scared to die; I was scared for Tom and Amanda. Now, I have never been a drug user, I've never had a blood transfusion, and I've never been promiscuous, but I dreamed and thought I had AIDS. One night I made Tom take me to the hospital because I thought I was having a heart attack. They put me on the EKG machine for hours, at 28 years old!*

I dreamed Amanda died and I wouldn't let anybody have her. I just kept carrying my dead child around. People would say, "Eve, you have to give us the baby," and my dad was telling them, "No. This baby is staying with her mother."

Right before I lost the baby, I dreamed I went into the hospital to have a C-section. When I woke up, the baby was fine, but they weren't going to let me see her because I was going to die. I remember it vividly, and it scared me then. I dreamed about Rebecca all the time. I still dream about her sometimes.

Amanda plays with our friends' babies, and she says, "Baby! Baby!" and she hugs them and I feel sad. I was sure that I was still going to be crying for three years without stopping. I was sure I was never going to be able to drag myself out of bed and put my makeup on again. After four months, I quit crying on an everyday basis.

Some raw nerves have been exposed during this interview. I still feel the pain of that loss really strongly. I still love Rebecca just as much now as I did then. I think about her all the time. I mean, every day.

If a friend were to lose her baby, I know at least one person that would help her . . . and that's me. *I'll never let anybody that I know go through something like* this *alone! I would be at her house, and I would grab her and hug her and cry with her. Nobody I know will* ever *go through something like this without somebody to talk to who understands, if I can help it! And I don't care if it makes me feel horrible all over again!*

I hadn't thought in a long time about the presents under the tree for the baby. Those presents are still here in my house. Tom hid them. I haven't looked at them since he put them away. But I know where he hid them. When I finish this interview, I'll go and get those out. That's really sad, isn't it?

CHAPTER TWENTY-ONE

Understanding Our Emotions

By now, if not already before, you know your feelings are a part of grief. But what do they *mean* and how do you get *through* them? In this chapter we will shed some light on these subjects. We will talk more in-depth about some of our feelings: denial, confusion and disorganization, guilt, anger, loneliness, panic attacks, and self-destructive thoughts and feelings.

DENIAL

Denial is an important defensive mechanism. When we deny, our unconscious minds shut out reality or pain in order to keep us from being overwhelmed with them. Being somewhat emotionally numb for a finite period of time is a functional necessity after great loss, which is too traumatic to cope with, express, or adjust to all at once. We protect ourselves while in the process of adjusting.

CONFUSION AND DISORGANIZATION

We have some degree of trust that things will happen a certain way. We assume the sun will come up in the morning, cars will stop at the red light, at some point in time it is going to rain, and libraries contain books. Each of us goes about our everyday life with countless assumptions we don't consciously think about but count on. For example, our assumption that cars will stop at red lights enables us to drive through intersections. Together these assumptions allow us to go about our daily lives. They are reassuring.

We also believe to a degree that we have life under control. We believe in our will and that if we work hard at something, we can make it happen. Usually these assumptions are correct. They, too, feel reassuring.

When a great loss occurs, things don't go the way we hoped or assumed they would go, nor the way we intended. We lose trust in many of our perceptions, assumptions, and beliefs. We worry that *other* things won't go the way *they* are supposed to go either. Many of our assumptions and beliefs or philosophical underpinnings are suddenly challenged and come into question. The world is no longer predictable. That feels scary.

Secondarily, our identities are wrapped up in certain traits, roles, and concepts like motherhood, being smart, being poor, being a schoolteacher, being beautiful or ugly, and so on. When one of these identifying factors is removed, we are faced with the task of developing a different identity, or redefining who we are. That is disorienting.

In addition, confusion and disorganization are fostered perfectly by the nebulous nature of miscarriage because there usually is not tangible experience of who our babies were or what unique qualities they would have had, nor of our babies' deaths.

In *When a Baby Dies,* Rana Limbo and Sara Wheeler write, "The struggle between the conscious and the unconscious to accept the reality of the baby's death causes bizarre thoughts and feelings." One-fourth to one-third of grieving people have a hallucinatory experience, according to Anne Kaiser Stearns and countless others who work with the bereaved. These experiences are normal. Part of us feels that these experiences are real. We are *also* intellectually aware that what we experience (such as sounds of our babies' crying or sensations of movement in our tummies) are not really happening. But we are not ready to cope with reality, so we temporarily create a different "reality." We may vividly remember the reality that existed before our losses and are not ready to let it go. Part of us feels that these experiences are real, and part of us knows, at the time or later, that they are not real. Perhaps some of these are even spiritual experiences.

It is totally unfamiliar to feel or express unpleasant emotions with such intensity as we may during bereavement. Sometimes our feelings are so powerful that it seems we may lose control of ourselves and go raving mad.

Yet in expressing intense feelings, we don't have a nervous breakdown or go crazy. We let go or lose control of our reigns on our intense feelings, which then come out, sometimes wildly. Such expression may be the best thing for us. We survive, and so much pain-energy gets released. Joan Borysenko, Ph.D., observes in *Guilt Is the Teacher, Love Is the Lesson,* "This is not craziness; it is the beginning of sanity." In the same vein, William Miller's book has a very telling title: *When Going to Pieces Holds You Together.*

GUILT

When we are grieving, we often experience feelings of guilt. The words "should," "ought," "have to," "supposed to," and "must" go hand in hand with judgmental thinking and result in guilty feelings. Psychological or physical self-punishment such as overeating, food deprivation, or accidental injury may be signs of guilty feelings, too.

There are different kinds of guilt. One kind stems from a general perception of being at least indirectly at fault for *whatever* happens, regardless of whether we can put our finger on anything irresponsible that we have done.

We may even wonder if our miscarriages were personal punishments. Yet people who have clinically died and were revived, repeatedly describe experiences of loving acceptance during those times.* Their experiences do not match up with the theory of a punishing God.

It is often difficult to see and appreciate our innocence. Yet sometimes when we observe someone else's undeserved guilt and are able to see clearly and appreciate their innocence, we can more easily recognize our own.

Even when our feelings of guilt are unfounded or not logical, we need to express them because they are there, bothering us, and need to be released.

Sometimes we feel a different kind of guilt—over something we have actually or accidentally done—but *without* a desire to hurt another person or our babies: "If I hadn't drank too much before I knew I was pregnant, fallen down the stairs, had a car accident, etc., maybe my baby would have lived." Such statements may possibly be true. Yet we did not know of or anticipate the eventual turn of events. We did not *try* to make things turn out as they did. Accidents in life are inevitable. Sure, we could *always* have done things more perfectly. But we are only human.

So many of us worry that our miscarriages occurred and were our fault because we were too stressed during our pregnancies. Stress is one of many factors that come together to affect our bodies and our health; yet stress alone has not been found to cause miscarriage and disease. In fact, all pregnant women and all people have stress in varying degrees.

***Life After Life* by Raymond A. Moody, M.D., and *Closer to the Light* by Melvin Morse, M.D., reveal the experiences of many adults and children who clinically died and were then revived. Over and over again, these people describe encounters with bright light, powerful love, and total acceptance.

Natalie Davis Spingarn, also without answers about the cause of her particular plight—cancer—addressed the theory that it is caused by stress. She wrote in her book *Hanging in There: Living Well on Borrowed Time,* "The seriously ill cancer patient desperate for clues, can be baffled by reports of studies attempting to link psychological factors, such as stress, and cancer. Common sense tells me that many people I know who are not depressed at all, including innocent children, develop ugly cancers; conversely many depressed, seemingly helpless, hopeless people go about their business, cancer-free. Common sense tells me I do not fit into Stephanie Simonton's description of the breast cancer patient: A 'nice' person who does not express her sadness and vulnerability (here I am writing about it all) and is confused about her role in life. Common sense tells me that my perky, barking Corgi dog Patrick died sadly and suddenly of lung cancer last winter, and he did not even smoke, much less suffer depression." (I loved that!)

In *The Dance of Intimacy*, Harriet Lerner, Ph.D., describes another kind of guilt that stems from knowing we did not or "are not taking a responsible position . . . congruent with our own values and beliefs as we have struggled to formulate them." Perhaps we used recreational drugs while we knowingly were pregnant, performed ski stunts, or practiced other risky behaviors.

To deal with this kind of guilt, we can acknowledge our legitimate acts of irresponsibility. We can express the depth of our sorrow to our babies, ourselves, our mates, and God (or whatever higher power we believe in), if any. We can realize that we did not desire to hurt or be unloving to anyone but rather were tied up with our own emotional pains. We can remind ourselves that every good person who has ever lived has behaved irresponsibly many times in his or her life (which does not make it okay but makes it human). We are still loving and valuable people. And we can come to forgive and develop sincere compassion for ourselves. If necessary, we can repeat this process until we eventually feel a genuine sense of resolve about our prior acts of irresponsibility, and we can know that we are still loving and valuable people.

Some of us feel guilty about our feelings of grief or guilty that our grief has not diminished as time has passed. Yet grief is the universal response to loss. Although we can choose what we *do* with our feelings, we don't "just" choose to have the feelings themselves. This currently popular notion can leave us feeling guilty for feeling bad because it implies we are just bringing it all on ourselves and could have chosen to feel otherwise. Ann Kaiser Stearns writes, "Human emotions cannot be ordered away from the arena like misbehaving fans at an athletic event." We hate experiencing grief, but it is there nonetheless. We cannot make it disappear even though it hurts so much that we would probably go to great lengths to make it do so if we could.

Expecting to feel good on an uninterrupted basis is not realistic. All of life is not an ice-cream sundae. We feel upbeat sometimes and low at other times. Nobody genuinely feels good all the time. Feeling bad is natural and part of the repertoire of every human being. Unrealistic expectations of ourselves are not kind. Feelings are not morally good or bad; they are merely pleasurable or painful. It is okay to feel bad and to accept all our feelings. We most need to accept the ones we label "negative."

Sometimes we feel bad about upsetting others with our grief. Yet it is okay to cry in front of others even if they get upset in the face of our tears. We are not causing them new pain. We are a mirror of their own pain. It may even be helpful for them to feel upset. They then have an opportunity to work out their feelings, just as we are working out ours.

ANGER

Anger is perhaps the least accepted emotion because it feels threatening. Sometimes we are afraid to express our anger because of potential outcomes such as hurting someone, feeling guilty afterward, or losing the acceptance or love of another. So sometimes we experience conflict and anxiety over our anger and mask it in withdrawal, critical thinking, sarcasm, niceness, or tears. Anger is closely linked to grief and sadness and often covers other too-painfully-vulnerable-to-face emotions such as hurt feelings, depression, anxiety, or guilt. Because anger feels less vulnerable than grief—even powerful—it is often easier to bear and express than the more vulnerable emotion underneath it. So sometimes grief covers anger, and sometimes anger covers grief.

It is okay to feel angry at circumstances, our babies, our doctors, our partners, strangers, acquaintances, God, life, and anybody and anything else. In fact, when our anger is suppressed, our dignity and our spirits can become diminished. Sometimes we even turn our anger against ourselves by berating ourselves or acting self-destructively. When we feel angry, we need to get our anger out or alter what we feel angry about.

We commonly feel angered by things people say about our miscarriages. Feeling angry does not mean we have to rage at our loved ones; sometimes we can take care of ourselves by saying honestly, "Please don't minimize how this feels to me" or "I know this may appear to be a passing disappointment to you, but this is a great loss in my life and I need you to treat it as such." We can express our anger constructively in a manner that does not push away those we ultimately love and need. For example, we can write an angry letter that we don't send, yell in private, or vent with a friend, spouse, or therapist who can handle our feelings without defensiveness or threat. Additional ideas are listed in Appendix A.

When we directly express our anger at human targets, we have a high likelihood of being received with *their* anger covering *their* vulnerable feelings, an interaction certainly not constructive or bridging of the relationship. No connection occurs between us, no one feels better, and it does not lead to what we really want: for both of us to feel okay about ourselves.

So when we feel angry at others, sometimes it is beneficial to take time apart from them, to ask of them what we really want from them (such as to listen or give us a hug), or to say "I feel ——" and name our vulnerable feelings rather than our anger in the heat of the moment. (For example, we can communicate, "I feel needy" rather than "You have been failing me.")

In each instance of anger, we can ask ourselves what will most likely help us accomplish what we really want: communicating with the person at whom we feel angry, venting alone, venting with a third party, altering the situation, a combination of these alternatives, or something else altogether?

LONELINESS

In *The Secret of Staying in Love,* John Powell, S. J., discusses the untold value of revealing our deep feelings and hidden vulnerabilities to other human beings. Our feelings, as opposed to our thoughts, are who we are. If we do not share our feelings with anyone, no one really knows us. Powell says, "The heart of my revelation will not be my thoughts. Everyone could know every thought I ever had and not really know me."

He explains that "to the extent that I have hidden myself from you the meaning of your love will be diminished. I will forever fear that you love only the part of me that I have let you know; and that if you knew the real me, all of me, you would not love me." He continues, "The pockets of privacy which we create for a place to run where no one can follow are death to the kind of human intimacy so necessary to the fullness of human life." When we and those we want to be close with withhold parts of who we are emotionally, we don't taste the rapture of feeling wholly loved.

The opposite of loneliness is connectedness, or unity. Risking the expression of our emotions with another human being—here on earth or in spirit—is the antidote to loneliness. When we open ourselves to another who responds to us with compassion, our loneliness dissipates.

We *can* find someone—a friend, a therapist, or a member of the clergy—who can listen to and accept all our emotions. And when we feel lonely for our miscarried babies, we can also communicate with them, for example, by talking or writing to them or by expressing our feelings to them through art, music, or dance.

PANIC ATTACKS

Panic attacks feel emotionally excruciating and can result in a substantial deterioration in the quality of our lives. They are characterized by an overwhelming feeling of being on the brink of death or doom.

Panic attacks are not considered medically harmful, yet it is a good idea to see your doctor in order to rule out any physical problems and to alleviate your worries. Tell your doctor that you are going through a time of grief and are suffering panic attacks. Emotionally, panic attacks are only harmful in that they feel so painful. Panic is highly treatable.

Unfortunately, a lack of information about panic attacks can lead to low self-worth in panic sufferers. We may judge ourselves for being "so irrational" and feel ashamed. But panic attacks are not our fault. In actuality, many of us are born with a genetic predisposition to anxiety that becomes triggered in the face of a death, separation, or change.

Panic attacks are commonly associated with grief. It is important that we become aware of this so we do not misunderstand and feel frightened by an onset of attacks. A lack of awareness about and a fear of the attacks themselves can inspire further and heightened attacks. One woman in our study said brilliantly, "If someone had told me that I might freak out, I might not have freaked out!"

Panic attacks can occur in response to frightening thoughts and to misinterpretation of natural bodily sensations associated with the "fight-or-flight" reaction. Our bodies naturally and instinctively respond to threat by preparing to run from or fight the threat. At one time, people lived among physical threats, such as wild animals and foes running at and attacking them, that literally necessitated their running or fighting if they were to survive. Some physical manifestations of the fight-or-flight reaction are a racing heart, increased pulse rate, elevated blood pressure and blood sugar, an increase in the depth and rate of our breathing, clenched muscles, and the evacuation of our bowels through nausea or diarrhea (so we will be lighter and can run faster).

Today we very infrequently encounter imminent physical threats to our survival or that of our loved ones. Although we can't run from or beat up pollution, the threat of unemployment, the crime rate, or people who treat us as though we are unimportant, we still respond physically to these and other nonphysical threats. Our brain stems instinctively respond with preparation for fight or flight.

We also go about our daily lives with preconceived notions about what will and won't happen to us. But when our babies die, we see that shocking and terrible things can and do happen. We realize we have limited control. This realization is scary in more ways than one. When one of our trusted and preconceived notions is shattered, we suddenly realize that our other preconceived notions can no longer be trusted either. If the unexpected can occur, anything at all may be around the corner. Our minds race with horrid possibilities. We visualize our worst fears coming to be.

But these catastrophes are not actually happening. In reality, it is our *thoughts* of these catastrophes that are frightening us. We are literally scaring ourselves with our thoughts, which invite and feed panic attacks.

These thoughts may also be an unconscious effort to anticipate, brace against, and protect ourselves from danger or "bad things." Such plans to avoid danger can appear prudent but cost us plenty. Our scary thoughts can be like a watchdog we buy for protection. But if the watchdog, in fact, bites us, how much do we benefit from and how much do we lose by keeping the dog? Robert Handly, who suffered terribly with (and won out over) panic attacks, wrote in his book *Anxiety and Panic Attacks,* "If anyone had told me I was being negative by worrying that way, I would have denied it. I was simply trying to spot problems before they happened, so that I could plan for them."

Unfortunately, there is a snowball effect. We think scary thoughts, our bodies respond to them, we misunderstand and feel scared about our body sensations, we feel even more scared, and our bodies respond even more strongly. When we understand this, we can pursue different thoughts and in doing so begin to settle the panic.

In addition, hyperventilating often accompanies a panic attack. Hyperventilation is commonly associated with grief. When we hyperventilate, our breathing is deep and rapid, and more carbon dioxide than usual is expelled. Our lips and fingertips may become numb and tingly, we may perceive that we can't get enough air, and we may become dizzy or pass out. But there is no danger even in passing out (as long as we lie down first and thereby avoid hitting our heads in the process of falling).

If we don't understand that we are hyperventilating, we may think that there is something radically wrong. The only thing that hurts us is the fear we feel in response to hyperventilating if we misinterpret our body sensations as the onset of a catastrophe such as a heart attack, "nervous breakdown," insanity, suffocation, or death. Thinking something is wrong makes us feel so much worse. The panic attack itself is not the problem; this thinking, or our *reaction* to the panic attack, is the problem. And here again the snowball effect occurs.

Panic attacks are manageable. We can learn to bring our bodies under control and gain the upper hand on the panic. Taking slower breaths or using relaxation techniques is often helpful.

Panic attacks can be set up and amplified by foods with caffeine including chocolate and tea (which we may crave more during bereavement). They can trigger a preexisting, genetic predisposition to panic in those of us who are hypersensitive to these stimulants of the nervous system.

The time following loss is prime for panic attacks because feelings of grief are so deep and numerous and we may naturally fear losing control of our restraints on those feelings. We also may hold back the truth of what we feel for fear that our expression will hassle, scare, hurt, or drive away people. But we may hurt ourselves when we hold back the truth. In the long run, it is often more helpful to face the fear of expression. John Bradshaw wrote in *On the Family,* "Tell the truth at all costs." As *I* did, my own panic began to dissipate.

It is helpful to talk about our panic attacks to another person. Talking about fear removes the power it has over us. Just as with grief, the more we communicate our feelings, access information, and understand what is happening, the less we have to fear.

SELF-DESTRUCTIVE THOUGHTS AND FEELINGS

During a time of bereavement, it is normal to experience feelings of despair, guilt, worthlessness, and to think that neither life nor we matter. Following loss, self-esteem is at a low. When we anesthetize ourselves or don't periodically let these and other feelings out, our feelings are not honored, and depression and sometimes anger grow. Sometimes we turn our anger inward against ourselves.

There are many means of coping with emotional pain. Some, like the excessive use of drugs and alcohol, are readily recognized as self-destructive behaviors. There are also many less recognized and less blatantly dangerous ways of hurting ourselves, such as not opening up when we need to talk, antagonizing and pushing away those we love and need, spending money unnecessarily to the degree that we create financial jeopardy, or depriving ourselves of needed closeness by watching hours and hours of TV or by working incessantly. All of us probably injure ourselves in ways we don't recognize. When we do, we are far from alone.

These activities usually lend us temporary distraction or hollow pleasure and leave us feeling empty, unsatisfied, sad, and lonely. They don't get us around pain; they defer pain until a later time. We still have our grief work to do.

The inclination to give up, self-destruct, or die comes out of hopelessness, despair, or seeing no bearable options for ourselves in the future. Yet no matter how bleak things look or how anguished we feel, a day will arrive when life is different from the way it is now. That's why Joan Rivers, who lost her husband to suicide, said on her television program, "Suicide is a permanent solution to a temporary problem." The only thing that life guarantees *is* change. Things always change.

The consideration of suicide or actions that could lead to serious injury or death are matters that need and deserve attention and care. If they persist for more than two weeks, professional help is needed.

Although most of us readily go to a physician for physical care, there is a major stigma in our culture about seeking emotional health care. Avoid the traps of thinking, "I should be able to work out my problems on my own," "It's too expensive," "I just don't have time," "My feelings are just too personal," "I'd be too ashamed," "It's no big deal (I'm not really important enough to make a fuss over)," "I saw a therapist and she was no good," and so on. Try other therapists until you find one who demonstrates sensitivity, awareness, and acceptance about miscarriage and with whom you can personally relate.

To utilize professional help is to make use of your resources, much like seeing a dentist to maintain optimal health of your teeth. The journey through therapy is extremely educational. In the process, we develop self-awareness, which is the most important tool for psychological growth. Seeking counseling is an act of integrity, strength, and self-value.

If you have been considering suicide, let someone know. There are lots of people and places to turn to. You can phone hospitals and ask their social services division about available in-hospital and community resources. Most cities offer counseling through government-subsidized family service agencies, for free or at a nominal cost to those in need. There are crisis intervention agencies in your phone book and listed with directory assistance. And you can phone the National Suicide Prevention Hotline from anywhere in the United States at 800-333-4444. (The National Crisis Center for the Deaf can be reached at TDD# 800-446-9876.)

You *can* help yourself: You can commit aloud to staying connected with a therapist and with a friend. There are people who are trustworthy. You are important. There is a way. And all of us who are honest with ourselves know that there are times in our lives when we need help. Get professional help if you want it or suspect you need it.

We hope that these pieces of understanding about some of the emotional components of grief help you in the process of accepting and coping with your own emotions. We hope you understand your feelings a bit better and that you see some of the sanity in all the insanity.

PART SIX

BELIEFS THAT GET IN THE WAY

CHAPTER TWENTY-TWO

Childhood Lessons

Some of us wonder why we feel what we feel or why our feelings are as strong as they are. We feel what we feel and as intensely as we feel, in part, because of who we are inherently. Stella Chess and Alexander Thomas, professors of psychiatry at New York University Medical Center, conducted 30 years of research on the subject in the New York Longitudinal Study, as reported in their book *Know Your Child.* They concluded that we possess recognizable, individual differences in our temperaments, including the intensity and character of mood expression, right from birth. So, part of how we respond to life and to loss stems from who we innately are.

But it would be simplistic to view ourselves only as products of our genes. Our life experiences, both pleasurable and painful, also clearly affect how and what we currently feel. We bring the total of our individual histories into our current lives.

Some of us recall wonderful childhoods. But realistically, our childhoods were two-sided: both pleasant and painful. Perhaps we had a babysitter who spoke to us in a demeaning manner, we got lost in a department store, we were humiliated by Mrs. So-and-So in the third grade, or our friend moved away when we were 10. Horrendous things occurred in many of our lives, too, like neglect, abuse, and the loss of loved ones. Each of us endured ache and loss as children.

As adults, many of us have a tendency to belittle or dismiss the significance of these losses. They may even seem trivial. We may say, "Oh, that was no big deal. It didn't affect me." But as children we were terribly vulnerable, and these events *were* a big deal—maybe even earth-shattering—if they felt painful to us on some level at the time.

We have grieved some of these losses to a point of resolution and healing; other losses we have not. Perhaps no loss is entirely and permanently healed and untouchable. Somewhere inside, we know and can re-sense old childhood losses.

Old pain has a clever and rotten way of reappearing when new pain is encountered as adults. One woman in our study reported, "I no longer had the energy required to deny what happened when I was young—not so much in the form of specific events, but in the form of *how life in general felt* for me then." New feelings of grief tap into old feelings of grief. We need not criticize ourselves when a new loss triggers grief about a loss that occurred 7 or even 70 years ago.

Luckily, grief is not picky about timing. In fact, it waits diligently until the time is right for us to express it. It is never too late to grieve. Sometimes we can ease present grief by acknowledging, experiencing, and expressing our feelings about childhood losses. We can nurture ourselves today by taking the little child of yesteryear seriously and by extending tenderness and compassion to her unhealed hurts.

When we were children, we were in somewhat of a bind. We needed to express freely who we were and, in turn, to be loved, accepted, and taken care of. Yet, although our parents were the ones on whom we were completely dependent, they often were not in a position to realize what we truly felt deep inside or to respond to those feelings with compassion.

This is not to imply that our parents were uncaring. They were humanly limited just as we are. There was not a societal consciousness about the importance of feelings before more recent years. Similarly, when *I* was a little girl, there was not yet a societal consciousness about taking care of Mother Earth. I can hardly fathom that I used to toss my McDonald's litter out the car window! In the same sense, our mothers and fathers were somewhat limited by the consciousness of their times.

Actually, most of our parents responded to our emotions in pretty much the same way their parents responded to their emotions. There is a saying: "We are all victims of victims." And as the Reverend James Carter, S. J., President of Loyola University of the South, so beautifully wrote, "There is far more to unite us than to divide us."

At the same time, their innocence does not change the fact that some of our parents' responses hurt at the time and still affect how we feel and how we treat our emotions today. We observed how they treated our feelings and how they treated their own innermost emotions. From our observations we derived values and beliefs about loss and about people in general and drew conclusions about the acceptability of our own feelings. We continue to live with those values, beliefs, and conclusions today. If our role models swallowed their *true* feelings and their inner pain, we probably feel predisposed to swallow ours, too. Many of us got the message on some level that our tears and our vulnerability were things to hide and, therefore, were somehow worthy of shame. Today that shame can still be associated in our minds with the expression of vulnerability and sadness. And it most likely is hard or scary for us to feel or express our deep pain today.

Also, if we sensed problems or unspoken feelings in our families and these were not acknowledged and discussed, we learned to question our sense or perceptions. To the extent that our sense of reality was denied by those around us, we felt that our thinking was distorted or even crazy and so needed to deny our feelings about our reality. Because miscarriage intrinsically is a nebulous loss and, in turn, is negated by most of society, miscarriage is very likely to ignite concerns in us about our sanity. Miscarriage is a "crazying" experience!

Along the way of life, each of us has developed some ineffective methods of coping with loss such as withdrawing, smoking, or arguing. Commonly in times of grief and stress, we revert to these old methods, even if we have already actively worked through many of our old losses, discovered the ineffectiveness of our old methods, and "know better" now. But if we examine and express our feelings of loss, our reverting will be only temporary.

Recent life experiences may be affecting our responses to our miscarriages as well. Grief and loneliness have increased for many of us as our extended families have divided and geographically separated, and substitute relationships tend to be brief and nonintimate. Sometimes crises are suffered in quick succession, set us up to feel even more overwhelmed, and make the prospect of griefwork intolerable. (For example, one woman in our study said, "My nephew was in a very serious accident the day after my miscarriage. His life was touch and-go. I could only focus on that. I didn't have time to deal with the miscarriage. We put it on a back burner and we went on.")

Whether from more recent experiences, childhood lessons, or our genes, there is a rhyme and a reason for all our seemingly irrational, mild, or intense feelings, thoughts, and behaviors even though we are not always aware of a basis for them.

It is important to know that our genetic predispositions and painful life experiences do not destroy our chances for feeling happy or peaceful tomorrow. These factors are very workable and manageable. When we identify them within ourselves and share and accept them with one another, they can even be a springboard for wondrous experiences in the future. In his book *The 7 Habits of Highly Effective People,* Stephen R. Covey tells a beautiful story demonstrating this. He writes,

> Another of those difficult times had to do with what I perceived to be a "hang up" Sandra had which had bothered me for years. She seemed to have an obsession about Frigidaire appliances which I was at an absolute loss to understand. She would not even consider buying another brand of

appliance. . . . She insisted that we drive the 50 miles to the "big city" where Frigidaire appliances were sold. . . .

This was a matter of considerable agitation to me. . . . When [the situation] did come up, it was like a stimulus that triggered off a hot button response. . . .

What bothered me the most was . . . that she persisted in making what I considered utterly illogical and indefensible statements to defend Frigidaire which had no basis in fact whatsoever. . . .

I will never forget the day we talked it through. We didn't end up on the beach that day; we just continued to ride through the cane fields, perhaps because we didn't want to look each other in the eye. There had been so much psychic history and so many bad feelings associated the with issue, and it had been submerged for so long. . . .

Sandra and I were amazed at what we learned through the interaction. It was truly synergistic. It was as if Sandra were learning, almost for the first time herself, the reason for her so-called hang-up. She started to talk about her father, about how, . . . to help to make ends meet, he had gone into the appliance business. During an economic downturn, he had experienced serious financial difficulties, and the only thing that enabled him to stay in business during that time was the fact that Frigidaire would finance his inventory.

Sandra had an unusually deep and sweet relationship with her father. When he returned home at the end of a very tiring day, he would lie on the couch, and Sandra would rub his feet and sing to him. It was a beautiful time they enjoyed together almost daily for years. He would also open up and talk through his worries and concerns about the business, and he shared with Sandra his deep appreciation for Frigidaire financing his inventory so that he could make it through the difficult times.

This communication between father and daughter had taken place in a spontaneous way during very natural times, when the most powerful kind of scripting takes place. During those relaxed times guards are down and all kinds of images and thoughts are planted deep in the subconscious mind. . . .

Sandra gained tremendous insight into herself and into the emotional root of her feelings about Frigidaire. I also gained insight and a whole new level of respect. I came to realize that Sandra wasn't talking about appliances; she was talking about her father, and about loyalty—about loyalty to his needs.

I remember both of us becoming tearful on that day, not so much because of the insights, but because of the increased sense of reverence we had for each other. We discovered that even seemingly trivial things often have roots in deep emotional experiences. To deal only with the superficial trivia without seeing the deeper, more tender issues is to trample on the sacred ground of another's heart.

CHAPTER TWENTY-THREE

Societal Myths

I learned my cultural lessons well. When a friend of mine had a miscarriage five years before my miscarriage, I said to her, "I guess it was for the best." To my surprise and confusion, she turned to me with pain in her eyes and said, "No, it wasn't!" The perception of miscarriage and grief that I held at that time is widely held.

In response to an article in *People* magazine that stated that actress Kirstie Alley had suffered a miscarriage, a reader who wrote in referred to the notion that miscarriage is heartbreaking as nonsense, as is any need for strength in the face of such a mundane part of childbearing. This reader's response came as no surprise to many women who have miscarried.

Although grief is something we all have to endure at times in our lives, we receive little or no education about the complexity of grief. We are a culture generally uninformed about what constitutes normal grieving, about the functional and healing nature of grieving, and about the grief of miscarriage specifically. We have much to learn about dealing with loss and grief in a manner that is conducive to healing. We learn, live by, and are hurt by many myths and misconceptions about grief.

For clarity and ease in reading in this chapter, we refer to the bereaved and to society as though the two groups were separate and distinctive entities. In reality, there are no boundaries between the two groups. We all have losses and attempt to console others' losses. Although we focus on some of society's hurtful myths and misconceptions about grief, it is important to point out that the bereaved are not "just victims" and society is not "just unaware and clumsy." Every last one of us is a victim of sorts, has limited awareness, and is vulnerable and human. Remember as you read that "there is more to unite us than to divide us."

MYTH: Emotions other than sadness, anger, and guilt have nothing to do with grief.

Most people realize that depression is a normal part of grieving but very often do not realize that so many other emotional, intellectual, physical, behavioral, and spiritual experiences are also common facets of grieving.

People commonly believe these other expressions are peculiar or unhealthy and unrelated.

MYTH: Some losses are trivial.

Sometimes people compare losses and trivialize what appear to be "lesser losses." In actuality, all losses are subjective and are relative to our completely unique realities. Therefore, they can't be compared. People may conclude that Mary should not feel bad about losing her bicycle because Lucy lost her husband. But if Lucy lost 40 husbands, Mary still lost her bicycle and still feels bad about it. Whatever any of us encounter, there will always be others who seem to have it worse and others who seem to have it better. We can always stand next to another and see our pain as better or as unjustified. So comparisons lose their meaning.

MYTH: We know how others feel.

It is easy for others to presume what and how deeply we feel or that our feelings match theirs. Thus, they may say things like, "It's 'only' a miscarriage" or "I'm sure she will be fine about her ex-husband dying; after all, they were divorced." Yet every loss holds unique meaning to each person, who in turn responds uniquely. Nobody knows for sure what another person feels unless that person has explicitly confirmed it for them.

MYTH: We know what others need to do in order to heal.

Sometimes people believe they can tell us what to do and thereby help us heal. They may offer unsolicited advice (sometimes in the form of "You should——" or "I would just——"), perhaps with the best intentions.

But in attempting to problem solve for us, they inadvertently convey that they know more about us than we know about ourselves, undermine and convey a lack of confidence in our abilities to think for ourselves, distract us from what we think and who we are as individuals, and invite us to be copies of them rather than our own true selves.

There is a saying: "A backseat driver never runs out of gas." Backseat drivers also have a completely different experience and point of view than the driver. Their opinion about how we should drive is probably very accurate relative to their point of view in the back seat. But our experiences, points of view, and realities are different and also accurate, and we have every right to them.

MYTH: Reminders of "the bright side" console grief.

Sometimes people attempt to ease our grief with reminders of the bright side or with intellectualizations like, "Well, it wasn't really a baby," "You have your other children," and "Thank God you weren't very far along in your pregnancy." But responses like these steer us away from our feelings, encourage suppression (and, consequently, depression), and encourage us to put our realities away and simply put on a happy face. Without our working through grief, future peace of mind may be made of pat-and-cheery phrases and cerebral bandages that can crumble in the face of future life crises. Sometimes we respond to these simplistic thoughts with additional guilt or with anxiety about whether something is the matter with us because we can't manage a happy face. Healing is not just a positive thought away.

MYTH: Grief over a great loss only lasts for weeks.

Our society does not appreciate that the process of grieving can take a long, long time. It is normal to grieve the loss of a loved one for years. We even grieve the loss of a loved one *on some level* all our lives.

We do receive support immediately following many kinds of loss, yet that support usually quickly falls away. We do not have control of our rate of movement through grief. When we hear comments like, "You probably should be feeling better by now" or "Are you still sad about that?" our anxiety, self-worth, and confusion usually increase. In turn, these increased feelings necessitate more time to process and heal.

Ongoing support, conveyed in very small and easy acts or in words of compassion, goes a long way toward helping us heal. (See Appendix A for specific things to say or do for the bereaved.)

MYTH: Showing sadness is weak or wrong.

In some cultures, people wail at funerals. In American culture, however, crying openly is often viewed as weak or even wrong on some level. When Jacqueline Kennedy did not publicly display tears after John Kennedy's death, she was tremendously "loved" and revered by the public for her "strength and courage." Jackie Kennedy very well may be strong and courageous but not because she didn't show her emotions during those days. Many people see those who openly express pain as "in bad shape" or even as "hysterical basket cases" and those who suppress pain as noble or as having maintained their strength.

Our culture does not appreciate the wonderfully efficient and functional nature of grieving. If we continually control the expression of our emotions, we control the flow of our very nature.

When we are admired only for who we appear to be (one who feels "just fine"), we are not admired for who we truly are. Deep inside, we feel we can't fully trust in or relish others' love of us because they don't even really know us.

Because we usually don't share our inner feelings with each other, many of us live with a belief that others manage better than we do. We hold an illusion that everybody else has nice, orderly, packaged-with-a-bow thoughts and feelings. In actuality, much of the time people don't feel fine. They feel afraid to show their true emotions, just like we do. Unless we recognize this, we are likely to feel painfully inferior to others because we can't measure up. When we grieve, we are likely to feel freakish, guilty, or ashamed.

The expression of one's true self before others or the expression of sadness or any emotion can feel deeply bonding and immensely healing.

MYTH: It's best to avoid the subject of loss. We may just upset the bereaved.

Sometimes people refrain from bringing up our losses because they are afraid that doing so will make us remember and experience the pain of those losses. But when we are bereaved, that pain is already present. When people don't bring up our losses, it appears they don't care, and we are likely to feel like outcasts or oddities and lonely or unloved.

MYTH: Crying in front of the bereaved will make them feel worse.

My friend Reta has been a widow for nine years. She has cried, written, and talked about her husband's death until she could do so comfortably, and she feels quite resolved about her loss. One recent evening, she told me that once in awhile someone will hear her tell her story and will say, "Oh, that's so sad," with tears in their eyes. At these times, my friend cannot hold back her tears. No one makes her feel sad by showing their own tears. Rather, their tears relate to and access or tap the tears already present in her. Also, by sharing their feelings of compassion, they make it safe for her to release her sadness. Reta explained to me that others' compassion helps her to realize, "Oh my God; I *do* deserve to still feel sad!" and her tears immediately emerge. It feels good to her to cry.

MYTH: We can best protect ourselves by altogether avoiding the bereaved.

Sometimes when we are bereaved, others avoid us completely, not because they are deserting or rejecting us personally as it usually appears but because they feel anxious and uncomfortable about the subject of pain and loss. They don't know what to say or do or they don't want to feel embarrassed. But they aren't avoiding *us;* they are avoiding *loss.* Our feelings of pain and loss evoke their own perhaps unconscious feelings of pain and loss. And they avoid pain and loss because pain and loss are painful!

It can be deeply painful for others to pay attention or extend compassion to our emotions when their own emotions have not been responded to with care and compassion and they, therefore, haven't yet developed an acceptance of their own feelings. In her book *Prisoners of Childhood,* Alice Miller points out that we all view and treat some of our own feelings with ridicule, belittlement, and telling ourselves that they don't even exist. How frequently we diminish ourselves when we feel bad with statements like, "Oh I'm fine!" "Don't worry about me" or "I know it's silly, but I feel——." Even though we, in all our grief, are beautiful, we are ashamed of our feelings. When we or others don't believe that our own feelings are deserving of attention and care, it can be too painful to extend attention and care to each other.

Also, it is natural for others to feel uncomfortable confronting the subject of death because they are reminded of their own mortality. A natural fear of death insures that we do what we can to remain alive and, ultimately, to survive as a species. Unfortunately, that fear also makes it difficult for others to approach us when we are grieving.

And the list of myths goes on. People behave as they do out of humanness or vulnerability. Yet, in not opening up and in not listening with unconditional acceptance, they take something away from themselves and from us. We still feel hurt. We all feel lonely and unloved. Life is passing, and we need each other. We miss (and still have) the opportunity to make our relationships with loved ones as healing, close, and fulfilling as they could be for us. We need to lend a hand or ask for support. Sharing our experiences and extending compassion to one another in grief leads to our and others' healing together.

John Powell, S.J., wrote, "While I am listening to you, you become the center of my world, the focus of my attention." Paradoxically, when we become attentive to and accepting of a person who is trying to communicate and who needs someone to understand, *we* gain something highly valuable.

Regarding my friend to whom I said, "I guess it was for the best," of course I truly meant no harm. In fact, she was very important to me, and I really wanted to say something comforting to her. Unfortunately, I automatically said what I had learned to say. Awkward gesture is born of vulnerability and humanness.

Fortunately, society is also comprised of people, each with personal experiences of loss and with inner wisdom to draw on, who sometimes make deeply loving gestures. After that reader's letter in *People* magazine about Kirstie Alley, yet another reader wrote, "As an obstetrician who is familiar with the high miscarriage rates for all pregnancies, I was still not prepared for the heartbreak my wife and I felt when we lost our first pregnancy a year before our son was born. Miscarriage may be a 'normal part of child-bearing', but it is always agonizing, and it is natural and appropriate to grieve over such a loss" (*People,* "Mail," 1990).

CHAPTER TWENTY-FOUR

Hannah's Story

My miscarriage occurred two-and-a-half months ago in the fourth month of my pregnancy. During my prior pregnancy I had spotted in the fourth month, but I went on to have a full-term healthy child. So when I spotted in this pregnancy, my first emotion was denial. I called the doctor but felt that miscarriage wouldn't happen to me. He said if I had any cramping, or if I lost a lot more blood, to give him a call because it could be a miscarriage. And I thought, "Uh-oh, he said the 'M' word." I did not want to hear it.

By the next morning I was fine. But I also no longer felt pregnant. Then I started bleeding real red blood. I went into labor and passed big clumps of black mucous and clots.

What I passed was not recognizable. That really hurt me—that I didn't have something I could pick up and hold. It was something that we had to flush. What a horrible way to end your life, being flushed down the toilet like junk. That's pretty bad. That really bothered me.

I wasn't prepared for that. I was but I wasn't. My doctor told me what you could go through physically. And he had said to stay at home and labor and come in for an appointment after delivering. That's what I did. I felt better doing it at home with no medication. If I had gone to the hospital, I would have had a lot of strangers invading me with procedures. This way I was with my husband and he was absolutely "textbook" perfect.

The worst thing was the panicky feeling that there was nothing I could do to stop it. I had to wait for the process to complete itself. It took from Thursday to Sunday to all happen. Immediately following, I was so numb, I don't know what I felt. Then everything hit me. I was devastated. I started crying.

I did a lot of crying at night though I was fine during the day. I was not prepared for the absolute sense of loss. That was so overwhelming. It was not fair. Something was taken from me. It's like when you're little and your big sister knocks you down and takes your ice cream cone and you think about the injustice like, "How dare you? I don't deserve this." I felt the injustice and the outrage of it all.

My 10-year-old was worried because she didn't understand. She understands the mechanics of reproduction but not the dynamics of the emotions. And she was worried that the process of death would continue in me and that I would die.

Our baby was already a part of our family. How could it be other than that? Already, this child had affected my eating and sleeping patterns. I had to be more careful about doing things. Many things changed. We bought a new home. These were things we did because this was a member of the family we were all preparing for. There was no doubt that this was a real baby. The baby had a name, a bedroom, and a college fund. It was a real person! Maybe it helps because I had had a child, so pregnancy is real cause-and-effect for me. You get pregnant and you go home with a baby. What a wonderful thing! So I was already in that mind set and I just couldn't wait to have the baby.

When our baby died, it had the blueprints for fingernails and toenails and fingerprints and major organs, even reproductive organs, so there was the promise of grandchildren. I thought of the baby as having curly brown hair and brown eyes. The only question would have been whose shape of eyes she would have, whose feet, that sort of thing. Or whether it was a boy or girl, although that didn't really matter. I thought it was a girl, but it didn't matter to me. Either way, I love it as much and I grieve it just as much.

We had names picked out for a boy and a girl, but we never really used them because we didn't know the sex. We had always called the baby "Bambino." It feels good to call the baby by a name. It wouldn't feel good calling it "it." That word always make me think of the TV show The Addams Family. *Bambino was the name we used in love.*

The miscarriage brought my husband and I closer. We have an unusually close relationship. My husband is so wonderful and completely and unreservedly there for me. He knew me enough to know what to say, and he touched my heart and soul when he did. He told me I had done everything to give the baby a good start and that nothing I did had caused the miscarriage. He reassured me. He believed in me as a good mother.

We grieved at different paces. He's sad when he thinks what the baby could have been. But he didn't understand how deep and how long I grieved. I had never felt this kind of grief before. We grieved the baby in different ways, but he's been there every step of the way for me.

While I was numb to everything for a time, he just took over the load of everything. He took time off work. He called in and said, "I won't be in. My wife needs me." Then when he went back, he called a couple of times a day from work. He made sure I got plenty of rest. He was solicitous of my total well-being. There was nothing more he could have done. He ran interference for me and acted as my buffer so nobody could run their horror stories on me. Those close to me pulled the wagons in real tight and protected me, and my husband was the wagon master.

My grief made me hang back from other people. This was not usual for me. Normally I'm very friendly and outgoing. People would ask me how many children I have. I wasn't sure how many to say. I never told anybody I was grieving or hurting because I had such a hold on myself. I didn't let others know I needed them.

When they questioned me about my miscarriage or about my feelings, it angered me more than it hurt me because they would ask, "Are you going to have another one?" or say, "It's all for the best." I felt like saying, "Don't you dare tell me it's a good thing my baby is dead!" They would ask me what I was crying for. I'd think, "What kind of monster do you think I am that I wouldn't cry over my dead baby?"

I felt very isolated. I felt there was something wrong *with me. I felt that nobody else in the world understood. I went over and over in my mind what I could have done differently, but I had no answer. I was confused, not because I wasn't sure what I lost, but why. Why? There was no reason. Therefore, why? I felt like I was losing my grip and having to hang on real tight. My brain went haywire. I was forgetful and indecisive. I was disorganized in my thinking. I couldn't make the easiest decision. I didn't trust my own decisions. I forgot things. Then it dawned on me, "Oh, hey, I'm depressed."*

My lowest point was six weeks after my miscarriage. I was no longer myself. I didn't want to do anything, talk, or socialize. I was not hungry. I had chronic fatigue. Sex drive? What sex drive? I was too depressed and fatigued to even consider it. Nothing cheered me up. I was really moody, extremely depressed. I had no nightmares, but I had champion insomnia.

I didn't allow myself to grieve. I severely underestimated my need to grieve. It hit me recently. The miscarriage was unfair. I didn't deserve it. There was no reason for it. It was especially bad for my husband because it was his first baby. Although it wasn't the end of the world, it was the end of our baby. We didn't have a memento of the baby. We needed to, though, because there was no little grave, no place to focus my grief.

To other women who have had a miscarriage I would say, "Go ahead and cry and screw the world if they say you are feeling sorry for yourself. If you feel the need to grieve, you've earned it. Your baby deserves that expression. No one can tell you you can hurt that bad and not grieve."

I used to always be the first to volunteer for things. I'm not doing that now. This is a protective mechanism until I'm finished with my grieving. I'm not finished changing from the loss. This experience has also made me stop before I am critical of other mothers of young children, and think, "Maybe she's lost one *and is so happy to have one."*

The baby was something my husband and I did together, something we were looking forward to together. Having a miscarriage is like having someone reach in and rip that out of you. A part of me died. Something was missing—a part of me, a part of my husband. It's like losing a part of your marriage. I have been touched by tragedy. I will never be the same. It lessens with time, but it is always there. It has left a hole.

PART SEVEN

THE JOURNEY

CHAPTER TWENTY-FIVE

Passage Through Grief

The natural thrust of our emotions is outward. Exertion is required to hold feelings in. That exertion consumes life energy. When grief is held back, our focus, attention, and abilities are tied up and less available for other things and to other people. For instance, we cannot feel very kindly when we are busy inside with anger or anxiety. We cannot feel very peaceful when we are drained by sorrow or confusion. Our freedom to feel the love that we have is diminished. Our ability to connect with others and to receive love is somewhat blocked.

When we suppress an emotion, we suppress emotion in general. When we bind feelings of loss, we bind all our other emotions, our intellects, our physical energy, and our spirituality. We stifle the life in us. We squelch our ability to access our inner resources: our energy, attention, love, talent, creativity, strength, and potential. Likewise, when we hold down pain, we also hold down pleasure. In the movie *Ordinary People,* a psychiatrist portrayed by Judd Hirsch told his grief-stricken client, who was scared to feel the pain, "If you can't feel pain, then you're not going to feel anything else either!" Wonderful things do not seem as wonderful anymore. Living with contained grief means living with a reduction in the quality of our lives. Grief held back is a loss in itself.

Sometimes bound and controlled feelings build inside us and escalate to great intensity. Borysenko graphically states, "The contents [of the unconscious] have been composting, getting wilder and wilder." Feelings can become like furious bees in a bottle.

Even when the prospect feels scary, we can take off the lid and let them go. It is okay to get hysterical. It is the alternatives that are more costly. Ole Abe Lincoln must have had a twinkle in his eye when he said, "When you have got an elephant by the hind legs and he is trying to run away, it is best to let him run."

The most effective way to let feelings go is to let feelings *go*—plain and simple in one sense. The expression of emotion is a tremendously productive venting mechanism and a highly functional part of nature. It is both freeing and life affirming. When we express our feelings, we are doing exactly what we need to do in order to take care of ourselves. We can only heal what we're willing to reveal.

When we do so, a weight lifts and we feel lighter and more energetic. There is a return of enthusiasm. Vitality is restored. Our attention and abilities are freed up and more available to us, to others, and to the rest of life. We are apt to feel more peaceful, loving, and loved. When we express emotion, we reestablish an inner balance and a sense of well-being.

Feelings long to be expressed; and once expressed, they can dissipate. Yet there are exceptions. For example, it may not be wise to express our feelings to someone who is likely to say to us, "What's the big deal? You're being ridiculous!" Second, feelings do not dissipate when we express one emotion yet feel a different emotion. When we feel hurt but express anger, we do not feel better because we need to cry, not yell. We are not expressing what we need to express. Third, feelings do not always dissipate when they are not completely expressed. For instance, we cannot witness extreme violence, mention "That was scary," feel relieved, and be finished. We haven't had time to work through the complex of our emotions. We feel better after expressing our feelings when we receive loving acceptance, when we express what is really bothering us, or when we fully relieve ourselves of what we need to for the moment.

One night after my miscarriage, I was tucking my son Jordan into bed. I could see that he was fighting back tears. I asked him if he felt sad about our baby. He expressed a very real concern: "Yes, but I don't want to cry because if I do, I'll never stop!" I held him in my arms and said, "Jordan, imagine a big pitcher full of water. And imagine that we poured just one little drop of water out of the pitcher. It wouldn't make any difference at all, would it?" He shook his head no. I continued, "Well, imagine if we continued to pour little drops out of our pitcher, just one at a time. After a long time of that, what do you think would happen to the water in the pitcher?" He answered, "Gets empty."

Sometimes when the pain of loss is great, crying does not seem to help, grief feels bottomless, and the prospect of healing looks hopeless. Yet over time, the "water level" does lower and the weight becomes lighter. "A drop at a time" grieving becomes less overwhelming and scary, and relief and good feelings come into view. Some of us are not accustomed to expressing our emotions, yet we can always start. The more we express them, the more accustomed we become to doing so and the more we learn we will survive and feel better afterward. We are surprised to hear ourselves genuinely laugh one day, we experience an enjoyable afternoon, or we get a good night's sleep several nights in a row. Progress is under way.

The analogy I gave to Jordan was not exactly accurate because it implies that we become completely "emptied" of grief over time, and we do not. Grief does not get emptied; rather, it emerges with generally decreasing intensity and with generally increasing intervals between eruptions. Working through grief takes time, but it can be so painful; we want to believe in a shortcut that will make us feel better quickly. We cannot heal in perfect entirety or as rapidly as we would like, but we do heal.

Because grief hurts so much, we may search for a shortcut anyway. But we cannot push and shove ourselves quickly through the grieving process. When trying to sort through thoughts or get in touch with feelings, if we are struggling furiously and it seems we are "banging our heads into the wall," we can be kind to and gentle with ourselves by setting the task aside for the time being. Working furiously at it will not force things into clarity or resolution any sooner. While we are patient with ourselves, our unconscious minds are working on prerequisite lessons. Then, when the time is right, we can come back to the task, and things will come together.

It is also helpful to seek a balance between dropping out on life (lying in bed all day every day or becoming self-destructive) and marching on with life (going back to work the next day and not looking back). The first approach brings about further loss as other parts of our lives fall apart. The second approach brings about further loss in the form of an absence of healing. There is wisdom in the old adage "All good things in balance." In addition, the principles of momentum and inertia are at play. The more we lie about, the more we feel like further lying about. And the more we are busy, the more we feel like being further busy. We need to grieve *and* function alternately.

The process of healing does not seem to move continuously straightforward. Shelly returned a draft of Marie's personal story with a notation that read, "This feels out of sequence." However, the sequence was right out of Marie's journal. Unfortunately, there are many dimensions, facets, and phases of grief, and they do not progress in a linear fashion. We take care of one issue and a second comes up; we take care of that issue and a third comes up; we take care of it and the first issue is back again! We may say, "I thought I was past this!" or "I thought I had dealt with this." Sometimes grief feels like we are just plain going in circles. We seem to be losing hold of some of the growth we have worked hard to accomplish.

When we revisit grief, we may feel disappointed in or even critical of ourselves if we are not aware that doing so is natural, sometimes inevitable, and productive. Grieving a loss again down the road does not mean we did an inadequate job of grieving the first time. Rather, we are grieving in a new way.

Timing is an integral factor in the scheme of grieving. Through our grief work, we grow over time in terms of how equipped we are to deal with loss. We possess new developmental and conceptual abilities and greater feelings of safety. We relate differently. Therefore, we reach a new level of readiness and ripeness. We also encounter and are affected by new events and experiences, and we need to rework loss in our minds in light of these experiences. A loss means different things to us at 26, 40, and 64 years old. And loss is worked and reworked in the face of new losses. We learn through repetition. We will always be growing, limited, and working toward mastery. We are never "there," finished, and neatly tied with a bow. So "setbacks" are not setbacks at all.

Grief is commonly reactivated briefly on the anniversary of the D&C or the due date and on meaningful holidays, regardless of whether we are consciously thinking about our babies or that it is that time of year. Last month I was depressed for several weeks and did not know why. Then I had a dream at 3 a.m. in which my friend Patti said to me, "Do you believe it was one year ago today that I told you I had to move away, and the next day your sister phoned and told you they found a malignant cancer mass in your father?" I awakened sharply and sat up in amazement. One year before, exactly that had happened!

After time has passed, shadow grief can be triggered by exposure to something strongly associated with or reminiscent of a loss, like a specific sight, a certain smell, or a song. It can also seemingly pop out of nowhere in a split second. My friend Chris lost her baby at birth. At a later point in time she saw a red stoplight through streaks of rain that ran down the windshield of her car. In her mind, she had returned at that moment to the delivery room, where she had seen the blood running down her doctor's glasses. She found herself on the side of the road, shaking and entirely disoriented.

Some of us feel acute grief down the road because we choose to. Sometimes there is much conflict surrounding holding on to pain versus moving past pain and feeling better. There is a need to hold on to it in order to honor our unhonored feelings, babies, or losses. We may fear we are betraying, disowning, or abandoning ourselves, our babies, or losses when we let grief go. Yet another part of us longs for relief from pain, to be healed, and for life again. At some point in time we may reinterpret what it means to let grief go. We'll talk more about this in subsequent chapters.

The pain of grief softens over the course of time. Eventually we even develop great comfort from focusing on and expressing our feelings. With innumerable factors involved in the timing of our growth, the range in time before resolution and healing is very broad.

It is also helpful to maintain a sense of humor and to laugh at ourselves. Dr. Elizabeth Kubler-Ross once said in a lecture, "If you have a sense of humor, you can be helped." One woman in our study laughed aloud during her interview at the fact that she could be in the midst of a primal scream, yet pull herself together to answer the phone in a perfectly lovely and dignified tone of voice. There is a saying, "We do not stop playing because we are old; we grow old because we stop playing." To that we might add, "and laughing and crying and seeking knowledge and . . ."

Finally, no one thing will heal us. Unfortunately, there is no short, simple system for getting through grief. Healing is born of a grand combination of things. There are many stones to be travelled in the road of grief. That road moves like a spiral. There are ups and downs along the way. Grief work is multifaceted and complex and requires time. Grief is like that; life is like that.

WHEN THEY FELT BETTER

The points in time when the women in our study felt "remarkably better" ranged from the time they learned their babies had died to three years after their losses. The average time was just shy of six months after their miscarriages.* (It is important to note that women were asked when they felt "remarkably better," not when they felt "healed." Second, a significant 12% of the women responded that they did not yet feel remarkably better. The average time from this group's miscarriages to their interviews was eight months [ranging from one month to three years], two months *later* than the average time for feeling remarkably better reported by the rest of the group.):

> *I was making a baby quilt. My husband was helping me with the batting. It was to be mine. After the loss, I would not give it away; I hung on to it very tightly. But by the time I finished it, I was ready to give it away. My husband still wanted me to keep it for myself. I said, "No, this one isn't mine." That was the most important thing I did. It was so pretty. I was so proud. I called it "my grief work."*

*One woman responded that she did not feel remarkably better until 16 years after her loss. Her responses, 5 "I don't remember when I felt better" responses and 12 "I don't feel remarkably better yet" responses, were omitted from calculations of the average.

As noted earlier, a significant number of women were interviewed very soon after their miscarriages. Their perceptions of emotional highs and lows reflect their experiences only up to the time of their interviews and without a long range view of their experiences. Because their responses were not calculated into the average, it is highly likely that the average would be later if they could respond from a broader perspective.

When a few mothers received answers to previously unresolved medical questions about their miscarriages, they felt much better:

My five losses occurred in the same week of each pregnancy. I felt better when I went to a specialist who confirmed I was right about the hormone levels causing all my miscarriages. Having the answer immediately made me stop blaming myself.

Some women felt better when they finally received compassion from others. Some felt remarkably better when they became pregnant again, when they heard their subsequent babies' heartbeats, had ultrasounds, passed the point in pregnancy at which they had previously miscarried, or gave birth to subsequent babies.

The women we interviewed felt pain *and* comfort while they were focused on their losses. On a typical day-to-day basis, many of them also felt happy in many ways and were leading full lives:

I tried to deal with it as best I could. Finally I was able to forgive myself and make peace. I kind of even feel good about it, if that's possible.

CLOSENESS WITH THEIR BABIES NOW

As time goes by, we remember our losses and our babies. Yet, there are also times when we feel distant or disconnected from our babies. Sometimes we need that distance in order to function. Other times the distance can feel very lonely.

Close to half the women said they sometimes still experienced a feeling of closeness or contact with their babies. Some sensed and drew comfort from the presence of their babies' spirits nearby:

I believe he's happy and that he's watching over me.

I often ask my baby to talk to someone in heaven about giving me another chance at motherhood.

For other women, the sense of closeness was experienced as painful, as though their babies were there yet forever out of reach:

Maybe I do feel closeness, but I don't want to deal with it, to feel the pain. It's haunting—she's out there but I can't touch her. She's too far to reach. All the pain catches up with me.

For some women who did not experience a sense of contact with their babies at the time of their interviews, the distance added to their pain and loneliness. Yet the distance provided relief for other women who needed to feel that their babies were wholly gone from their lives and who needed to close a door on their relationships with their babies to try to ease the pain.

Some mothers felt they could not remain close with their babies directly, because they had little or no memories of or experiences with their babies. So some mothers thought of their babies as being with deceased and loved relatives whom they could see and know in their minds. The idea that their children were taken care of by these relatives felt comforting:

I said to myself, "You don't have that baby now, but that baby is with your mother." That was very comforting to me.

Both of my babies are in heaven with God and my parents. They never got to see my other two children. I'll see them when I die.

I had a dream right after my miscarriage. My grandma (who had died one year earlier) was sitting and rocking a baby. I know that's where my baby is. [crying] I have smells I remember my grandma by, and there was a song she sang to me as a baby. It's their *song now. She swaddles my baby. It's very comforting.*

We may even wonder with sadness if our babies' spirits exist anymore or if they ever did exist to begin with. The separation can feel very lonely. Sometimes it feels good to reconnect with our losses and to bond again with our babies' memories or spirits by thinking about and expressing our losses again, feeling the pain, and remembering.

Mementos serve purposes for us in healing. They hold tribute to our babies' lives and help us know that our babies are remembered. By doing so, they help us move in the direction of letting go and developing a feeling of peace. Although there are usually few or no mementos associated with babies lost in miscarriage, we can create them.

MEMENTOS

Many of the women in our study created mementos of their babies. These included, among other things, objects that symbolized their babies (such as pieces of crystal or sculpture), personal journals or poems about their babies, and flower gardens in their babies' memories. Some women held formal or informal memorial services alone, with family and friends, or with clergy. The creation of these mementos and memorials brought closure to their losses and was crucial to their healing:

We planted a tree in the back yard. All my husband's family came and helped dig the hole for it. The tree is my youngest son's size, and it will grow with him. It felt very very very very very good that I had something that represented my loss which I could go to, which I could have. It gives me a warm, comforting feeling.

We bought a yellow blanket and put it in a memorial box. We buried the letters we each wrote to the baby, pictures from the sonogram, and a copy of the verse we said. After the service, I felt that a weight lifted.

I had a journal of my pregnancy, the hospital band, and the blue stick from my pregnancy test. After the miscarriage, I wrote a letter to the baby. I put them all in an envelope with the cards people had sent to us.

One of my best girlfriends bought me a gift when I was pregnant—a box of baby Dior socks. They stay on my dresser. Those little socks will always be there. They are comforting.

We put a gravestone marker by his brother's.

On the three-year anniversary of my loss, I wrote to my son,

This is the day of your passing on
to a new plane
a hundred zillion miles from home,
your new home.
I shall stand in tribute to you
for a hundred years or more
'til tomorrowland appears.
And someday we'll float together there
gentle son of mine
nameless, faceless
and dancing on clouds.

One mother's letter of healing (from *Ended Beginnings* by Panuthos and Romeo) touched our hearts:

And to Elizabeth and for all our Children . . .

Whom I've never held or physically seen.

For years, now, I have talked to you in that old rocker. I have seen you sitting there. I've told no one. Today, I am free to give the old rocker to someone I truly love. And you, my child, live in my heart forever. I am free to let you go, to find your way.

I am grateful that you could stay so long on this plane, to guide this [grief] work before beginning anew your purpose. God bless you always.

Love, Mom

CHAPTER TWENTY-SIX

Elizabeth's Story

I had two miscarriages in the second month of pregnancy and a third in the fourth month. They occurred 8, 9, and 10 years ago.

I didn't take the first miscarriage so badly. I looked at it like a medical statistic. I was upset but not completely devastated. I wasn't devastated until after the second miscarriage. With the second one, I had passed the second-month point at which I had miscarried before. My water broke in bed. I went into the bathroom and delivered my baby. I was hemorrhaging.

I don't know what happened to the baby. The paramedics put him in a little container and sent it to pathology. We got separated. I don't know what happened to him.

The doctor on call was extremely gruff. I had tissue stuck in my cervix. He did what amounted to a manual D&C. It was very, very difficult.

At that point I experienced a reflex action of going back over the first miscarriage. I had buried it and pushed it into my subconscious and was not thinking about myself and my feelings. I began to emotionally feel the first miscarriage as well as the second.

I worried that I had caused the miscarriages. My body was not performing the way it should. If I had a better body or organs or something, I would have been able to just pop them out.

I wish the professionals had acknowledged that I had a baby and had given me the option of burial or seeing the baby again. I wish I had not been treated by the physician like I was stupid. I wish he had talked to me like an adult and told me about my condition, what it meant, and what actually happened. I wish they hadn't treated me like I delivered a piece of tissue. A human being *was lost. I wanted the dignity of being treated like a person who miscarried, not like a surgery patient.*

I did nothing to take care of myself after the miscarriage. It was just so "black" there. I did not care about anything, and I did not want to care. If I could have done anything differently, I would have nailed the doctor and sat on him until I got the answers. With the second loss, I would have seen the baby, named him, buried him, asked for handprints and footprints, written a poem, and buried it with him. I would have liked to have been more of a participant.

When I had the third miscarriage, I went to the hospital myself. I was numb. I was depressed for awhile. Afterward, I made a lot of changes—in my doctor, my job, and my attitude. I became very determined that I was going to have a child.

From the second I got pregnant each time, I had envisioned them graduating from Harvard, and I envisioned my being a grandmother. I know the second one was a boy. I don't know the sex of the other two. That makes me feel really uncomfortable. I'd really like to know. They were prospective family members. It would have been nice to have known the complete person.

I experienced my lowest point after each miscarriage right away as I walked out of the hospital door. At that time I felt the worst physical pain that I ever experienced in my life, a real big hole in my heart, a sinking emptiness and pain. Your heart hurts. It hurts. Your whole chest hurts. It's awful. The pain from the cramps wasn't bad enough. I wish I had been cut from the top of my head to the bottom of my feet so people could see I was suffering, so I could say, "See, I'm ripped apart." I would have welcomed that.

Every time I got in the shower I heard a baby cry. I'd turn off the water to make sure. It was a very distinct, definite baby cry. I didn't have to "search" for my baby. It was right there. The crying stopped after the birth of my subsequent baby.

It was difficult because my husband and I didn't grieve in the same way. We did in the beginning. But then I was still stuck behind, and he couldn't understand where my anxiety was coming from. He could sympathize but not empathize. He wasn't on the same plane I was. He wouldn't say anything. I knew I was driving him nuts, but he wouldn't say I was driving him nuts. I felt him closing up.

I worried that he was going to die. I wanted him to go and I wanted him to stay at the same time. My poor husband. My sex drive changed. I told him to get away or I'd cut it off. I was not into intimacy for a really long time.

I experienced confusion. "What am I feeling? Is this real? Is this warranted? Is this a normal reaction to what I've experienced? Was I overreacting?" Everything I felt was illogical. Nothing made sense. I was losing my mind.

I used to have a lot of friends. They were not really friends. Most depended on my being happy and up. I realize most relationships were "one way": my helping them. As time went on I whittled them down. Now I don't put up with bullshit. I don't have any relationships with people who are phony or greedy or who take advantage. I'm very selective. I felt absolute loneliness. I felt totally alone on the planet. Nobody else felt this way. I felt completely isolated.

I didn't really have any spirituality. As far as I was concerned, everything sucked. I didn't have any feelings about anything. Sometimes I wish I had died instead of them. When someone you love dies, a piece of you dies.

Miscarriage is like falling into a deep well and you hit the bottom and you have to work your way out. You can get help, but you still have to do it yourself.

To a woman who has had a miscarriage I would say, "I can feel your pain. I can feel your sorrow. I have been there." I'm so changed. I don't take anything for granted. I make sure at the end of each day that I tell the people I care about that I love them. I try to settle any beefs at the time. . . . It completely changed my life.

PART EIGHT

UNFOLDING

CHAPTER TWENTY-SEVEN

A Common Grief

I read an article about a woman artist whose 21-year-old son was killed in the December 1988 crash of Pan Am Flight 103. I was struck by similarities between her grief, our own, and that of the women we interviewed. To help keep her son's memory alive, she created and dedicated sculptures to him. She had raised and lived with him and had photographs of him and memories with and of him; yet *still* she worried that she and others would forget him, just like we worry that our babies will be forgotten.

The article went on to describe the difference between her and her husband's expressions of grief. Whereas she felt a need to talk, give interviews, and express her grief through sculpture, he dealt with his pain more internally. As I read the article, I saw that the experiences of grief we weathered were not confined to miscarriage. We were not peculiar or alone. We were in perfect sync with this couple who had undergone a different kind of loss.

Then someone shared a book with me called *The Wall: Images and Offerings From the Vietnam Veterans' Memorial.* It is a beautiful book of photographs of the visitors to the Wall, loved ones of those who lost their lives in Vietnam, and of the accumulation left there—their mementos and letters to the soldiers. In the photographs, I saw the anguish in their eyes. I heard the heartache in their words.

I never knew anyone who died in Vietnam. Yet I felt both torn apart by and drawn to the grief revealed in the mementos and images pictured on those pages. I felt and identified with their sorrow and pain. Each page brought forth more tears, and by the end of the book I felt flooded with an overwhelming sense of sorrow.

Even though my loss was so different from theirs, I felt tied to the people. The book touched my heart, and I learned again that grief is grief is grief, regardless of its source:

> This is the suffering that connects us with all suffering. (Stephen Levine, *Meetings at the Edge*)

We had similar experiences while reading the books of, among others, Anne Morrow Lindbergh, whose one-year-old child was kidnapped and murdered; C. S. Lewis, whose wife had died; Dr. Joyce Brothers, who lost her husband; and others:

[While living with long-term cancer] It's amazing how that gnawing feeling in your stomach goes away when other patients tell you some of their friends avoid them too; it's not just miserable old you. (Natalie Davis Spingarn, *Hanging in There: Living Well on Borrowed Time*)

[11 years after the deaths of her father and brother in a car accident] I know there was nothing I could have done to prevent it. But I couldn't get over the question "What if?" What if I had been home to pick up John? What if I hadn't been shopping? The "what ifs" were so unanswerable; I felt so out of control. But I lived in the what-ifs because that way I could keep control, keep them still here in the what-if. Finally beginning to let go of the what-ifs was the first step in—letting go. Time heals a bit, but when you're down it's right there like it just happened. [crying] I treasure that I still remember and feel so deeply, because then they are still here with me. (Antoinette Cepe-Thomas)

[As her 16-year-old son lay in a coma] All the concerns of "normal life" are meaningless to me now. I talk to people and think, "I am living in a world these people know nothing about." They might as well be from another planet; they seem so alien. They have no idea, haven't a clue. I go through the motions and try to keep my perspective as normal as possible, but everything has become so simple in the face of death. (Cathy Atadero, *From Tragedy to Triumph*)

We were struck by the universality of their words and feelings. Wherever we turned were people who shared similar pain from altogether different kinds of loss. We have come to realize that we are one with those who share our grief not only today but yesterday, a year ago, a century ago, and a millennium ago, and we are one with those who will share our grief into the far reaches of the future. We are in communion with the universe in a way that transcends time. In this way, we and all humankind are each other's echoes of mourning.

CHAPTER TWENTY-EIGHT

Marie's Story

On the morning of December 29th, 1986, I awakened from a powerful dream which told me of the presence of a new baby son. In the dream, he looked fat, healthy, and about three months old, and he was naked and lying on his back with his feet in the air. I had had the same kind of dream (of a baby girl) when I was first pregnant with my daughter, Terese, eight-and-a-half years before. These two dreams felt very different from my regular dreams, in that these felt utterly real.

I was still using the same method of birth control I had used successfully since the birth of my son Jordan five years before. Regardless, the nurse said my pregnancy test was clearly positive. I sat there looking at the curtains, expressionless. She asked, "Are you okay?" I burst into tears and cried, "I feel like you said the moon is blue and made of cheese!"

She asked worriedly, "Do you want to be pregnant?" I answered, "Sure!" It took me about five minutes to begin to absorb the information and to have the heavenly, honored, privileged feeling I have with pregnancy.

When I am pregnant, I have an acute sense of a tiny, powerful presence in me. I feel deeply blessed. I feel like my baby and I are in a private little fort together, and no one knows we're there but the two of us. I feel I am very special. I feel like I am walking five inches off the ground and I thoroughly enjoy the extra attention I receive.

I had not thought I would ever have another child. My husband, Greg, previously felt it best to stop at two children. I, on the other hand, wanted more children but felt it would be best if they were welcomed by both of us, so I grew accustomed to the idea of no more. Our two were the "end of our line."

Because I was on birth control, this seemed to be a miraculous conception. God simply vetoed the birth control. Nobody could argue with "The Ultimate Authority" about whether or not this baby was supposed to be here. It was fate. And I was elated!

I remembered the euphoria of giving birth to Terese and Jordan. I remembered their infancies—the preciousness of those times, the miracles, the abounding sweetness. I could already imagine the peace of being alone all day with our new baby.

I thought about the powerful experience of holding him at two in the morning in the quiet and the darkness. I had this feeling that all was well in the world; everything was the way it should be. I had a sense of well-being and fulfillment and that this is what makes all of life worth living.

In my mind, the baby I was carrying looked like Jordan. I "saw" him at two years old, having an absolute ball in an inner tube in my dear friend Patti's pool with Terese and Jordan, who played and swam like fish there all summer long, each summer. I felt joy and great love in my heart at the thought of this little boy of mine having so much fun out there and feeling so terrific about himself.

I was so excited about choosing a name for him and getting a bigger station wagon—the symbol of family to me. He would be darling, and I would be the proud mother of three.

Greg was shocked by the news of the pregnancy. He was deeply moved by the presence of the tiny new baby inside me. He clarified that his feelings about a potential baby and his feelings about a baby who was actually on the way were entirely different matters.

Three days after my pregnancy test and five weeks pregnant, I experienced some pain in my side. Greg and I went to the OB covering for my own Dr. Michaelson, who was out of town. The OB felt I might have a tubal pregnancy, so he did an ultrasound but couldn't locate anything on the screen. I had never heard of a tubal pregnancy. He told me that in a tubal pregnancy, the baby is implanted in the fallopian tube. It still didn't enter my mind that anything might happen to my baby. The doctor explained that if it were a tubal pregnancy, I would have to have major surgery. I figured that meant moving my baby into my womb. He explained it meant the removal of my tube and my baby.

BAM! I felt my world crashing in. I began shaking. He told me that if I felt intense pain, I should get to the hospital right away. I pushed him to explain why. He said that if not taken care of, my tube could burst and ultimately I could die. My baby was threatened and I was threatened. I felt fear and deep, deep sorrow about forthcoming loss.

I phoned Patti and told her the news. She recognized how sad this was. She personally felt and shared my sorrow. She burst into tears and said, "Oh how sad; oh how sad!"

Around that point in time, Greg emotionally disconnected from the pregnancy until he had reason to believe it would work out. When he disconnected, I felt left to parent our baby alone.

I had a horrible feeling of doom. I lay in bed at night and worried about the potential intense pain. I worried about the logistics if my tube burst. How I would get to the hospital? Would I get there on time? And who at any given moment of the day or night would be available to take care of my two children? I worried that so much worrying would harm or kill my baby.

The future looked bright when two weeks passed and I hadn't felt pain. Greg and I were to see the covering doctor for a second sono (because he had ultrasound equipment in his office and Dr. Michaelson did not). I wore a festive shirt in anticipation of good news.

The doctor said, "The amniotic sac is in your uterus. But it looks two weeks too small. It has probably ceased development." I thought, "Ceased development. Ceased development. . . . Stopped growing? DEAD!? Is he saying my baby is DEAD??"

I was devastated. I began shaking. He asked, "Do you really want this baby?" I was very confused by his question. I answered, "Yes." He asked again, "I mean, do you really want this baby?" I answered, "Yes, I really want this baby." He continued, "Because it could just be younger than we figured, although I doubt it. We could schedule a D&C now, unless you really want this baby." My shaking was obvious, and to save face, I announced, "I'm shaking." He touched my leg and said, "You are shaking! Why?" I said, "Because I'm nervous." He responded, "You really are nervous, aren't you?"

The doctor was a highly educated man, a high risk perinatologist who delivered life every day. I figured he would know better than most that this was a life inside me. Obviously there was some doubt about whether or not that particular life was gone. Yet, regardless of whether or not it was gone, he was ready to take it away for sure, even if its mother wanted it. He apparently felt that to lose this life or even to actively destroy it was nothing to "shake" about. In fact, for him, the basis of the decision was whether or not I even felt like hassling around for two weeks. Was my baby's entire life not even worth two short weeks of waiting? I found his concept of the reality of my baby completely baffling and mind-twisting! After all, he would not suggest I throw out Jordan if he were suspected as dead but no one had verified him as dead, nor if I were having problems with him! I could not see the difference between the two. To him my baby was not a real and actual human being. That life was no big deal. But that life was MY SON.

Days later when an acquaintance heard about my pregnancy, she said to my friend with impatience and criticism in her voice, "Marie's having a problem pregnancy? Well, why on earth doesn't she just abort it?!" I felt furious! How dare she! This baby was real to me. This baby was my son. How could people suggest I wipe out my child? Again I felt so confused and so undermined in my perception that my baby was a real person.

About a week later, I saw my own Dr. Michaelson, who advised that we not jump to any conclusions yet because ultrasound technology was not yet so precise. He suggested that we just sit tight.

For the following two weeks, I desperately clung to the possibility that my baby was just younger than we had thought. I had had some nausea, fatigue, and a little bit of colostrum, which continued. My belly seemed to grow thicker, and I sometimes thought, "I've had babies before and I know that this is pregnancy." Interspersed were growing feelings of despair. Near the third sono, I stopped emitting colostrum.

Greg and I were waiting in the OB's outer office to have the sono when a song by Rick Ocasek came over the speakers. The words were, "I would do anything to hold on to you . . . until you pull through. I'd hold onto you 'til the mountains crumble flat. I'd hold on to you. . . .You're emotion in motion." I was emotion in motion. In my mind, the singer seemed drawn to his lover and found her appealing because of her emotion. While she felt so pained, he was pledging to love her, to hold fast and never let go until she was ready, to never abandon her. To me, the music was strong, persistent, and securing. In the face of this situation I deeply needed to be protected and loved that way, while I wailed for a hundred years. I concealed my sobs from the other pregnant women in the waiting room.

The doctor said, "The amniotic sac has grown but not enough." Grown but not enough? I just could not believe I could receive more nebulous news. How could that be? I felt anguished by more ambiguity.

The next day Dr. Michaelson called me in. He gently told me that he now felt as sure as he could that my baby had died. He also said that if I wanted, I could have a fourth sono in another week for my own assurance. Greg and I couldn't yet feel certain in our heart of hearts that our baby was positively gone, so we elected to wait as a safeguard against error.

That final sono showed minute growth of the sac and no visible body. (By then I should have been 10 weeks pregnant and the baby should have been perfectly visible on the screen.) Afterwards, Greg and I stole down the hall to find the radiologist in his lab, where I said, "I have to ask you something. In your opinion, is there a snowball's chance in hell that I'm going to have a baby?" He looked at the floor and softly said, "No." I finally felt sure. I felt relief from cruel uncertainty.

The D&C was scheduled for the next morning. I asked Dr. Michaelson if I could see the sac afterwards. I needed to see the surroundings that had housed and touched my child. But he explained that following the procedure, the sac would no longer be intact. I also asked if Greg could be with me during the D&C. I needed my husband. But husbands were not allowed in the room during D&C's.

That evening my sister Martha phoned from Dallas. She did not know all of what I had been through. She asked several times if I were certain the baby was dead. Her questions threw a wrench into my fragile sense of resolve. Only hours from a D&C, I could not cope with the thought that my baby might still be alive. I couldn't stand it anymore. The implication that I should wait longer felt cruel and inhumane and I exploded. Then I explained that I had been through grueling pain in my already exhausting effort to be sure that the baby was dead. She apologized, and we cried together.

At 6:30 the next morning, Greg and I arrived at the surgical center for the D&C. It was my very first surgery. I thought the story and the trauma were all finally coming to an end. I teased the nurse, who really liked my hot pink suede boots, that they had better still be there when I returned from surgery. She made a note in my records that I was in good emotional condition. (HA!)

The anesthesiologist explained that I had to sign a legal document stating I understood some people don't survive general anesthesia. That was all I needed to hear!

It was time. I kissed my husband and walked away down the hall. Climbing onto my own surgery table felt bizarre. Everything was happening very quickly. The surgery staff looked at me as if they knew what I was going through, and felt awkward and bad for me. They were trying to be really nice to me. But all I could see were strangers' eyes behind masks and under caps, and part of me felt like they were about to kill my baby.

The IV containing general anesthesia went in. Then came the final moment of good-bye to my child, and I was flooded with the greatest sadness I have ever known in my life. As I was about to SCREAM a cry of sorrow from the center of the earth, I felt my head fall to the right and my eyes close. . . .

. . . There was a realization that it was over, but there was no sadness attached to the realization. I only felt like lead, physically. I was in the recovery room. Within minutes after awakening, they had me sit up. I was in a lake of blood. They had me dress myself and moved me by wheelchair to a lounge where they were to finally let me be with my husband as promised. But they had sent him downstairs to the pharmacy for my take-home medications. The comfort of his presence was another thing taken away.

Surgery had begun at 7:40 a.m., and by 9:50 a.m. I was walking up our driveway. The quickness of it meant that this was not a big deal.

After five hours of contractions, the entire process was over. I lay in bed in my prettiest nightgown and fresh sheets. I felt a perfect and deep peace, like I had been lifted up into heaven.

The next morning, Greg went back to work and the kids went back to school. There I sat in my bed. ALONE. A shocking void was rapidly moving up inside me. Enormous pain was flooding in. There was no companion, no presence; my child was dead; I was emptied. Oh my God. I felt bottomless sorrow. It hit me so quickly and it felt so deep; it was frightening.

I phoned Patti and asked her to come over. With the pregnancy over, she thought I would be putting the experience behind me. She said she wanted to stay home and do her laundry. I told her I felt great emotional pain. She was surprised and thought she had better try to "snap me back." She said, "Pain?! For God's sake, Marie, the thing was four cells!" I was enraged, and I cried, "It was not! It was MY CHILD!"

She did come over. I knew that underneath all, Patti possessed an amazing capacity to be empathetic, and I needed someone. While she honestly believed I was overreacting, she could also feel the authenticity of my pain. We argued and then cried together, yet our friendship was in a state of disrepair.

Several days later, I secretly wondered if the doctor had really performed the D&C. After all, I had been asleep during the procedure and sometimes I still felt I was pregnant. But I didn't dare tell anyone. I thought they would put me in a psych ward.

I wore the bandage from the IV for two weeks. The weather was warm out, but I wore long sleeves anyway in order to hide it. (I knew people would think it was weird to wear a bandage for so long.) But I didn't want to take it off because that bandage was my only connection to my baby.

During those first weeks, I was hit with waves of profound feelings of loss and anguish without limits. My world went black. The realization struck: My baby was gone forever and ever and ever. With that realization I felt dizzy and like my face would explode.

Within only a couple of days, Greg told me I was milking the loss and it was time to move on. I couldn't let my grief out, and I couldn't hold my grief in. I began hyperventilating. I would shake at night, and I was to realize later that the shaking was from the struggle to hold in my grief. I felt that if I expressed my feelings, I would die because they were so intense that my heart would burst and my insides would explode and I would disintegrate or fly away and never return. I couldn't give myself permission to grieve at all. It was too scary and too "not okay."

I think the healthiest thing for me would have been to have had my mother, my husband, or other loved ones there at the D&C holding me, to be awake, and to go ahead and wail and feel the emotional pain . . . to have the loss. *Somehow it would have been right. I had to have the loss, but I couldn't have the feelings of loss. I had to lose the baby, but I couldn't have the feelings that go along with losing the baby, and that made losing the baby five times worse!*

I had nightmares regularly: the world was ending; the United States declared nuclear war on Russia; I had brain cancer. Two weeks after the D&C, I wrote in my journal, "I feel much better now, but I'm shaking at night and I'm having nightmares." I didn't realize I was trading my feelings from the day to the night! They were all just coming out in my sleep!

I misunderstood sensations of dizziness, shortness of breath, and chest pains to be indications that something was drastically wrong with me physically and that I was actually dying. I was absolutely terrified.

I wanted someone to want to *hear all about my miscarriage 10 hours a day. But of course everyone had their own lives to live. I felt like such a bother dragging everything down. I thought that no one else experienced grief over miscarriage, let alone that depth of grief. I felt grossly embarrassed that I was just this out-of-control freak, flipping out like a fish out of water in front of the whole world over this thing that made no sense. I felt I was just* acting *like I lost a baby, but* really *I had gone through just this little disappointment.*

One evening I was shaking and I couldn't contain my grief anymore. I had to go out of control or over some kind of edge. Patti picked me up, and we parked in an empty lot. I began to spew thoughts and to thunder grief. I told her I felt nothing in common anymore with anyone on the earth and that I was a million miles from anywhere, alone, in a bottomless black hole out in space forever. I cried because I felt like my son was out in space somewhere, too, or he was lost and he needed me, just like a missing child. Patti was not afraid. She listened with acceptance, cried with empathy, and held me in her arms until I was limp. She was a lifeline. It was the first time I allowed myself to vent my grief in the way I needed. That night was the beginning of my journey back to life.

My sister Mary developed alarming, incapacitating symptoms and soon after was diagnosed with multiple sclerosis. Multiple sclerosis, miscarriage—I thought these things didn't happen in our family. I felt overwhelming grief about the permanent loss of my sister's health.

My mother, with two daughters in crisis, was suffering. She was very loving to me, and she kept calling me from St. Louis. She did not brush my grief aside in the face of my sister's MS. I felt important to her. I felt such love for her. In one conversation she said, "Sweetheart, you have a little angel up in heaven." With those words, she recognized my baby as a real baby. The acknowledgment felt so good; it made me weep.

Across a T-shirt, I drew stick figures of our three children and printed their names. Later, I wrote in my journal, "I am a farce in my shirt with the baby's name on it. People would be confused and annoyed and critical if they knew I put a miscarried baby on it. You don't count a miscarried baby publicly. But you don't discount them in your heart, either. How can I live with that discrepancy? How can I publicly not have my child, yet have him in my heart? Am I not automatically a farce? No matter what I do, I feel so fake."

Patti ran across an article in the L.A. Times *about a support group. She phoned me and said, "My God! At their meetings they lump together parents who have had* stillborn *babies, with parents who have had miscarriages! I had no idea that other people feel that depth of grief over miscarriage!"*

At the first support group meeting we attended, Greg learned through listening to others, that my feelings were real and not "melodramatic." He cried and said he felt like a heel for urging me to "get on with it." I felt tremendous support from him then.

After the meeting, I dreamed there was a drinking straw going right through my head. "Understanding" was coming in one end of the straw and "misunderstanding" was going out the other.

I never cared for stuffed animals, even when I was a little girl. But every night for several months after the loss, I found myself holding my son's soft stuffed puppy as I slept. I didn't even think about why. When I did think about it, I realized the puppy "was" the baby.

At another support group meeting, we listened to parents of stillborn babies talk about having held their babies and having said good-bye to them. Driving home after the meeting, Greg pulled off the freeway and cried about having had no chance to hold and say good-bye to his own baby. He deeply missed the opportunity. He also cried, "He was just a little guy who never had a chance," and expressed his feelings of helplessness in the face of trying to protect his baby boy.

I realized that until Greg cried about our baby, I had been mourning that my baby had no father. When Greg finally cried over him and, in that way, acknowledged his baby as his son, I was able for the first time to forgive him for not "fathering" his dead son with his grief.

I also felt sad that Terese and Jordan did not have a mother. All I did was lie in bed all day, and in that way they were abandoned. One day Terese came in and asked how I was. I cried and told her I missed my mother 1,400 miles away. Terese cried, too, probably because she understood all too well. She missed her mother, too. I held her and kissed her cheeks softly until she had spent her tears for the time being. It was a tender and loving encounter that was bonding and healing for us both.

At another support group meeting, I met Peggy. She had lost her 13-month-old son to a degenerative neuromuscular disease 12 years before. I felt like a snivelly little drip with my loss next to hers. But she only conveyed great acceptance and compassion to me. She put my loss right in the same league as her own. She helped me to "get it" that my seemingly crazy and immeasurably intense feelings of grief were not only real but undeniable. It felt good finally coming to terms with the fact that I could judge my feelings for a thousand years, but they would still be there and they would still need to come out.

Then I was flooded with the feelings again, but away went the shakes and the nightmares. And the feelings weren't so frightening anymore. In fact, it felt so good to grieve.

At times I would phone Patti and ask, "Can we meet at the office?" "The office" was a joke. It was a dead end street by her house where we would sit in the car and I would bawl and she would listen and usually she would cry with me. You know, we can share our joy with anyone. But we are lucky to have one person in our whole lifetime with whom we can share our misery.

I had a dream that Greg, Terese, Jordan, and I were lying on our sides like stacked spoons across our bed, all dying together peacefully. It felt like we were drifting on a leaf along a stream, gently, slowly, safely, and warmly. It was a letting go, and we were going to be with our baby.

I came to realize that the feelings and dreams of my imminent death were also expressions of my partial desire to go to my baby and be with him in death. But they were conflicting with my desire to remain here with Terese and Jordan. I felt ripped between death with one child, and life with the other two.

I dreamed that I had a large hole in my body that extended from under my breasts, down to my pelvis, and out to my hip bones. I only realized the meaning of the dream when I described it to Peggy and saw myself demonstrate the boundaries of the hole.

I recorded in my journal, "To have a child die is to be weak and powerless and defeated. It's like dying. Other spirits live while their bodies die; my spirit died while my body lived."

My miscarriage erupted anxiety in me about whether or not my nonreligious ways would cause me to be forever damned. In the midst of all of my philosophical gropings, I felt the need to resolve on a deeper emotional level my feelings about some of the religious teachings ingrained in my head as a child. Yet even as a little girl, I felt distrustful of claims to religious righteousness made by faiths, each with supposed dibs on the line to God. I felt that people were divided in religions, and division of peoples was so contrary to the fundamental and common goal of religions—love—so simple, universal, and so shared. My sense was that God was entirely too vast to be confined to only one image or one faith. I wrote to a beautiful, elderly, and scholarly nun whom I trusted and who taught me theology in college 12 years before. She wrote me letters and sent me articles affirming my conviction that no church holds any franchise on God, and that all of us in all of our different ways are loved, accepted, and welcomed by God equally. That perception felt so much more kind. Her letters helped.

Over the course of many meetings with Patti at "the office," I learned to let go, to fall over the edge into the land of all-encompassing pain and to wail with abandon of restraint. The healing power of those encounters was extraordinary. Patti recalls that time in our lives with her own tears. It was, in many ways, a meeting of souls.

I regularly wrote letters to my baby in my personal journal. Three and a half months after my miscarriage, I wrote, "I feel much better. And I still miss you, my baby, throughout most of the day. But it isn't frighteningly awful anymore. And I feel the beginnings of peace again."

About five months after my miscarriage, a day came when I could finally speak the unspeakable. With tremendous pain, I confided to Peggy that during one of my sonos, the covering doctor had said to me, "Maybe there never was a baby." Over the past five months, I had anguished over his statement. It took away my child's having ever existed.

I felt so painfully distant from and lonely for my son. I had no sense of contact with him until one day when I spoke to him aloud, directly, and without censoring myself. I believe his spirit was there in the room. At that time, I experienced a tremendous relief from the excruciating loneliness I had been carrying for him all along.

But it was temporary. Later, one night when I again felt a really sorrowful distance from him, I went outside and sat in my back yard. It was quiet. Ethereal, transparent clouds were very rapidly moving across a full moon. As I looked at the moon through the moving clouds, I felt the presence of my son. There was a great peace. He was not gone. He was present. He had stayed close at hand.

That night I learned that I could speak aloud to him whenever I wanted and feel his presence there with me. I realized that I would be able to sense him again after a month, after a year, or after 20 years.

I had a dream. It was not a dream of images but only of the words, "There are five," over and over again. With the dream, I felt a powerful sense of peace. In it, I was claiming on a deeper level, not four, but five members in our family, including its fifth member: my baby son.

I wrote the following, which today hangs in a pretty frame on my bedroom wall:

Andrew Tyler Allen,
You lived in my womb
I felt your presence
I knew your soul
You were my friend
Then, my child, you died
Your spirit,
as real and as complete as my other children's,
lives in my heart
You are, now and forever,
my son.
My precious baby,
I need to tell you
that I love you.
Mom

Old wounds from over the years of my life had been opened. One of these was the great loss of a very dear neighbor lady, Pat, who died quite young of a brain tumor when I was about 20. Grieving the loss of my baby crossed over into grieving the loss of Pat, too. I wrote her a long letter. Then I had a dream that Pat was helping me get through my grief, via my dreams.

I began working as a volunteer for the support group. I was asked to be a resource for a newly bereaved mother. That particular day was uncomfortably busy, but I made the call anyway. Thank goodness I did. Her name was Shelly Marks.

Even though Greg previously felt that two children were enough, once I had become pregnant, he had felt very tenderly about and protective of the presence of our newly conceived baby. Six months after the miscarriage, he confided to me that his reservations about having another child had been based on his concerns about finances and not on a lack of desire for another baby. He agreed to another baby. Four months later we conceived.

In November of 1987, I wrote to the subsequent baby I sensed growing in me, "I feel so filled with calm. I am waiting to learn the results of my pregnancy test. I feel so special. Together, our family will be so happy about you. I feel very lucky. You will be a breath of heaven. . . . Pregnancy test: 'POS'."

Yet I felt afraid to fully trust that all would go fine and to let my joy out, so I had an ultrasound at seven weeks of pregnancy. The baby was alive and well. The ultrasound technician didn't want to give me a copy of the image of my baby in case the pregnancy didn't work out. I had to do a lot of talking and to use my experience working for the support group to persuade her that it would be helpful to have a copy even if something did happen to the baby. Against her judgment, I got a copy and was greatly relieved.

Someone asked Jordan if he had any brothers or sisters. He answered simply and matter-of-factly, "My Mom has four kids: my sister and me, one up in heaven, and one in her tummy." His words felt good.

Baby Grace was born to us all, fresh from heaven, a year-and-a-half after the death of our son. In a conversation with Greg one day when Grace was several months old, I equated how I felt after the miscarriage, with how I would feel if Grace died. Greg was completely floored at the analogy. His eyes welled up just conceiving such a thing. At that moment he appreciated for the first time that I had actually gone through the death of a real, living child. He understood the unspeakable depth of my pain. That felt healing to me.

I wrote to my lost baby, "Somehow my grief and all my suffering feels like a gift that I have wanted to give or go through for you who were my son. You are worth that price."

In working through so much grief, I had to refine my ideas about life and about myself, and I had to grow so much through the process. There were many unlived parts of me that had clamored to be expressed. I fostered my talents, discovered more of my competence, and realized more of my yearnings. I emerged from the struggle with a greater sense of my natural ability to create what is important to me in the world.

I had a dream which I feel represented my labor of grief and my resultant, expanding sense of who I was. In the dream, we acquired a house that was absolutely majestic. Every room in the house had a different kind of floor, and each floor was one you might see once in a lifetime in some grand museum. One was an elaborate scene made out of intricate and tiny pieces of marble, the next floor was the same but in fine woods, the next in tiny ceramic tiles. Each floor was born of incredible human labor, persistence, and creativity. The house had a secret winding staircase to a loft above, which was right over the ocean. The staircase "railing" was actually an ongoing harp, and the strings were strung in such sequence that if you put your hand out as you ascended, you would play a beautiful song.

There is a line from the soulful movie Field of Dreams* *that jumped out at me: There comes "a time when all the cosmic tumblers have clicked into place and the universe opens up . . . and shows you what is possible." I related to it. It was what I had gone through.*

It's been four years and four months since my miscarriage now, and Shelly and I are in the final stages of writing this book. Except for certain rare times, my sense of loss feels healed. So what is it I cry with now? It is remembrance—remembrance of a time. It is remembrance of the loss and sorrow that a mother of a dead child knows.

Sometimes I remember my son and sometimes I do not. Regardless, I know his spirit is entirely too vast to require memory among the living in order to continue to exist. I know that Mother Love *persists without waver, even when my mind is consciously focused in other directions. I know that my relationship with him will never end, even when he is out of my thoughts, for our relationship is not built of memory. When we have both been dead and gone for a hundred years, we will still and always be . . .*

Mother and Child.

*The line came from the book *Shoeless Joe* (W.P. Kinsella) from which the screenplay was written.

CHAPTER TWENTY-NINE

Opening to Life

Beyond grief lies hope, and beyond darkness may lie a life of purpose and meaning. Just as death is the birth of a new state of existence and a point of transcendence onward, so too is grief. In neither can we see the light ahead. Nonetheless, it is there.

When we undergo the loss of someone we love in life, the place in the world that belonged to that someone is forever vacant, and we are forever changed. Great losses make us different people than we were before.

With the death of our babies, we died inside, maybe a little or maybe a lot. We may feel shaken all the way to our roots. In eventual healing, some of us undergo a kind of rebirth into new life. By this we do not mean a religious rebirth. By transformation we mean profound spiritual growth that arises from being open to the pain of grief, from allowing the pain to move through us, and from expressing it. Whereas loss changes us, grieving loss transforms us. Through the process of mourning, we are reshaped into more highly evolved souls than we previously were:

> I can be inspired to grow, but more often I grow because I have been broken by certain unyielding realities. (Hugh Prather, *Notes on Love and Courage*)

Over the passage of time, we do more than survive the journey. We go through the labor of self-discovery and give birth to the being deep within. We seek, explore, formulate, express, and cultivate our thoughts, feelings, values, dreams, and desires. We emerge from the struggle with a unique combination of ideas about ourselves, God, life, and the world. Our talents are fostered in the process, we grow to understand better what we value and want in this world, and we know ourselves better. What develops down the road is an evolution of who we are. We break past boundaries, we come to see ourselves and our worlds from a different point of view, and pain is transformed into new meaning. We emerge more enriched, empowered, and evolved women, connect with the spiritual* wisdom that lies deep within us, and experience the more whole life we deserve.

So, grieving opens a door into our souls that might otherwise not have been opened. Grieving is a pathway to our inner core and to the connection with the presence of God within:

> I will welcome happiness for it enlarges my heart; yet I will endure sadness for it opens my soul. (Og Mandino, *The Greatest Salesman in the World*)

Before we let go of control over our emotions, grieving often feels strenuous and frightening. When we do fully let go of our restraints on our emotions, perhaps grieving at that point in time is no longer work, struggle, and effort. Perhaps the *work* of grief is allowing the containers that have held our emotions to shatter, surrendering to the grief, and letting our hearts break or be torn open by the pain. This is life's grand and challenging paradox. Perhaps the *work* of grief is letting go and giving way to grief, to its release, and eventually to what lies beyond grief. Great loss sometimes pushes us to a brink. We have the option to go over the brink and give way to grief. If we feel the threat of "the black hole," we can fall into the darkness in order to pass through it to the peace, love, and universal wisdom that exist in the core of each of us. Through unreserved grieving comes a freeing of the soul.

The prospect is so scary. Levine wrote in *Meetings at the Edge:*

> Some may feel unprepared to face this much suffering. We have so much doubt and so little confidence in our own natural greatness, in our original nature. . . . [Yet] we have within us, all that it takes to face the immensity of this pain, to let it soak in, to learn to breathe it into the heart, to let it burn its way to completion.

In addition, Levine writes, "Growth is measured by . . . the openness with which we continue and take the next unknown step, beyond our edge . . . into the remarkable mystery of being."

Sometimes I think of people in terms of a core surrounded by two layers. I see the outer layer as our illusion of who we are, which we reveal to ourselves and for the world to see. This outer layer is labeled something like "I am fine. I am nice and neat and packaged with a bow." The middle layer is made up of our emotional pain and grief. The very center or core

*We use the term "spirituality" to refer to closeness with the heart and with our inner voice of wisdom or higher consciousness. This sometimes includes but is not confined to religion or a belief in God.

is labeled something like "I am valuable and loving. I am attuned with a greater knowledge. I am a spiritual being. I am safe. I know that everything is okay and as it should be." This center is truth.

Much of the time it seems we don't get from our outer layer to our center because our middle layer stands in the way and the prospect of traveling through it feels too scary and painful. Yet we can get to our center by going through the pain in our middle layer.

Within the confines of our outer layer, we are restricted by our perceived limitations. We believe that we can accomplish certain things and not others, and that we have a fixed degree of talent, wisdom, and ability. We do not envision ourselves beyond those confines. We all, to one degree or another, are unrealized potential.

When we are grieving, we are moving through our middle layer. Grieving a crisis or great loss can enable us to recognize and even break apart some of our confining illusions. Sometimes we evolve through grief only to look inside ourselves and find secrets of our souls that have been hidden away, to recognize more of who we are and who we can be, to become more realized.

In a way, I feel like I spent my life locked inside a body cast. I absolutely believed I could not do many everyday tasks that most people consider simple. I felt paralyzed and tremendously inept. I lived with guilt over my lack of contribution and with anxiety over how I would survive. Meanwhile, also locked away in that body cast were marvelous talent, potential, and creativity.

When I had my miscarriage, I felt completely shattered. In mourning the trauma, I felt like I was mourning the ills of the whole earth. It was so scary and so difficult to go through that grieving. Yet through grieving, the cast (my confining illusions) shattered, too, and fell to the floor. I feel so much less encumbered. I feel freer now. And I can actually *feel* my ability, my competence, and my power.

What I hadn't realized was that when we feel weak, our power is there to actually be claimed in opening ourselves to the feelings of weakness and to all our feelings. Through giving way to our "weakness" and expressing our feelings, our power and ability eventually come forth.

And I've thought about the concept of the "ills of the whole earth." Perhaps we all carry a universal sorrow inside: the sorrow of never having been wholly loved by parents who were humanly limited and, therefore, could not love us perfectly, the sorrow of never having realized or experienced all the beauty inside of us, and the sorrow of never having fully felt or expressed the boundless love that we have inside to give.

Over the course of our lives, we cannot consciously be focused on all our feelings. At different times we focus on different emotions while the others remain tucked inside. Along the road of life, we may not have been able to fully see or grieve our universal losses. Whereas some of our grief over these losses necessarily remained tucked inside, other parts of us remained tucked inside, too. When our feelings remained unexpressed, who we are also remained unexpressed. We did not have access to pieces of ourselves. Much of our talent, our intelligence, and our energy never evolved and lay dormant and untouched.

When we are shattered by loss, new grief awakens this universal grief. We are faced with our lifelong feelings of sadness, helplessness, and vulnerability. Yet, at the same time, grief also rattles the lid that holds down our potential, our talent, and our energy. When we allow ourselves to feel and express our grief, something magical and holy happens inside. Because our losses and lifelong grief are tied together, when we shed pain over our miscarriages, we also shed old pain over other parts of our lives; then more of those unlived parts of us that had clamored to be expressed are awakened.

We have an option to take the road into the shadows: to look at our grief (old or new), to stay with our feelings of grief, and to provide them an avenue of expression. In doing so, we reclaim pieces of ourselves. There is a returning to some central place inside of us that got lost long ago along the road. There is a coming home.

> Change is the return of something once known, something that will not be abandoned. I look down the line of my life and I see it surfacing again and again. I recognize it. I am that thing. (Hugh Prather, *Notes on Love and Courage*)

All the emotion we held for our babies, all the force with which we loved them, is still here inside us. That energy yearns to go some life-affirming direction. Grief is an energy or a force needing to emerge from within us. While in grief we experience a diminished vitality, paradoxically, grief holds inherent within it the promise of life and future. When we give expression to our grief, we join life again. We access our energy and awareness of the life force within us. These may come forth in an instantaneous and force-filled bang, in small bursts, or in countless tiny pieces like silent planets in the distance.

We can come to experience great spiritual moments—powerful, free of pain instances of knowing we are safe, connected, and loved. These moments may occur rarely at first but then may occur more frequently.

Even during the most dismal and bleak night of the soul, we are carried or guided along our path by spiritual knowledge like a tiny light deep inside us. Sometimes we can hardly see it. Sometimes we don't see it at all. But when we have once caught a glimmer of it in our lives, somewhere inside we remember its mysterious and compelling presence within:

> Jung talked about . . . knowledge beyond words, these stories in our bones . . . that are part of every person's consciousness at birth. They are the heritage of universal wisdom that resides in the Self—an instinctual pattern that reveals the path of return. (Joan Borysenko, Ph.D., *Guilt Is the Teacher, Love Is the Lesson*)

> . . . the soul's wisdom continues to guide us in the same way that the sun still lights our way when it's behind the clouds. (Borysenko)

As working through grief unleashes more of what we can *be*, it also unleashes more of what we can *do*. Grief is impetus, attempting to spawn new life both within us and through us, out into the world beyond us where it affects all of life. The pain of grief can be a catalyst that thrusts us into action and unleashes our creativity out into the world and toward the nurturance of life and the future. When we respect and honor our grief, we feel more love for others. Grief work may lead us to remarkable deeds.

We can come to live in response to our experience of loss in a manner that holds expanded meaning for us and gives us a greater sense of purpose, contribution, and making a difference in the world. We come to live in celebration of our babies' souls. The possibilities are endless.

For the two of us, our labor of grief led to this book, which was accepted by our publisher on the three-year anniversary of Shelly's miscarriage. That evening Marie asked, "What on earth does this mean to you?" Shelly answered, "I'm not quite sure yet, but I can't think about it without crying. I think that . . . this has all been . . . a gift."

Had we not gone through our miscarriages and all our suffering and grief, or had our miscarriages been just brief disappointments to us, we would never have had the impetus to write this book. And the thousands who will be reached by the women we interviewed would not have been touched, nor would we all have been a part of one another's lives.

All our growth has deep and penetrating ramifications, for even what may seem to be the tiniest of changes in one of us affects the lives of all we meet. We touch so many lives even with our thoughts, which spill out into everything we say and do. In this sense, not only are *we* transformed but our world is, too, for transformation of any size and shape is global:

> The most minute transformation is like a pebble dropped into a still lake. The ripples spread out endlessly. (Pat Rodegast and Judith Stanton, comps., *Emmanuel's Book*)

Clues to our own personal transformation lie in the dreams and longings we as individuals hold for ourselves. In those rare and holy moments when we dare to dream wondrous dreams of ideas, miracles, dances, or creations, we catch a glimpse of what we are capable in our lives and perhaps of what we are designed to do. There is a coming home to who we are deep inside. The kind of person we long to be, the things we dream of doing—perhaps these are our yet-to-be realized and hidden truths, our purpose. Those little voices in our heads and hearts of love and hope and faith in ourselves, in life, and in the future are the voice of the universal spirit in us telling us what is possible.

So we hold the opportunity to use our experience of loss as a tool for growth that pushes us to new depths and eventually onward to new heights. Grief is life's calling us, spurring us on to a personal unfolding. It is a force, or an energy to move masses within us that propels us to higher levels of awareness, depth, compassion, power, commitment, action, and impact.

The journey through grief is a spiritual excursion, a life-affirming movement toward that to which all of us are drawn: a sense of communion and peace with ourselves, with one another, with a greater spiritual being, and with all the universe.

In moving through grief, we learn, grow, and expand, and we discover that something lies beyond. There is a finding of self, and an evolution of who we are. As we access our potential and creativity, we transform not only ourselves but our world. We move closer to the soul-spirit within us, to the center that is still, where we are all one, and where, lastly,

. . . Love abides.

CHAPTER THIRTY

Gifts

Through their lives and deaths, our babies affected us in profound and unseen ways. They brought us gifts that touched not only our lives but also the lives of countless others. We have been changed by the lives that resided within us and our love for those lives, and we are changed by working and growing through the pain of the loss of those lives. From those changes we reap the blessings of emotional and spiritual growth. And with that growth—now a new part of who we are today—we touch the world around us through our everyday interactions.

How does miscarriage lead to our growth as individuals, women, wives, mothers, daughters, and friends?

WE ARE NOT SAYING IT'S A GOOD THING YOUR BABY DIED.

Turning our babies' deaths into something good may well be impossible. Our babies have died; our hopes and dreams for our future with those children are gone forever. Our lives will never again be the same, nor will they ever be as we envisioned them to be with our children. Yet making something good out of experiencing, expressing, and growing through our love and grief over our losses *is* possible.

The writing of this chapter presented a dilemma. We did not want to deny pain or imply that we can or should "think positively" and that pain would then turn into happiness, nor did we want to send a message that "your miscarriage was for the best." When I was told at a support group meeting after my miscarriage that something good would come of my loss, I felt furious at the notion. I thought, "*Don't* try to make something *pretty* out of this!"

Yet we want to share what many of us have experienced as a result of our miscarriages: the fact that our babies' lives and the process of grieving our babies' deaths brought us emotional, psychological, and spiritual gifts that changed our lives.

These gifts do not compensate for the loss of our children's lives. They do not make miscarriage a good thing. They do not take away from the sadness we feel when we think of what we have missed by not having, knowing, and growing with our children. They do not erase the love or the pain. Rather, our growth is born, in part, of the sadness that we feel. Through the process of grieving, growth does occur and is there to be appreciated. But how could we share that with you, perhaps still in the midst of pain and grief?

Sometimes when we are close to a thing and looking directly at it, we think we see it most clearly. When we are in the midst of a situation, we may think we have the clearest perception. But not before the night hours arrive can we appraise the day. When we are able to view life events from a broader perspective, the larger picture is often quite different from the view up close.

One evening after my miscarriage, I was lying in bed with my left hand resting on a book I was reading. As I looked past my hand at the words on the page, the diamond in my wedding ring appeared to turn a beautiful, radiant blue. I am sure there is some simple scientific explanation for this phenomenon. But that evening, it had a special significance for me. When I looked directly at the diamond, it looked the same as always. When I looked past it to the pages of the book so I could see the stone only in my peripheral vision, it again looked bright blue. At that moment I could feel the presence of my grandmother, who had passed away two years before, and I could hear her as though she was speaking to me in my mind, saying, "Sometimes we can only clearly see a thing when we are able to look past it."

Part of our transformation process involves coming to view life's experiences from this broadened perspective. Whether or not we are aware of them or can yet feel or understand them, there are hidden gifts from our miscarriages that often come to us in the form of inner changes, new awareness, and spiritual growth:

> Bless this pain
> for it will bear its perfect gift
> to you in its perfect time
>
> (Rusty Berkus, *To Heal Again*)

Some of our growth comes even before we have time or energy to work through our grief. Carrying life inside our bodies gave birth to beautiful changes within us. We are different women than we were before because we are mothers, whether we have living children or not. We carried and nurtured our babies within us the best way that we knew how. They were and are our children. We were and are their mothers. We gave them our blood, our breath, and our love, and we love them today and forever (even if we didn't realize we were pregnant or were focused on the hard realities of raising them rather than on our love for them).

In this sense, we and our lost children experienced a lifetime together. Our children were conceived, they grew, and they died. Their lives are no less important because they weren't born in the middle of the life cycle. Life matters, no matter how brief. That we didn't experience them in the world of our five limited senses as we had hoped does not change that. They lived and they died, far too quickly for us to feel comfort in that life, but life it was. As the poet Ben Jonson wrote:

> It is not growing like a tree
> In bulke, doth make men better be;
> Or standing long an Oake, three hundred yeare,
> To fall a logge at last, dry, bald, and seare:
> A Lillie of a Day,
> Is fairer farre, in May,
> Although it fall, and die that night;
> It was the Plant and flowre of light.
> In small proportions, we just beauties see:
> And in short measures, life may perfect bee.*

Some of us find comfort in the belief that our babies came to us for a purpose: that their souls fulfilled their life work in a very short time and returned to God. They held meaning for us. They gave love and they received love. They touched our lives and our hearts. Perhaps their lives were, in this manner, complete.

Over a period of time and as part of the process of grieving, we turn inward and explore our losses within the overall scheme and pattern of our lives. We examine, challenge, and develop our thinking, values, and directions. Some of us come to feel more in touch with what really matters to us:

> *I went through fire and it burned off some of the junk. I'm a more pure person now. I feel a real connection with the earth. I feel more of a "woman-ness." I'm not so much concerned about going to the finest department store and buying another outfit, versus being at home and enjoying the sky and the earth and grass and what I have here.*

> *I realized I had to start reading books I like and taking time for myself. I've become more aware of doing what I want now—living life as I want to.*

*From "To the Immortall Memorie and Friendship of that Noble Paire, Sir Lucius Cary, and Sir H. Morison," *The Complete Poetry of Ben Johnson*, William B. Hunter, Jr., (ed.) (New York: New York University Press, 1963).

I'm not searching anymore. I am more comfortable with not knowing. I feel at peace.

I am philosophically affected. I am more sympathetic. I appreciate things more. It woke me up. I am more calm.

In my journal, I wrote:

I'd like to linger on the beaches in the sun, to hear the waves and to look into the distance and just experience the beauty and power of nature—the breeze on my face, the quiet, the simplicity, the stillness inside. I'd like to fall asleep on the shore with sand in my hair and stuck all over me. I'd like my hair to be a mess. I'd like to feel the sun sizzle on my skin. I'd like to read at night and to write. I'd like to realize that there isn't a damn thing I can do to make the world safe and all-loving for my children, and I'd like to cease trying to make it that way. I'd like to make love a lot. I'd like to hear music. I'd like to talk and talk and talk. I'd like the house to be wooden and for it to have a screen door that doesn't shut right.

Some of us learn through our miscarriages that there are aspects of our lives that we cannot control with will or through might, and some of us learn to let go of the attempt to control them. I remember saying when I was pregnant with Jamie that *no* one would take this child from me. When she died, "the universe" said that I was not the one in control of my children or the lives of those around me. In fact, I think my biggest lesson (and one that I am still learning) was that I do not have control over every aspect of life. I used to feel that I *had* to control everything. People remarked about how organized I was, how I paid attention to every detail, and how I thought about each aspect of each situation. I tried to run my own, my child's, and my husband's lives. I felt not so much like a woman holding a whip to the world as a woman holding the world on her shoulders. My miscarriage was a first step in seeing that not only do I not have to hold up the world, but I *cannot* hold it up. I feel freer to live my life without the tremendous and painful burden of feeling responsible for everything. Through our miscarriages, many of us begin to learn to let go of some of the control we have so futilely attempted to maintain over life.

Although few of life's experiences can make us feel as broken and as weak as the death of a child, great strength comes through meeting life's despairs. Some of us find for the first time that we can survive tremendous hardship:

Those miscarriages are the most monumental things that ever happened in my life. They were major turning points like marriage or the loss of a parent. It's amazing I've made it through. It's an accomplishment I have survived. I feel good about myself. I handled it. I found out I was a stronger person than I thought.

It gave me the strength to trust and go with grief and loss. I am more capable of being in the presence of things unfair.

Growth occurs in other areas of our lives as well. Following loss, our relationships often change as we see ourselves and others through the filter of our new experience. Some relationships that felt painful needed to grow or be given space. Those that feel honest and loving we hold with increased appreciation and cherishment.

Relationships made or strengthened at this time have the potential to be deep and caring ones and are based on who we truly are deep inside. When we really express or listen to one another's true inner emotions and embrace one another's hearts, we feel genuinely accepted, valued, and loved. Sharing who we are deep inside and appreciating one another connects us and brings us both closer to the soul-spirit within us. In a powerful and holy sense, we are both transformed.

The pain and grief of miscarriage make us become more attuned to our feelings and the feelings of those around us. With hearts softened by our own sorrow, we feel tenderness toward others, with the chinks in their armor, and in all their pain and vulnerability. The women we become or find within ourselves are more compassionate toward our fellow human beings than we previously were. Borysenko writes, "Compassion, which is the interpersonal bridge, is the union of the temporal and spiritual planes. It is the place where Divinity enters human relationship":

I'm more in tune with others' pain like an instrument (a viola or a cello) that has a deeper, richer sound.

I feel more of a sense of the family of mankind, that we really are all kind of a family of humans.

I am changed in that I am more understanding of other people's pain. I am less judgmental. I listen more. I wear my heart on my sleeve now. My heart is like radar. I am more gentle. I really do care. When I say, "How are you?" now I mean, "How are you?" I am not reborn, but I am redefined!

In healing, we continue to remember and love our babies. We do not forget our babies when we are transformed through our grief. We carry our love for them always, regardless of whether they are in our conscious thoughts. And we remember our babies for the gifts they brought us and for the enormous impact they made on our lives and the lives of others:

I feel joy that I had her for a while and she was created. I know now that I have an enormous capacity for love. I feel blessed that I experienced this child and that I could experience the love of that child even for a very short time. My child's life caused me to grow and my life to change. I understand now: There is nothing like A Mother's Love.

Our babies profoundly impact our lives, yesterday, today, and forever. These are some of the many gifts our babies have delivered to us, and these are some of the many possibilities our babies' lives have opened to us. As poet Rusty Berkus wrote in *Life is a Gift:*

> There comes that mysterious meeting in Life,
> when someone acknowledges
> who we are
> and what we can be,
> igniting the circuits of our highest potential.
> I see this as the appearance of an angel,
> and know it to be
> a moment of Grace.

Dear Mother and Fellow Journeyer,

We too are following a path. We have tripped over the stones and gotten lost many times along the way. Hand in hand with you, we are learning the lessons of life.

We know that there is a place of stillness deep within each of us, because we visit there. It is a place free of suffering, a place of infinite peace and love. There we are united and connected with who we really are, God, each other, and our children.

Keep your heart open in grief. Allow yourself to unfold and honor the being within you. Risk the journey through the pain, for without fail, love lies at the journey's end. As you travel the path through your emotions to the holy places in your heart, we wish you grace and Godspeed.

Marie and Shelly

To every woman we interviewed, we feel deeply grateful for the gift of revealing themselves and allowing us all to look into delicate and private places inside their hearts. We feel deeply respectful of them. We have cried over and remain moved by their poignant stories. We are struck by the beauty of these women who gave a part of themselves to help other women. It is their love and their courage that have made this book possible.

Alexia Scheele
Alix Barbey
Amy Cousins
April Fout
B. Murray
Barbara Harris
Barbara Combs
Barbara Zaslow
Beth Bresnahan
Betty Ebert
Beverly Marston
C. Q.
Carol G. Link
Carole Osier
Caroline Jaques
Caryl Matzel
Cathi Lundy
Charlo Zauss
Connie Rice-Allen
Deborah Moretti
Deborah Nalbandian
Deborah Plotkin
Denise Mauriello
Elaine Ballengee
Elaine Tutterrow
Estelle
Freddi Lindsay
G. Ellerkamp-Harris
Jackie Gutowitz
Jamie Johnston
Jamie Wolinsky-Blumenthal
Jan von Euen
Janice Swift
Jeanne Franklin
Jill Green
Jody A. O'Konski
Judith Ann Kingsbury
Judy DiGennaro
Judy Tapper
K. S. Harvey
Karen Campbell
Karen Young
Kathy McCoy
Katie Powers
Kay Pflueger
Kelly J. Dennis
Kerri A. Shepherd
Kristen Nelson Spathas
Kristen Linden Hill
Kristia Smith
Laura Gross Weiss
Laura Kitson
Laura Riley
Leslie Marks
Linda M. Dunn
Linda Hamel
Linda Harmon
Lisa Giandoni
Lisa Yamamoto-Tadokoro
Lyn Linden
Lynn Larue
Lynn Packer
M. G.
M. W.
Madonna R. Smith
Margie Somers
Maribeth Doerr
Marilyn Van Winkle
Martha Tassi
Mary L. Rudiger
Michele Merchant
Michele Tamayo
Michelle Kwik
Mickey Strasner
Myeva Brett
N. Levy
Pam Scheunemann
Pat Melzer
Patricia Yates-List
Patti Andreoni
R. Brownell

Rebeca Griep
Rebecca Burfield
Reena Deutsch
Robin Rastello
Rosemary Brinig
Sandra W. Groebner
Sandy Fry
Sara Ellen Vance
Shannon Morris
Shawn L. Crane
Sheryl Angeloni
Sheryl Gerbracht
Susan Latina Sterrett
Susan Reed Clayton
Susan Quick
Susn Penn
Suzy Foster
Tammy Sims
Vickie Johnson

Walking about
day after week after month
in an on-going state
of holding back one scream
from down in the center of the earth
up through the center of my body
never quite out through my throat.
The struggle to hold it down
chokes the life out of me.
It is two years and eight months now,
and interviewing these women is freeing me
to welcome up and embrace and thank the pain.
It is my friend;
it is my freedom;
it is my love for my spiritual son.
They are the ones who give me permission
and I thank every last one of them.
Holding it back hurts excruciatingly forever.
Pouring out my pain with dignity,
standing tall,
arm-in-arm with these hundred voices grieving,
resounds my strength.
I love them all
and those never interviewed.
We are all
a living tribute to each other,
to our Motherhood,
and to the immortality
of our power to love
our sons and daughters
on whatever planes.

APPENDIX A

Taking Care

> And so at a certain point 'helper' and 'helped' simply begin to dissolve. What's real is the helping—the process in which we're all blessed, according to our needs and our place at the moment. How much we can get back in giving! How much we can offer in the way we receive! But even 'giving' and 'receiving' now seem artificial. Where does one begin, the other end? (Ram Dass and Paul Gorman, *How Can I Help?)*

When one of us hurts, we are all affected. In helping ourselves, we help each other; and when we help one another, we help heal ourselves.

Following is a list of ideas and examples of ways you can best take care of yourself, and ways others can help take care of you. We offer these like choices on a buffet table. No one will find everything at the buffet inviting or useful. We invite you to pick and choose what feels right to you. We begin with suggestions for you who have miscarried. Others now can turn directly to page 227.

THE MOTHER

> The ultimate lesson all of us have to learn is *unconditional love,* which includes not only others but ourselves as well. (Elisabeth Kübler-Ross)

Respect Your Needs

Do whatever you need to do in order to heal. Open up to whatever you feel and need. Stay with your feelings and needs—do not abandon them and do not pretend to feel okay when you don't. Then move with your feelings and needs as they change over time. Go with what your heart tells you would be good for you in each new moment.

Express Your Emotions

Emotional expression is your lifeline. Expression not only relieves pain over time, but it helps you know and understand yourself better and directly leads to emotional independence—to the inner strength for, and the ability to cope with, whatever life might deliver. Express your feelings and thoughts in your own way and in your own time. It doesn't matter how; it matters that you free yourself of the pain.

- Talk. When you do, don't constrict your facial muscles or wear a tight smile. Instead, let your face and tone go limp, and automatically they will communicate what you feel. Your feelings can escape more easily that way.
- Tell your baby aloud or in writing that you love him or her.
- Write letters to your baby.
- Record a journal, perhaps in a book or on video or audiotape. Keeping a journal has been shown to lower blood pressure.
- Write an article about your experience.
- Write to us through our publisher about your experience and your feelings about what you have read in this book.
- Draw, sculpt, paint, or express yourself through music.
- Read sad books, listen to sad songs, or watch sad movies that help you cry.
- Go somewhere where you won't alarm anyone and scream.
- Vent your anger: rip up old magazines or phone books, slap water, wring a towel, squish "Play-Doh®," beat your bed or a pillow, or write angry letters to people and later decide whether to save them, send them, or throw them away.
- Run, walk, or jog. Physical movement often helps feelings come out. It also releases brain proteins within your system called endorphins, which help you feel better.

Create Memories, Mementos, or a Ritual

- Get copies of your medical records, your baby's lab records, or ultrasound pictures if there are any. Keep them in a special folder or envelope.
- Keep hospital bracelets, a bandage from an IV, and/or OB appointment cards in a special container.
- Press and save flowers you may receive from others. Save letters or cards.
- Write out the story of your pregnancy. Have it bound.
- Fill out a pregnancy book with the facts of the pregnancy.

- Draw your family tree and include your baby's name on it.
- Refer to your baby by name, even if it feels funny at first to you or others. It won't once you get used to it.
- Find a special toy, pretty pink or blue decorated or marble eggs, a sculpture or other piece of art, an angel ornament or some other article that will remind you of, or signify to you, your baby.
- Make something out of needlepoint or another craft in remembrance of your baby.
- Have a plaque engraved with your baby's name on it.
- Place a headstone or plaque in honor of your baby at a cemetery whether or not you buried your baby's remains.
- Wear your baby's birthstone in a special piece of jewelry.
- Place a written letter or poem to your baby somewhere special to you—frame it, bury it with some flowers, burn it, or place it with your baby's remains if that is possible.
- Choose a special song to commemorate your baby for you.
- Hold a memorial service. You might want to write the service yourself. You, your clergy person, or a loved one can conduct it. Play your special song.
- Place a memorial notice in the newspaper.
- Every year on the anniversary day of your loss, do something special to celebrate your child.

Take Care of Yourself Physically

- If it won't jeopardize a needed job, take as much time off work as you need.
- Remember the basics: good nutrition, regular exercise, and sleep. No matter how much you don't feel like taking care of yourself, your most basic needs can't be totally forgone. Get on a healthy routine.
- Get extra sleep to fortify yourself during this incredibly fatiguing time.
- *Can't* sleep? Get up and write, paint, play music, create something, or watch a movie. Hint: Crying during the day helps sleeping at night.
- Push your body into the shower and put on something clean and pretty.

- Go outside—walk, jog, or sleep on a blanket. Sit in the sun. The sun is a natural antidepressant.
- Pamper yourself with a massage, facial, manicure, or pedicure. If you can't afford these, ask a friend to give you one or give yourself one.
- Soak in a warm tub with nice smelling bath oils or bubbles.
- Get a physical checkup with your internist or family physician if you want. Your body is depressed and worn and this is a good time for one.

Take Care of Yourself Socially

- If you don't want to bear the news of your loss to others, ask someone you love to do so for you.
- Draw close with others by sharing your innermost feelings. Talk to those who are likely to be accepting. Open up with them unless they have demonstrated a lack of acceptance of your feelings.
- Tell people who are uncomfortable or nervous around your tears that crying helps you.
- Plan how you want to handle tough questions you'll receive such as, "How many children do you have?" "When are you due?" and "How is your pregnancy going?"
- When someone you love or value says something that feels hurtful to you, say when you feel able, "When I heard you say ——, I felt —— [name an emotion]. It would be really helpful to me if you would —— [name what you want]. Will you please?" They might then feel bad and respond with defensiveness. Reassure them that you love and/or value them. You may have to "actively listen" before you get any compassion because they may not be able to listen to you until *they* feel heard. (How to actively listen is explained on page 227.) Once they seem satisfied that you do understand, perhaps they'll be ready to hear *you.*
- Kindly say to people who give unwanted or hurtful advice or comments, "I'm not asking for your advice/input on this; I just need to get this off my chest. What I would really love is for you to just lend me an ear and try to understand."
- When loved ones are insensitive, hold on to the fact that, underneath all, love is probably there.
- Nurture others' nurturing of you by telling them what specific things they do that you appreciate.

- Spend time with a good friend doing whatever you would like.
- Recognize that your partner cares deeply and has the capacity to share vulnerable feelings. As you do so, you encourage that capacity in him to expand. Show him your tenderness and affection.
- Seek out other women who have miscarried and with whom you can talk.
- Visit a support group.
- Contact "Pen-Parents" for their newsletter and/or a pen pal by writing to Mary Beth Doerr at PO Box 8738, Reno, NV, 89507–8738. Submit an article to the newsletter.
- Send for *Shattered Dreams,* a newsletter that offers support, information, and sharing. Their address is PO Box 2225, Vancouver, BC, Canada V6B3W2. Submit an article.
- The different feelings of other women who have miscarried are okay just like yours are. Come to respect and accept all feelings of all women equally.

Take Care of Yourself Spiritually

- Sense God's presence nearby.
- Talk to God or nature about anything on your mind.
- Express your anger at God.
- Talk with a member of the clergy.
- Ask your clergyperson where you can attend a memorial service for miscarried babies.
- Tune in to your baby's spiritual presence. Talk aloud to him or her in spirit.
- Read the spiritual books on our Additional Reading list (Appendix B).
- Find a relaxation meditation you like. There are books on these in your library and bookstore. A nice one is *Creative Visualization* by Shakti Gawain.

Give Yourself a Break

- Ask less of yourself. Give yourself time. Have short-term, quickly achievable goals. Set priorities and be concerned only about what is at the top of your list.

- Ask someone to pick up items you need at the store when they go.
- Take breaks to indulge in something that is pleasurable to *you.*
- If you can afford the luxury, now is the time to hire someone to clean your house for you.
- Give yourself permission to take time off from sex without guilt if that is what you want. Talk with your partner about any anxieties you may feel about sex.
- When you are ready to give sex a try, talk first with your partner about how you want to handle it if you become uncomfortable in the midst of sex.
- Consider avoiding major decisions for up to a year. Also consider before taking long or far trips that some women in our study felt relaxed while away, yet other women desperately needed the security of home.
- Get your name off mailing lists for baby products. Write to Direct Marketing Association, Mail Reference Service, 6 E. 43rd St., New York, NY 10017.
- Take a class in a subject in which you have had an interest.
- Do something you've always dreamed of doing.

Reach For Help

- Ask for help and be specific about what kind of help you do and don't want. Say, "It would be helpful to me if you'd ——."
- For any reason that strikes you, get counseling. It can be extremely valuable.
- Read. Having knowledge about miscarriage and grief helps you understand yourself.
- For materials and information about tapes, support groups, workshops, or talks, write us at PO Box 22711, San Diego, CA 92192-2711.
- If you are thinking about suicide, phone the National Suicide Prevention Hotline from anywhere in the United States at 800–333–4444. (The National Crisis Center for the Deaf can be reached at TDD# 800–446–9876.)
- Talk with someone at the Grief Recovery Helpline (800–445–4808), which operates from 9:00 to 5:00 (Pacific Standard Time) Monday through Friday in the continental U. S. only.

Express Your Love and Energy

Do something meaningful and creative with your love for your baby:

- Nurture something living such as a pet or a garden. Hug, listen to, express appreciation of, or take flowers to someone you care about. Take care of other children.
- Hold a friend's baby and cry if you feel like it.
- Start or volunteer in a support group. Educate the medical community or the public about the emotional impact of miscarriage.
- Make a donation to a charity in your baby's name—of time, money, or things, maybe on the due date or the anniversary date of your loss.
- Send flowers or cards to other bereaved parents.

Cope with the Prospect of Subsequent Pregnancy

- You may want to resolve the main bulk of your grief before trying to conceive again. Women who become pregnant within five months of their losses sometimes experience more grief later on. Yet for some women, conceiving sooner works out beautifully. There is no right decision on this very personal matter.
- Although there are no guarantees, be aware that even after three miscarriages, you have a 70% to 80% chance for a successful subsequent full-term pregnancy, and even after four or five losses you still have a 65% to 70% chance. (*Current Medical Diagnosis and Treatment 1991,* by Schroeder et al., published by Appleton and Lange.)
- Think about other options, too, such as adoption, foster parenting, big sister programs, and childlessness.
- The following may be considered if you are pregnant again:
    - Find an attentive and sensitive obstetrician.
    - Anxiety is normal in pregnancy, even for a woman who has never had a miscarriage! Talk to your doctor about coming into the office between scheduled visits if you need to feel reassured by hearing the baby's heartbeat.
    - Keep a current list of concerns. Talk about or take care of the items on your list.
    - Get an ultrasound to reassure yourself.
    - After the after 20th week of pregnancy, purchase a stethoscope to comfort yourself that your baby is alive.

THOSE WHO CARE FOR HER

> The most helpful people were those who were not afraid to talk about the death. They did not look the other way, or change the subject, or run off to some important task. They stayed with me. They held fast. They were afraid, but they were not so afraid that they could not be with me. . . . Thank God for them. (John DeFrain, *Stillborn*)

The mother who has miscarried needs people. You are in a position to make a tremendous difference both in how she feels and in her healing. Be part of what John DeFrain calls a "circle of love" around her. The most powerful things you can do for her are to care about her truly and in some way to let her know that you do.

View and Respond to Her as an Individual

When my mother said to me, "Sweetheart, you have a little angel up in heaven," I felt so good that I wept because she acknowledged the reality of my baby. But when a woman in our study was told the very same thing, she angrily thought, "I don't want my son up in heaven! I want him right here!" To assume the thoughts, feelings, and needs of a grieving person can be like walking through a field of land mines! One woman sees miscarriage as a disappointment while another woman sees it as the death of a child, and one mother needs to be hugged while another mother needs to be alone. Because each woman is an individual, sidestep further upset to her by *asking* her how she feels, what she thinks, and what she wants. Learn what the world is like from her unique point of view.

Be a Good Listener

Practice constructive or "active" listening. Identify what appears to be her emotion, and check out your assumption by saying, "Sounds like you felt misunderstood" or "So you felt lonely?" or "You must've felt so angry." Sometimes you'll be accurate and sometimes you won't. Keep trying until she seems satisfied that you do indeed understand how she feels. She will probably feel somewhat calmed and settled for awhile.

In the process of active listening, you learn how her experience feels for her, appreciate her feelings as real, unconditionally accept them (whatever they may be), and give her compassion and respect with carte blanche. Suspend all judgments, offer no solutions, and don't talk her out of her feelings. Instead, be a safe receptacle for her grief:

- Tell her you would like to listen if she would like to talk. Invite her to talk over coffee or on a walk.
- She may or may not respond to your invitations to talk. Proceeding with further conversation on the subject can be based on how she responds to your lead.
- If she wants to talk, let her speak for as long as she wants.

Validate the Reality of Her Loss and Her Grief

- Say the words "baby" and "died" rather than "fetus" or "is no longer viable."
- Send a sympathy card or flowers.
- If she seems to feel grief but also seems to feel confused about why, say, "You lost a baby. You are grieving." Tell her that miscarriage is frequently experienced as the death of a child.
- Say, "It's okay to be sad and cry." Tell her that to talk about the feeling *is* the healing.
- Ask if she would like to have a memorial service for her baby. If so, tell her you would like to be there.

Honor Her Baby and Her Motherhood

- Remind her that she is a mother.
- Ask if she wanted to name her baby or if she preferred not to. If she did, call her baby by name.
- If she knew her baby's sex, say "him" or "her" when you talk about her baby.
- Send her a card on Mother's Day.

Express Your Care

Mother Teresa once said, "Kind words can be short and easy to speak, but their echoes are truly endless." Here are some things you can say and do:

- "I care."
- "You're in my thoughts, my prayers, my heart."
- "I love you."
- Showing your vulnerability helps her accept hers. Share your own feelings of sadness. Say "I'm sorry," "I'm sad for you," or "I'm so sad about your baby."

- Say these things in a time and at a place that are comfortable for her and won't put her in a compromising position (such as in front of a group, when she really needs to get work done, or in front of someone with whom she feels emotionally unsafe).
- Show your affection through touch. Hold her hand, touch her arm, put your hand on her back, or hug her.
- Write her a letter about what you value or appreciate about her.

Connect Her with Other Women Who Have Miscarried

- Give her the name and number of a support group and invite her to use it, keep it, or throw it away, as she wishes.
- Ask her if she would like you to introduce her to another woman you know of who has also had a miscarriage.
- Refer her to this book.

Help Her Function

- She may feel lost and not know what she needs. So rather than ask, "Is there anything I can do for you?" give her specific options from which she might choose. Then ask if there is anything else she can think of.
- Do some of her chores or clean her house or a room in it. Do a load of laundry or offer to repair things around her house. Run errands or grocery shop for her.
- Cook a meal and take it to her home or have a pizza delivered to her at mealtime.
- Offer to take her other children somewhere pleasant or fun for an afternoon.

Give a Gift

- A flower or plant
- Needlework, embroidery, or other craft item you make for her
- A new or library copy of this or another carefully selected book
- A certificate for a massage, facial, manicure, or pedicure
- A poem written by you; a published poem
- Prayers—silently or noted in a card

- Donations in her baby's name: money, a Bible, a book, a tree or plant, toys, clothes, food to a befitting charity perhaps of her choosing, for example, shelter for homeless families or a church preschool
- A tape of beautiful, peaceful music

Refrain from "Helping"—Trust in Her Ability to Heal

As you quietly recognize and relate to her as a person with inner resources and the capacity to heal, you encourage that capacity in her. Do not try to fix her grief. Rather, provide quiet in which she, herself, can begin to find resolve. Demonstrate your confidence in her ability to think for herself. Listen and allow her to develop her own solutions and views. At this time, when her sense of self-worth is at an all-time low, encourage her to be herself. Know that her way is the best way for her.

Give Her Time

Support is needed down the road because she still grieves. Be open to listening to her talk about her miscarriage and her feelings, days, weeks, months, or years later. Paradoxically, being there for her over time actively helps her move through her grief more efficiently and quickly.

Remember as Time Passes

- With the passage of time, ask her, or send her a card that asks, "How are you doing since you lost your baby?" "Thinking of you since your miscarriage" or "I'm remembering the loss of your baby and I want to tell you I care."
- Each year remember the anniversaries of her baby's death or due date or remember Mother's Day.

Take Care of You, Too

- You are also affected when someone you care about loses a baby. How are *you* doing? Honor your own feelings, too.
- If you're overwhelmed by her feelings, tell her you feel bad and don't feel capable of being helpful right now and that you'll get back to her when you feel better. Take a break and recoup. Then follow through with your promise.
- For materials and information about brochures, support groups, and talks, write us at PO Box 22711, San Diego, CA 92192-2711.

Additional ideas follow tailored for fathers, medical professionals, morticians, support group leaders, members of clergy, mental health professionals, and present and future children.

FATHERS

Commit to Growing Through Grief with Her

Use this time of grief as an opportunity to deepen the bond between you and your partner. It's easy and wonderful to share the highs of life with your partner, but often you draw closest and become most solidified when you share the lows. With loss comes a chance to pull together, to express pain together, and to accept each other's feelings. As you do, you nurture the relationship, bolster the two of you for future blows, and reap the benefits throughout the years to come.

Be Present for Her

Your love and support helps her profoundly.

- Be with her at the D&C, doctor visits, healing rituals, and so on.
- Take time off work if you possibly can in the days to follow and spend the time with her.
- Hold her, look at her, and ask her to tell you what she is going through emotionally.

Acknowledge the Baby and Her Motherhood

- Give her a flower—perhaps a white rose—on Mother's Day or the anniversary of the baby's loss every year.
- Give her a card *from the baby* on Mother's Day.
- Buy a locket, put half of it on a chain for her to wear, and place the other half in a special place—such as in a lake or the ocean, a forest or a garden—with other mementos or with the remains if possible.
- Give her a baby ring in memory.

Share Your Vulnerability and Grief in Words or Tears

Open up with her and share your grief whether it be for your baby, over seeing her in pain, or over your loss of her emotionally. Tell her what you are grieving. Don't make your partner the target of your anger about the miscarriage. Don't hold back any tears. *Sharing your pain with her is the single most powerful gift you can give her.* With it you lend her unspeakable comfort and let her feel united with you in shared grief.

You can communicate feelings, even if it has not been your pattern historically. Your capacity to be expressive of vulnerable or sad feelings may not be evident to you, but the capacity is in you. Trust in that capacity. As you believe in it, you draw it out.

Take turns with her at being the comforter and the "comfortee," the functioner and the "basket case," the nurturing parent and the needy child, and the listener and the one unloading emotional pain. Don't be concerned about tallying equal time in these roles.

Helping her helps you. Ram Dass and Paul Gorman wrote, "We work on ourselves . . . in order to help others. And we help others as a vehicle for working on ourselves." Part of tending to yourself is tending to your partner because in the process of doing so, you are nurturing her ability to be loving back to you.

Be Aware of the Impact of the Miscarriage on Her Sex Drive

- Because of the association between sex and pregnancy, your partner may link sex with the loss of a baby at this time. Ask her how the prospect of sex feels to her and try to be compassionate to her feelings about it.
- Decide together if you are both ready to make love and how you want to handle it if one of you feels the need to stop midway through.
- Do not bury yourselves in sexual activity to the exclusion of your or her opportunity to grieve.

MEDICAL PROFESSIONALS

Acknowledge Miscarriage as a Loss

Often women don't show their feelings about their miscarriages, but *they do feel.* Although first-trimester spontaneous abortion is considered a routine medical emergency, it is never a good idea to treat miscarriage as a lightweight event. To any woman, a miscarriage may well be the death of her child. It is crucial that you be ready to treat her miscarriage as a profound loss. Quick personal attention from you in the time surrounding miscarriage markedly increases her likelihood of grieving in a healthy manner, healing from her grief, and healing sooner.

Be Sensitive to Her Grief

Good emotional care is good business. Sensitivity or insensitivity is communicated by patients to other patients, and business is gained or lost as a result.

- In the hospital, list her as an obstetrical patient rather than gynecological. To her, the word "gynecological" erases the pregnancy and, worse yet, her baby.
- Do not place her near the hospital nursery or with maternity patients because the sounds of other new babies crying is too searingly painful.
- Put a card on her door to denote to staff that her baby died so she isn't approached as a happy new mother.
- Offer to bring in a clergy person and/or a social worker.
- Remove her name from the list of women to receive baby products.
- Do not discharge her without talking with her at length and answering all of her questions, or else she may feel abandoned by you.
- Scheduled follow-up appointments during times when you are seeing gynecological patients, not obstetrical patients, so she doesn't have to face the painful sight of happy pregnant women.

Involve Both Parents

- Allow the baby's father in the room with her at all times including during all medical procedures. Include them both in decisions that must be made.
- Explain to the father that he can best take care of her and help her heal by sharing his care and sadness with her in words or tears.

Provide Information

- Give patients information when they become pregnant, and again when it appears they may miscarry, about the incidence of miscarriage, signs of miscarriage, what to expect at each step, and what to do.

- Keep your information simple and clear and your tone gentle. Parents may not be able to absorb much or absorb well right now. Repeat the information again later.
- Be careful of terminology. For example, the word "abortion" is confusing and has connotations that may be disturbing to parents. If you suspect a blighted ovum, don't say or imply that there may have been no baby. This rules out the life of their baby and can lead them to believe that they have no right to their feelings of grief.
- Encourage their questions.
- Go over every concern they may have about the cause of the miscarriage, so they can trust you when you then reassure them (if you can) that it was not their fault.
- Offer and explain all available tests including genetic studies or an autopsy.
- Explain and help them through hospital procedures for obtaining their baby's remains (when possible and if they so choose).
- Tell them where their baby's remains will go if they choose not to retrieve them.
- Give them information verbally and in written form (a typed sheet, pamphlet, or brochure) about support groups and about grief. Recommend that they read this book.
- Suggest the option of a funeral or memorial service.
- Tell them that, following miscarriage, women commonly reach their emotional low point within the first 30 days, but there is a range.
- Tell them they might expect to feel significantly better emotionally after about six months, but there is a range.
- Offer the community periodic lectures on grieving the loss of babies.

Give Parents Experiences, Memories, Memorabilia

In many people's minds, "real" mothers deliver, see, touch, hear, and care for their children. *Any* experience of delivery or seeing or touching the remains of her pregnancy can offer her the opportunity to go through the mothering process, to somehow know and care for her baby in some form, validate her motherhood, make it more real and complete, and help her heal. One woman in our study who was under general anesthesia during the D&C expressed great sorrow over never having experienced the emergence of, nor touched, the remains of her pregnancy. She said, "I never *mothered* my baby."

We can experience someone we love through our five senses. Our experiences of them become our memories of them. Without some experience of her baby, a woman possesses almost nothing by which to remember her baby; she has no *memories*. She has nothing to mourn. Yet, memories are crucial to mourning. In addition, through memories and mementos to hold on to, we can "keep" someone we have lost close to our hearts always.

- When applicable, explain and offer options of natural expulsion versus a D&C. Some women need to go through the process of labor and delivery to experience the reality of the pregnancy and their motherhood and to grieve the loss. Other women need to push labor and delivery away or may not be ready to realize or grieve the loss.
- In the event of a D&C, offer the option (if possible) to have the procedure immediately or to wait a few days or several weeks. Some women need to get it over with right away, and some women need to hold on to their pregnancies or babies until they are more ready to let go.
- In the event of a D&C, offer her the option to undergo general versus local anesthesia. Some women need to avoid the physical and/or emotional pain altogether right now, while others need to experience the process of losing the baby and to feel and express the emotional and/or physical pain.
- Allow parents to keep a piece of their baby's existence. Offer them a drop of the blood on a white card with a sentiment or poem on it (such as the one on page 213) in a pretty script.

If there is a visible fetus:

- Offer parents the opportunity to view or touch the body or tissue. Viewing and/or touching the remains of the pregnancy, as well as communicating to her with sensitivity about her loss, are central to aiding a normal grief reaction.
- How the baby or tissue is presented is very important. Treat it with dignity. Offer it in a tiny baby basket or cradle, in a doll blanket or a piece of blanket, or cradled in your hands.
- Ask if they want to be alone with their baby. Allow them the length of time they need.
- Ask them if they want anyone else (family members, the social worker, or the member of clergy) to see or hold the remains.
- Provide them with a "memory packet" containing, when possible, a photograph, measurements, the tape measure, a lock of hair, birth

and death certificates (keepsakes as opposed to legal documents), and handprints or footprints. Include places for the baby's name, dates, written memories of the pregnancy, information about the stage of pregnancy, and family information.

If there is no visible fetus:

- Ask the parents if they want to see any remaining tissue or blood.
- Show pictures and relay information from *A Child is Born* or a similar book containing photos and facts about babies at the gestational stage at which their baby died.
- Offer a shorter memory packet curtailed for earlier losses. The packet should not contain sections for specific items or memories not available such as the baby's handprints. (Their inclusion would further highlight her lack of memories and memorabilia.)

Encourage the Expression of Emotion

- Tranquilizers and sleeping pills clog the release of grief. Let her fully feel and overtly vent her grief.
- If you feel unsure about how to communicate with the bereaved, a nearby hospice may offer a training seminar on how to do so helpfully.
- Inquire about her emotional well-being and encourage her to talk about her feelings to you, a friend or loved one, and/or a support group.

Offer Follow-up Care

After the passage of one year, bereaved people who receive follow-up care manifest fewer emotional and physical symptoms and take fewer medications. Those at high risk for distorted or delayed grieving show marked progress when they receive follow-up care (see "Bereavement Counselling: Does It Work?" Colin Murray Parkes, *British Medical Journal*, July 5, 1980).

- Include the father and their other children in follow-up visits.
- Call her one week after her loss, four weeks after, on her due date, and on the anniversary date of the loss:
    - Check on basic functioning: sleep, work, play, and relationships.

    - Check on her emotional condition, that she has been able to talk to someone about her feelings and that she has a support network. Be ready again to refer her to a support group or bereavement counselor.

- Determine if she is at risk for an abnormal grief reaction. Risk factors are: having an uncertain or tumultuous relationship with her mate, being single, widowed or divorced, having felt conflicted about the pregnancy, prior miscarriage, becoming pregnant within five months following miscarriage, lack of support from family, and prior psychiatric problems.
- If she is at risk for an abnormal grief reaction, keep in close contact and suggest the benefit of a support group as well as counseling.
- Refer parents to any regular memorial services for bereaved families.

Ease Subsequent Pregnancy

- There is no right answer to the question of when to try to get pregnant again. Explain that she may want to resolve the main bulk of her grief before trying to conceive again because there are sometimes more problems with grief later on for women who become pregnant within five months of their losses. Yet for other women, conceiving sooner works out beautifully.
- Provide statistics on the success of subsequent pregnancies.
- Although statistics are in her favor, nobody can promise her that miscarriage won't happen again. Be aware that subsequent pregnancy is likely to be a highly fearful time for her.
- Offer to let her come to your office between her regular appointments when she needs the reassurance of hearing her baby's heartbeat.
- Solicit and provide ample time for her questions.

MEMBERS OF CLERGY

- Use a symbolic object such as a white cloth, a candle, a seashell, or a piece of silver to bless the baby (whether or not the baby is present) and then give that object to the parents.
- Offer a certificate of blessing or baptism.
- Provide parents verbal and printed information on grief.

- Hospital clergy can offer to contact the family's own clergy.
- If the parents wish, you, the parents, or all of you can create a memorial service for their baby.
- Invite them to be an active part of the service—to deliver a eulogy, read a personal letter or Bible passage, and so on.
- With permission, videotape or audio record the service and give the tape to the family or invite them to record it.
- Include the baby's siblings in what you do.
- Tell the mother it's okay to feel angry at God and talk about why.
- Invite the parents to name their baby aloud during a regular service.
- With permission, remember their baby aloud in prayer during a regular service.
- Hold, and invite parents to, monthly memorial services for all miscarried babies.
- Establish time following those services for the families to meet the other families.

MORTICIANS

- Help parents retrieve their baby's remains or tissue from the hospital or pathology lab.
- Explain the options of burial (alone, with a relative, or with other babies) and cremation, and help with a memorial service or an obituary if they choose these options.
- If the parents choose to hold a service, tape it (with permission) and give them the tape.
- Have a special garden in the cemetery dedicated to miscarried babies.
- Have a wall in the cemetery for plaques naming individual miscarried babies and the dates of the losses.
- Offer cards parents can send out to make their loss known to friends and loved ones.

SUPPORT GROUP LEADERS

- Confine the group to miscarriage only.
- Hold meetings for an hour and a half to two hours and at least every two weeks.

- Break the group into smaller groups or "sharing circles" consisting of three to no more than six women. That way each woman will have ample time to express herself and will not feel she is speaking before the public about her very private grief.
- If you include fathers on a regular basis, consider separate sharing circles for them in another room. (Because fathers often grieve less and usually grieve differently than the mothers, mothers often feel most comfortable with other mothers who have miscarried.)
- Encourage fathers' support of mothers: Invite fathers to join their partners at a specific meeting each month so that fathers have the opportunity to discover that *other* mothers express the same thoughts and emotions as their partners.
- Consider holding a sharing circle on separate nights for pregnant women coping with the anxieties of subsequent pregnancy.
- Newsletters, special speakers, and a supply of books to lend to members are nice additions but are not necessary for an excellent support group.
- Provide community education on miscarriage.

MENTAL HEALTH PROFESSIONALS

Based on the findings of our study, we recommend the following issues be addressed in future studies:

- A study of the significance and impact of prior experience with infertility on women's emotional responses to miscarriage
- A long term longitudinal study of women's grief beginning at the time of their miscarriages
- A study of the relationship between religious background and womens' emotional responses to miscarriage
- A study to determine the factors that affect the intensity of fathers' grief
- A comparison of the emotional responses of women who have had particularly dysfunctional or abusive childhoods with women who have not, to ascertain and describe any relationship between childhood experiences and difficulties with grief following miscarriage
- A comparison of grief over miscarriage with grief over elective abortion
- A comparison of the emotional responses of women who have had and who have not had previous elective abortion

- A similar study with balanced demographics
- A study of the emotional responses of women who report feeling no grief over their miscarriages

PRESENT AND FUTURE CHILDREN

In this final section, we convey what we can all do for the children of families who have lost babies.

Because children operate on a feeling level, they are extremely aware and intuitive. They sense our emotions and absorb the feeling in the air, even when they are not informed of the events associated with the emotions. On some level, children know the truth.

Help Them Heal Through Talk

Even when the truth is upsetting, talking about the truth is reassuring. What they *know* happened is often easier for them to handle than what they *imagine* happened because it is finite and they can talk about it together with us. As Anne Kaiser Stearns put it, "Mystery and deception are psychologically harmful to a child; honesty and tenderness bring comfort." Be honest about your own feelings, too (and let them know that it is *your* job, not theirs, to take care of you emotionally and get through this).

Next to providing basic care, presenting truth to our children and accepting their emotions about that truth may be the most valuable gifts we can give them. Their being aware of the truth and expressing their feelings about it lead directly to the development of inner strength, competence, and the ability to cope in the world.

As we communicate honestly with our children, we convey our confidence in their strength and their ability to cope with and master life's hard realities. As we believe in their competence, they, too, come to believe in their competence.

We also teach children how to cope by role modeling how to cope—facing, expressing, and accepting our feelings of loss. Through witnessing our movement through the grief process and our eventual healing, they learn to do the same.

Because they are so closely identified with us and see themselves as extensions of us, they conclude that they, too, are strong and able enough to face and deal with *their* feelings of loss.

Ease the loss for them through togetherness. Grief can be a time of great closeness when we share and accept one another's sorrow and pain.

The grief becomes a source of unity. Support your children. Be with them. Hold them. Touch them. Kiss and hug them and tell them they are loved, safe, and protected. Tell them that no matter how bad you feel, you still love them and always will.

Invite them to ask anything and then let their questions guide you in terms of the amount and kind of information you share. When they are young, keep the story simple. Your terminology needs to be very clear. For example, "I lost the baby" can be taken to mean that you literally "lost" and cannot locate the baby. Tell them you feel sad because you miss the baby. You don't want them to think you are sad for the baby because the baby is now experiencing something awful.

Children usually want to go over information again and again. This is not only normal but very functional, as we all learn through repetition. Keep answering their questions truthfully. They are going through the loss in their minds, like you are when you talk it through, and they are trying to make sense of it.

Tell them about grief, too—that in grief we feel sad, scared, confused, and maybe angry, that we do feel better after time passes, and that it helps to talk about it and to get our tears out.

See Appendix C for a list of children's books on death that you may find in your bookstore or library. They can be used not only as teaching tools about grief but also as a springboard for conversation.

Children may ask why the baby died. If you aren't sure why, tell them you aren't. Some children are comforted to hear the analogy that some seeds grow into flowers and other seeds do not—a very natural part of life that perhaps has no "why." Assure them that the miscarriage did not occur because of them.

Your child's emotional needs may feel overwhelming to you now. If you are not yet ready to talk about your loss, explain so to your child, and let him or her know that you will talk about it at another time. Then be sure to follow through later. If you can't talk about it yet, find someone who can. Your mate or a sensitive friend can spend an afternoon with your child and gently and respectfully invite discussion.

Help Them Heal Through Play

Through expression, children reestablish balance and flourish as individuals. They often express and work through their emotional energy in play, writing, drawing, and more—alone or with another child, you, or another caring adult.

Violet Oaklander, child psychologist and author of *Windows to Our Children,* tells us to invite our children to draw a time when they felt "bad, mad, or sad." Asking them to draw and to tell about what they have drawn conveys that it's okay to feel and express their feelings. Children usually don't verbally elaborate about their drawings, so ask specific questions about what they have drawn. Oaklander suggests that we say, "Tell me about the ——" (naming an article in the drawing). Or ask, "Where are you in the picture?" and then "What does it feel like to be a ——?" (naming what they just pointed to). *Keep your tone light and casual* so the discussion doesn't feel too intense or threatening. *And do not interpret!* (The interpretation tells more about the interpreter than the artist.) The goal is simply to help them express themselves and to let them know that you are interested in whatever they express.

Children are commonly afraid to express anger. But their answers to the question "What don't you like?" will often reveal the focus of their anger. Oaklander says that they need help finding acceptable ways to express anger without getting into trouble. She suggests that we give our children opportunities to be aggressive and to "demolish" something. For example, sometimes it is useful and fun for young children to express anger through a puppet or doll. They may have fun attacking another puppet or a stuffed animal. Give your children old magazines or phone books to rip up, or let them slap water, or you can do these activities with them. In these ways children vent their feelings constructively and feel some of the power they lost through the miscarriage.

Let children write their own book about the miscarriage. If they are too young, you can write down their words and they can draw the pictures. Chapters can be added over time as they continue to deal with their emotions regarding the loss.

Help In Other Ways

- Tell children, "I'm sad for you" or "I miss your baby and I'm sad."
- Include children in the planning and delivery of services and rituals.
- Invite children to choose or make a gift of their choosing for the baby.
- Buy a commemorative of the baby for the children such as a stuffed animal or a charm.
- Get away with the children to the park, to a movie, to an amuse-

ment park, or for an ice cream cone; or ask someone else close to them to do so.

- Get professional help for you, your children, or all of you, if you are struggling with one another.
- Know that it is never too late to talk about or work through a loss with children.

Additional Reading

In addition to the many books and movies referred to throughout the text, we recommend the following reading:

A Return to Love: Reflections on the Principles of "A Course in Miracles" by Marianne Williamson (Harper Collins Publishers, 1992).

The Castle of the Pearl by Christopher Biffle (New York: Barnes and Noble, 1983) is a workbook for self-knowledge and growth.

Celebrate Your Self: Enhancing Your Own Self-Esteem by Dorothy Corkille Briggs (New York: Doubleday, 1977).

Coming Back: Rebuilding Lives After Crisis and Loss by Ann Kaiser Stearns (New York: Random House, 1988).

Don't Take My Grief Away by Doug Manning (San Francisco: Harper San Francisco, 1984).

Getting the Love You Want: A Guide for Couples by Harville Hendrix (New York: H. Holt, 1988) is a helpful book for couples who are struggling in their relationships.

Gifts From the Sea by Anne Morrow Lindbergh (New York: Pantheon Books, 1991) is a book for women about finding tranquility in the chaos of the world.

The Grief Recovery Manual: A Step by Step Program for Moving Beyond Loss by John W. James and Frank Cherry (New York: Harper and Row, 1988).

Healing a Father's Grief by William Schatz (can be ordered from Medic Publishing Co., PO Box 89, Redmond, WA 98052) is a booklet that fathers have found very helpful.

Healing Into Life and Death by Stephen Levine (Garden City, NY: Anchor Press/Doubleday, 1987) assists the reader in opening the heart to healing physically and emotionally.

How to Meditate by Lawrence LeShan, Ph.D., (New York: Bantam Books, 1974).

Illuminations: Visions for Change, Growth and Self-Acceptance by Stephen C. Paul (San Francisco: Harper, 1991) is a book of paintings and sayings about moving from pain to the possibilities of the future.

The Road Less Traveled: A New Psychology of Love, Traditional Values and Spiritual Growth by M. Scott Peck (New York: A Touchstone Book published by Simon and Schuster, 1978).

There's No Such Place as Far Away by Richard Bach (New York: Delacorte Press/Eleanor Friede, 1979) is a book about a kind of love that does not depend on time and space.

The Three Minute Meditator: 30 Simple Ways to Unwind Your Mind Anywhere Anytime! by David Harp (San Francisco: mind's i press, 1987).

Transitions: Strategies for Coping With the Difficult, Painful, and Confusing Times in Your Life by William Bridges, Ph.D. (New York: Addison-Wesley, 1980).

Visualization: Directing the Movies of Your Mind by Adelaide Bry (New York: Barnes and Noble, 1978) is a how-to book about using visualization "to improve your health, expand your mind, and achieve your goals."

Way of the Peaceful Warrior: A Book That Changes Lives by Dan Millman (Tiburon, CA: H. J. Kramer, 1984).

When Bad Things Happen to Good People by Harold Kushner (New York: Avon Books, 1981).

There have been many articles published in medical journals about studies of women's emotional responses to miscarriage. These can be found in medical libraries.

Many films (available for rent on video) that deal with grief include *Born on the Fourth of July, Ordinary People, On Golden Pond,* and *Paradise.*

Bibliography for Children

There are many books for children about death and grief in bookstores and libraries. Here are a few examples:

Better With Two by Barbara Joosse (New York: Harper and Row, 1988).

First Snow by Helen Coutant (New York: Alfred A. Knopf, 1974).

Goodbye Rune by Marit Kaldhol and Wench Oyen (New York: Kane/Miller Book Publishers, 1987).

I'll Miss You, Mr. Hooper by Norman Stiles (New York: Random House, 1984).

Lifetimes by Bryan Mellonie and Robert Ingpen (New York: Bantam Books, 1983).

Losing Someone You Love by Elizabeth Richter (New York: G. P. Putnam's Sons, 1986).

The Two of Them by Aliki (New York: Greenwillow Books, 1979).

Films for children about grief, such as *Charlotte's Web*, are available for video rental.

Statistical Findings

Statistical responses to pertinent interview questions are listed here in ascending order of percentages.

- 30% of the women interviewed said that, after their miscarriages, they had thoughts about **suicide.**
- After 31% of the miscarriages,* women said they experienced **conflict about the reality** of their babies.
- 32% of the mothers **named** their babies, some before they were pregnant, some during their pregnancies, and some after their miscarriages.
- 36% of the women said their losses triggered thoughts about **their own mortality.**
- 38% of the women recognized in themselves a sense of **searching** for their lost babies.
- Although less than 10% of the women experienced what they labeled as panic attacks *before* their miscarriages, 38% of the women said they experienced **panic attacks** *after* their miscarriages.
- 41% of the women said they felt desires or yearnings to do things that seemed **odd or irrational** to them.
- 42% of the women recalled having **nightmares.**
- 43% of them felt a **closeness or contact** with their babies **at the time of the interviews.**
- 44% of the mothers felt concern about their own **sanity.**
- Following 48% of the miscarriages, women at some point in time doubted they would ever **get through their grief.**
- Although almost none of the women had physical evidence or medical verification of their babies' genders, 50% of them **"had a feeling" about the sex of their babies.**

*Because the women who had more than one miscarriage were asked to respond to some questions as they pertained to each of their miscarriages, some statistics reflect the percentage of total miscarriages in our study rather than the percentage of women interviewed. These are worded accordingly.

- 50% of the women felt a sense of **closeness or contact** with their babies **after their miscarriages.**
- 55% of the mothers created **mementos** of their babies.
- 58% of the women remembered **dreaming** about their babies after their miscarriages.
- During 62% of the pregnancies, the women **thought of themselves as mothers** to their babies.
- Following 63% of the miscarriages, women said they felt **devastated.**
- 64% of the women said their **sex drives changed** following their miscarriages.
- 64% of the women described thoughts that seemed **illogical or strange** to them.
- 64% of the mothers interviewed, consciously **visualized their babies** during their pregnancies.
- 69% of the women felt that the **pain** from their miscarriages would **never completely go away.**
- Relative to 70% of the miscarriages represented in the study, women said that when they had been pregnant, they had experienced their babies, in their hearts and minds, as **whole and living human beings.**
- 71% of the miscarriages were experienced by mothers as **the death of their children.**
- 73% of the women felt a sense of **internal chaos or disorder.**
- 73% of the women worried that they had somehow inadvertently **caused the demise** of their babies.
- At the time of or after their miscarriages, 74% of the women felt **out of control** emotionally and/or physically.
- 79% of the mothers talked of feelings of **confusion** about emotional *and* physical experiences, both during and after their miscarriages.
- Following 81% of the miscarriages in the study, the mothers felt that **a part of them had died.**
- After 83% of the miscarriages, mothers felt **loneliness.**

Blighted ovum refers to a fertilized egg that died.

Cervix is the name for the neck-like part of the uterus that projects into the vagina, and through which a baby passes during delivery. An "incompetent cervix" is a condition in which the cervix opens too soon, causing miscarriage by allowing the baby and placenta to leave the uterus.

Colostrum is the first milk or thin white liquid secreted by the breasts during pregnancy, at the completion of pregnancy, or in the first days following delivery.

D&C stands for "dilatation and curettage." It is a surgical procedure in which the cervix is artificially expanded and the inner lining of the uterus is scraped with a spoon-like instrument. In the case of miscarriage, this procedure is performed to obtain tissue samples or to remove tissue remaining in the uterus in order to stop bleeding or prevent infection. At the time of this printing, it appears that the D&C procedure is being replaced with the newer hysteroscopy procedure, which enables the physician to see directly inside a woman's uterus and precisely direct the scraping to the areas that need it.

Ectopic pregnancies are commonly referred to as "tubal" pregnancies because the embryo implants outside the uterus and usually in the fallopian tube. The fallopian tube does not have the capacity to expand and successfully house and nurture the growing baby. The mother will experience pain as the tube is overextending or bursting, at which point emergency surgery must be performed to remove the baby or both the baby and the tube. If the ectopic pregnancy goes undetected, the tube will burst at about six to eight weeks' gestation. Ectopic pregnancy can be life threatening; the mother's life depends on timely surgical removal of the baby. Usually the tube is removed as well. Following the surgery, fertility is maintained yet is somewhat reduced.

Embryo is the term used for an unborn baby from the time of conception to the end of the eighth week of pregnancy.

Fetus is the term used for an unborn baby from the end of the eighth week of pregnancy to the moment of birth.

Gestation is the duration of time that a baby is carried in the uterus.

Hemorrhaging refers to excessive bleeding and necessitates immediate medical attention.

Missed abortion is a miscarriage in which the baby has died but for some reason has not been expelled. This term is sometimes used synonymously with "blighted ovum."

Ova are female reproductive cells; a woman's eggs. "Ova" is the plural form of "ovum."

Perinatal death is the death of a baby from the 20th week of gestation through the 28th day after birth.

Stillbirth is pregnancy loss after 20 weeks' gestation, at which point babies sometimes sustain life outside the womb for at least a brief time. A loss occurring after that point in time is thereby differentiated from a miscarriage.

Sonogram refers to the image produced by ultrasound and is seen on a monitor or film.

Tubal pregnancies See **"Ectopic Pregnancies."**

Ultrasound is a procedure in which high-energy sound waves are used to create a visual image of the baby and the uterus on a screen or monitor. Still photographs of the image are sometimes available. The general public commonly interchanges this term with the term "sonogram," or "sono."

INDEX